THE NEW
EMAIL REVOLUTION

THE NEW EMAIL REVOLUTION

SAVE TIME, MAKE MONEY, AND WRITE EMAILS
PEOPLE ACTUALLY *WANT* TO READ!

ROBERT W. BLY

Skyhorse Publishing

Skyhorse Publishing books may be purchased in bulk at special discounts for sales promotion, corporate gifts, fund-raising, or educational purposes. Special editions can also be created to specifications. For details, contact the Special Sales Department, Skyhorse Publishing, 307 West 36th Street, 11th Floor, New York, NY 10018 or info@skyhorsepublishing.com.

Skyhorse® and Skyhorse Publishing® are registered trademarks of Skyhorse Publishing, Inc.®, a Delaware corporation.

Visit our website at www.skyhorsepublishing.com.

10 9 8 7 6 5 4 3 2 1

Library of Congress Cataloging-in-Publication Data is available on file.

Cover design by Rain Saukas
Cover photo credit iStock

ISBN: 978-1-5107-2791-5
Ebook ISBN: 978-1-5107-2792-2

Printed in the United States of America

Dedication

To Andrew Linick—friend, teacher, colleague

Acknowledgment

I'd like to thank my agent, Bob Diforio, for connecting me to this project and its publisher; my acquisitions editor Michael Lewis for suggesting this book and then agreeing to have me write it; and my editor Michael Campbell for making it much better than it was when the manuscript first landed on his desk.

Also, thanks to all the digital marketers who provided sample emails, ideas, and strategies for the book. I appreciate Bob Reina of Talk Fusion, who took the time to educate me on the benefits of using video email. I am also grateful to Jennifer Holmes, Marilyn Pincus, Kim Stacey, and Justin Cassata for their invaluable editorial and research assistance. A few sections of the book appeared, in slightly different form, in articles published in *Target Marketing* and *DM News*.

Contents

Introduction

Despite all the buzz about Snapchat, Twitter, Instagram, and other social media, email is still the most widely used way people communicate at a distance in writing, whether personally, as consumers, or in business—the "killer app" of digital communication.

According to market research firm The Radicati Group, in 2015 there were over 205 billion emails sent and received daily worldwide[1]—about seven million emails zipping around the digital superhighway that is the Internet in the time it took you to read this sentence.[2] The average office worker gets 121 emails a day.[3]

Fierce CMO reports that 98 percent of consumers ages 18 to 64 check their email address at least one to three time per day. An article in *Chief Marketer* reports that millennials expect email to remain their preferred method of communication at work for the next five years.[4] Some 86 percent of professionals surveyed by HubSpot prefer email for business

---

1   http://www.radicati.com/wp/wp-content/uploads/2015/02/Email-Statistics
    -Report-2015-2019-Executive-Summary.pdf.
2   If you read it aloud at a moderate pace, it takes about thirty seconds.
3   http://expandedramblings.com/index.php/email-statistics/.
4   http://www.chiefmarketer.com/millennials-still-favor-email-survey/.

communication.[5] Since 2015, email use by business-to-consumer (B2C) marketers has more than doubled, increasing by 106 percent.[6]

The New Email Revolution is the definitive guide to writing effective emails both at home and at the office. It covers email messages for personal and social correspondence, business communication, and email marketing.

With this book in hand, you will be able to quickly and easily:

- Find model correspondence you can use to create emails for many different situations.
- Know the right wording and optimal word length for email communication.
- Get recipients to read and respond to your email messages.
- Understand when it is legal and not legal to send email to a person you do not know.
- Incorporate photos, graphics, sound, and video into your email messages.
- Avoid spam and get past spam filters and other blocks to increase email deliverability.
- Measure the bounce rate, unsubscribe rate, open rate, and click-through rate to every marketing email you send.
- Write clearer, more engaging, more persuasive email copy for every occasion.

I do have a favor to ask. If you have a particular email tactic or writing tip you've found useful, or a successful email that generated a positive result, please send it to me so I can share it with readers of the next edition of *The New Email Revolution*. I can be reached at:

---

5   Ray Schultz, "Email Still a Top Channel," The Email Edge (MediaPost.com), 5/19/17.
6   http://www.thedrum.com/news/2017/06/23/email-marketing-up-83-2015-b2b -marketing-grows-200.

Bob Bly
Copywriter
31 Cheyenne Drive
Montville, NJ 07045
Phone: 973-263-0562
Email: rwbly@bly.com
Web: www.bly.com

CHAPTER 1.

The Science and Mechanics of Sending and Receiving Emails

Over 2.6 billion people today use email as a quick and easy way of communicating with others, according to Radicati Group's *Email Statistics Report* 2015–2019. By their projection, in 2019 there will be nearly 2.9 million email users, with two to three accounts for each person. Email is fast, simple, and you do not need a stamp to send it—just an Internet connection through a service provider.

So what exactly is email? In some ways, writing an email is similar to writing a letter. But the communication is delivered digitally over the Internet, usually within minutes of hitting the send button. Your message transfers electronically, from your computer's email service, to another recipient's service.

Email messages are usually shorter than postal letters, and much shorter than those long, handwritten letters people composed years ago. Sending email is faster and easier than mailing a letter with enclosures through the U.S. Postal Service, and much less costly than FedEx.

The bonus for using email is that you can also send pictures, animations, videos, or links to content where people can go view these on an online repository or cloud-based service. Files of nearly every type can be attached to an email, getting business documents to recipients much faster than sending bulky envelopes with a hard copy tucked inside.

How Was the Concept of Email Created?

Samuel Morse invented the telegraph and a "language," Morse code, for sending coded messages with it.

With Morse code, telegraph operators use a series of short taps, called dots, and long taps, called dashes, to send coded messages over the wire long distance. The telegraph became the nation's first electronic messaging system in the mid-1800s. The telegraph is a two-way communicator, consisting of two copper wires and a needle, with each device capable of both sending and receiving signals.

Before there was early commercial email, such as provided through dial-up CompuServe and AOL services, there were some smart people in the private sector who figured out how to get a message to another person in the same company. Otherwise, climbing up and down the stairs, or taking the elevator to that floor, was the only way to get that message there, particularly if it had sensitive information in it. This would have been time-consuming, time that should have been spent at the office desk instead.

Large corporations circulated interoffice mail throughout the plant, delivered by a mail room worker with a mail cart. When I was at Westinghouse in the late 1970s, we began using a robotic cart for interoffice memo delivery, and it worked very well.

When it comes to emails, while there is significant and ongoing controversy as to who actually created the first email, the most common story is that someone figured out how to place a message to another worker in the same company in their directory. It took knowing and writing the code, read by the computer system's operating platform, which could read where that file should reside.

In 1978, Shiva Ayyadurai created an electronic message system for the University of Medicine and Dentistry of New Jersey (UMDNJ), with the typical Inbox, Outbox, Subject, Cc, and Bcc header form, still seen today in regular emails. This version was internal, for those that worked at UMDNJ, as a way to communicate rapidly with each other, within the system. As time went on, more users were added on within that system.

Essentially, this was the first Intranet, a private network comprised of a business's many departments in the organization. (An extranet in today's business world, as a private network, incorporates communications with outside vendors, partners, client, who wish to send invoices and other documents, vital to a business, but within closed secured parameters, thus bypassing telephones or conventional Internet emails, which might be unsecured.)

The first email as we know it can be traced back to the 1970s.[7] Just a few decades later, email is all-pervasive in our lives, and email has become one of the most popular forms of communication. Not only does email save time and money, it's also a great tool for personal as well as business communications. These statistics reveal even more about how much we depend on this channel of communication.[8]

- The total number of email users worldwide is 3.7 billion[9]
- 92% of online adults use email, with 61% using it on an average day

---

7   See: "Email Timeline," https://www.theguardian.com/technology/2002/mar/13/internetnews.
8   See: "70 Email Marketing Stats Every Marketer Should Know," https://www.campaignmonitor.com/blog/email-marketing/2016/01/70-email-marketing-stats-you-need-to-know.
9   See: "How Many Emails are Sent Every Day," https://www.lifewire.com/how-many-emails-are-sent-every-day-1171210.

- 30% of subscribers change email addresses annually
- 17% of Americans create a new email address every 6 months[10]

Whether you're sending "one-to-many" emails (where a large list of people are sent the same or very similar emails from a source to which they've intentionally subscribed), or one-to-one emails, the basic anatomy of the message remains the same.

That being said, many people now have more than one email account. If you are working for a company or have your own business, you likely have an email account for business. At home, you probably also have a separate personal email account.

It is estimated that there were 205 billion emails sent and received a day, globally, in 2015, and these amounts are only reduced when you choose to unsubscribe or deregister with these emails. But many like having the notifications of sales, special events, and offers, that one ordinarily would not receive any other way. Who would have time to daily visit favorite websites to find out what the special of the day is? Therefore, it may be beneficial to continue to receive these email notifications.

Business emails in 2015 range at 122 billion sent and received, indicating that there is quite a bit of success coming from these send outs and, therefore, should be a major consideration in marketing/advertising strategies conducted by any business in the Internet marketplace. Direct mail strategies are still very popular, but email strategies in alignment with direct mail, serve to bolster the message. I believe that in digital marketing, email, and not social media or Search Engine Optimization, is truly the "killer app."

---

10 See: "15 Email Statistics that are Shaping the Future," http://www.convinceand convert.com/convince-convert/15-email-statistics-that-are-shaping-the-future.

Who Offers Email Services?

The first step to taking advantage of email's speed, functionality, and power, whether for personal or business use, is choosing an email services provider (ESP).

Appendix IV lists a few of the most popular ESPs for both personal email and business emails. The main difference is that personal emails are typically sent to one individual, though a few other recipients may receive it when they are "cc'd" or "bc'd." The names of recipients who have been cc'd are visible on the email while the identifies and email addresses of those who have been bc'd are not visible to other recipients.

Business emails too can be sent to a primary recipient and others who are cc'd or bc'd. But in addition, many business email messages are mass distributed or "broadcast" to lists of dozens, hundreds, or even thousands of recipients simultaneously, using some of the business email services listed in Appendix IV.

You can get started in email with a free account set up with a major browser, such as Google's Gmail, which offers many capabilities for attachments, storage, and also sorts mail for you into three categories: primary mail, social mail, and promotions. You can also star those emails which are important to you, or mark all emails as read or unread, sort by sender or date, and place into category files, created on the left side index section. Those sent to trash or spam are with some services deleted automatically in 30 days or so.

With some services, when you click on an email, the folder, trash, and action buttons pop up above the email columns, allowing you to conduct whatever option you need to do with that email, or a series of emails. Consider archiving emails of importance, which you may want to access much later on, for one reason or another.

If you use Google calendar, you can also click on a link from an email verification you signed up for, which automatically takes you to the calendar date for the seminar, conference call, or other event scheduled on the calendar. There, you can edit the notification further for an alarm to be sent to you as a reminder, along with a number of other options.

Google is only one option, Yahoo! is another. Both have paid versions as well, which may work better for your needs, especially if you have a business website and need a contact email.

There is also Microsoft's Outlook program, which comes with a trial or purchased version of any of its office suites, and is integrated with a calendar. Outlook has a great directory structure for storing emails by client, project, activity, source, topic, and any other way you want.

A problem with Outlook is that when you reach a critical mass of stored emails, it starts malfunctioning. The solution is to connect it to Microsoft Exchange, which solves the overload problem and can store a virtually unlimited number of emails.

Outlook also gets wonky when you have too many emails in your sent or delete folders. Clear these when there are just a few thousand. If you allow the volume of emails to get too big in these folders, Outlook may be unable to receive more email until you clear them. And when they are very full, the automatic clear function may stop working, forcing you to remove messages manually, which is time-consuming.

Microsoft Live has a free email program, using your Microsoft account that you need, initially, to sign into your new Windows 10 update or licensed platform version on your computer. Download the app (short for application) for it on your phone, and you can access your email anywhere. Yahoo! and Gmail also have downloadable apps for their mail services as well. You can find these apps through the Google Play phone app, or the Microsoft Store phone app. Alternatively, you can go to the Store app in your computer's Windows menu, or just type in the Microsoft Live name on a web browser to get it online.

Consider that getting your emails on your phone is great, but if you want to easily respond back with a letter, you may want to carry a portable keyboard rather than using the phone's keyboard. It just depends on your needs, unless you are a whiz at tapping or typing on phone keyboards. If a response is needed, maybe calling or texting a short note would be better, or wait until you get to your laptop, tablet, or desktop to send a longer response back.

Business vs. Personal Email

As noted in the previous section, the main difference between personal and business email services is this: personal emails go only to a few individually selected recipients vs. business emails are often mass-distributed to large lists of recipients that include both names and email addresses.

An important consideration is that, if you have a business, your email can come from your web domain, or has your domain name within the address you created for your email service, for that site. Example: my site URL is www.bly.com and the email address and the email address from that server is rwbly@bly.com.

Also, create a personal email address in one of the free or paid services to connect with family, friends, and others. I have a Gmail account as my second address. Sometimes if you have problems with your primary address, a backup address can keep you in business until it is fixed.

A benefit of email in communicating with clients in your business is that you can keep track of projects through sequential mailings in a chain of emails, generally called a conversation. Each new email, chains to the previous one, and both you and the client, are current on any changes to the project, what was previously discussed, and it all goes in your pre-designated folder. You can also archive these, for later access, if you need them. Doing so, frees up space on your service provider's server.

Recently, a client called to complain that the website designer quoted a higher figure for doing his site than I said she would. When he told me the website designer was HL, I replied that I had recommended someone else, WB. He said I did not. I quickly went into my saved emails for that client in the Outlook directory I created. Sure enough, I found my original email recommending WB, whose estimate was exactly what I said it would be.

The Etiquette of Emails

While personal emails are two or more people sending messages in a tone that is familiar to the others, marketing and business emails should observe certain forms of etiquette, also called netiquette. There should not be any cursing or foul words used in your messages. You never know who you will offend. Messages should never be typed in all capital letters. That is equivalent to shouting in someone's ear if they were standing next to you. The same is true in social media messages.

When you write your body of content, you should provide as much information as possible, in the least amount of words used. Be direct and informative with every word. Boasting about yourself or your work as being the best on the marketplace may raise eyebrows. Not everyone may agree with you on that count, unless you can prove it in some manner. Imparting information is the main focus of your message, but do provide interest, such as a story about how your product or your service improved someone's life or work habits, for example.

Some messages work very well with emails, depending on what is being offered. Sometimes, the message in words can be enhanced with a video that shows more about the message, such as testimonials, or showing how a product works. It is a judgement call, as to how to design your message for your unique product or service. In recent years, email greeting cards with animated videos, which include words, music, and animation, have become increasingly popular; in 2016, Americans spent $393 million to send e-cards.[11] However, for most of us, our personal emails

---

11 https://www.ibisworld.com/industry-trends/specialized-market-research-reports
    /online-retail/lifestyle-services/online-greeting-card-sales.html.

are text only, eliminating unnecessary distractions while the recipient is reading the email.

If you can be found on social media sites, such as Facebook, LinkedIn, Pinterest, Instagram, or Twitter, you should add those icons from your site, directly into your email at the bottom. This expands your coverage and the opportunity to get your message out to those who are following you. Use only those social media site icons that allow you to market effectively to your customer base and communicate with your friends or others in your online community.

Best Word Length for Emails

Almost everyone agrees that emails should be brief. But let's quantify how much shorter online copy is than offline. Should you compress your personal, business, or sales letter to half its length for email transmission? Less?

Kathy Henning, who writes extensively about online communication, says, *"In general, online text should be half as long as printed text, maybe even shorter."* Not a precise formula, but a good starting point for estimation.

When deciding on the word amount of an email, using between 50 to 125 words is reasonable for greatest response optimization at 50 percent, based on Boomerang's research analysis of forty million emails. Customer service emails, like the ones shown in this chapter, may need more words because it is outlining or solving a problem. Alternatively, emails with ten words or less barely get off the ground, as per Boomerang's analysis. Longer emails can work when:

- You have an existing business or personal relationship with the recipient.
- The topic is interesting, important, or both to the reader.

- You need to offer some proof of claims, arguments, or ideas presented in your email; for example, citing a scientific paper that demonstrates global warming is real.

Keep your writing level for readers at a seventh-grade level for most occasions, to garner the highest response rate. Use simple words and avoid run-on sentences. A sentence with too many words may lose the reader about three-fourths of the way through. Have you ever had to go back and reread the first part because you forgot what the writer was first writing about? Keep it short, simple, and easy to read.

"What works best in email copy length for business and especially online marketing?" I was asked for the umpteenth time the other day. "Long copy or short copy?"

For routine business and personal correspondence, short emails typically work best. Email is a quick, casual medium, much more "in the moment" and "on the fly" than postal mail was in the pre-Internet and especially the pre-PC days.

When I entered the corporate world in the late 1970s, writing and sending a letter was a big production. We agonized over the writing. Professionals and managers did not have typewriters on their desks, so a secretary typed the letter. You made edits. She typed it again. Then she put it in the outgoing company mail. The post office took a couple of days to deliver it to a recipient, for the price of a first-class stamp.

Now, we all have keyboards. We type our own short, quick letters and memos. Hit the send button. And our recipient has it in seconds. Cost to send? Nearly zero.

However, as for the optimal length for email *marketing* campaigns, the answer as to what works best, long copy or short copy, is a bit more complex. Let me explain.

There's a widely held viewpoint that, on the Internet, the less copy the better. Web marketing experts tell us that the Internet is faster paced than the "snail mail" world, that attention spans are shorter, and long messages get zapped into oblivion with the click of the mouse. "Keep it short!" they extol in countless advisory e-zines.

General advertisers, for the most part, also believe that when it comes to copy, the shorter the better. Often their print ads have large pictures and only a handful of words. So they have no trouble embracing the "people don't read" mentality the web marketing gurus say works best.

But traditional direct marketers whose products are typically sold with long copy direct mail packages and self-mailers—newsletter publishers, seminar promoters, magazines, book clubs, insurance, audio cassettes— have a problem. It goes something like this:

"In print, I have to use long copy to make the sale . . . or I just don't get the order. We've tested short copy many times—who *doesn't* want a cheaper mailing piece with less ink and paper? But it has never worked for our product. Now my web marketing consultant says the email should be just a few paragraphs. If a few paragraphs won't convince people to buy offline, why should things be any different online?"

And they are right: Just because a person buys online doesn't change the persuasion process. If he or she needs the facts to make a decision, he needs them regardless of whether he or she is ordering from a paper mailing or a website.

Yet we also have a sense that the web marketing gurus have at least a clue as to what they are talking about. We sense that our four-page sales letter, if sent word for word as a lengthy email, wouldn't work. People would click away long before they got to the end.

I think I have some sensible guidelines to answer this puzzle. The answer is that in online marketing, though long copy may often win the day, the promotion's text is divided between two messages. The first is the email you receive, and the second is the remainder of the sales copy posted on the web page you go to when you click on the call to action hyperlink in the email. Because this needs some explanation, I will take up the matter in detail and with precision in chapter 8, where the issue of copy length in email marketing will, I promise you, be made clear.

CHAPTER 2.

CAN SPAM Laws, SPAM Filters, Junk Folders, ISPs, and Other Barriers to Email Deliverability

Forty percent of all emails in the United States are spam.[12] Globally, estimates are as high as 86 percent.[13] Despite the CAN-SPAM Act passed by Congress in 2003—as well as state-of-the-art spam filters—spam remains an everyday reality for anyone with an email account. You've probably received spam this very day, offering you a "free membership" perhaps—or worse, someone from Nigeria asking you to send money so he can help you claim a fortune waiting for you.

---

12 "Global Spam Map," Trend Micro (as of December 15, 2016), http://www.trend micro.com/us/security-intelligence/current-threat-activity/global-spam-map. In Canada, the numbers are even higher, at 65 percent.

13 cf. "E-Mail Spam Goes Artisanal," Bloomberg, https://www.bloomberg.com/news /articles/2016-01-19/e-mail-spam-goes-artisanal.

But spam is of special concern for business owners, marketers, and anyone who *sends* emails. Email authors may be unaware of when they can and cannot send emails to people whom they do not know—and what they are allowed and not allowed to say in them.

Laws, spam filters, junk folders, ISPs, and other barriers to email communication can undermine your email campaigns if you aren't careful. Email communications can cause big problems for you if they break the law or aren't getting delivered

When you follow the simple guidelines in this chapter, you'll know just what you're allowed to email and what not—and how to get it delivered.

Defining Spam

Spam is defined differently. Some define spam as unsolicited bulk email, in which an identical or almost identical message is sent to multiple recipients.

For instance, Spamhaus identifies spam as follows:

An electronic message is "spam" if (A) the recipient's personal identity and context are irrelevant because the message is equally applicable to many other potential recipients; and (B) the recipient has not verifiably granted deliberate, explicit, and still-revocable permission for it to be sent.[14]

Others define spam as unsolicited *commercial* emails.

As email authors, however, we should primarily be concerned not with the definition of spam, which is somewhat subjective, but simply with what is regulated by law. And the law regulates commercial

---

14 "The Definition of Spam," Spamhaus, https://www.spamhaus.org/consumer /definition/.

messages in general, whether solicited or unsolicited, spam or no. The Federal Trade Commission (FTC) defines a commercial message as "any electronic mail message the primary purpose of which is the commercial advertisement or promotion of a commercial product or service."[15]

The CAN-SPAM Act passed by Congress in 2003 covers commercial messages of any kind, whether solicited or unsolicited. So commercial emails, not spam per se, should be the central focus for us.

The Difference Between Commercial Emails and "Relationship or Transactional" Emails

The basic distinction is the message's purpose. If it's an advertisement or promotion for a commercial product or service, it's commercial. If the purpose is to "facilitate, complete, or confirm" a previously agreed-upon commercial transaction, it's transactional or relationship. Included in the latter definition are warranty information, product updates or upgrades that regard the previously agreed-upon commercial transaction, and benefits and other communications information to your own employees.

It is primarily *commercial* messages that are regulated by the CAN-SPAM Act. While there are some less rigorous requirements for transactional/relationship emails, nonetheless, it is commercial emails that are of greatest concern.

The CAN-SPAM Act

In 2003, Congress passed the Controlling the Assault of Non-Solicited Pornography and Marketing (CAN-SPAM) Act[16] to regulate commercial

---

15 "CAN-SPAM Act: A Compliance Guide for Business," FTC, https://www.ftc.gov /tips-advice/business-center/guidance/can-spam-act-compliance-guide-business.
16 15 U.S.C. sec. 7701–13.

messages. This was a result of the onslaught of unsolicited emails of a commercial nature—and particularly those that were sexually oriented.

The CAN-SPAM Act does not prohibit commercial emails, it merely regulates them. The Act applies to any commercial message sent electronically. Again, a commercial message is "any electronic mail message the primary purpose of which is the commercial advertisement or promotion of a commercial product or service." That means business-to-consumer (B2C) *as well as business-to-business* (B2B). B2B emails are *not* exempt from the CAN-SPAM Act.

Nor are *solicited* commercial emails exempt from this Act. If someone has "opted in" to your email list through a signup box on your website or has otherwise asked to receive your emails, your email messages are still regulated by the CAN-SPAM Act and you must follow its restrictions. These solicited emails are sent to those who have given "affirmative consent" (opted in) to receive your commercial messages. As you'll see, the restrictions in this case are slightly less rigorous, though these solicited emails must still adhere to the majority of restrictions for commercial email.

Compliance Basics: A 10-Point Checklist

Many of these points are basic and already second nature to opt-in email marketers: no fraudulent transmission data, no harvesting email addresses. Others are more complex, such as rules regarding inclusion of a physical postal address. These are good starting points in ensuring your email program is in compliance with the law:

- Don't use fraudulent transmission data, such as open relays, which are Simple Mail Transfer Protocol (SMTP) email servers that enable users to send emails that hide the source of their emails. Also avoid using false headers, which deceive recipients as to the source of the email.

- Don't use misleading sender or subject lines.
- Add your postal address to all email. The signature or "sig file" is ideal for this. Your email provider almost certainly allows you to create and then automatically add to all your outgoing emails a sig file with your name, address, and any other information you wish.
- If your email list isn't opt-in or double opt-in ("prior affirmative consent"), include a clear notice that states the email is an advertisement or solicitation in commercial messages. Please note that if your list is opt-in or double opt-in, you're exempt from this provision. Double opt-in is a process of gaining permission to send an email to someone during which the recipient confirms that the email address is theirs—typically by clicking on an email link they receive from the sender. Double opt-in isn't required, but it's ideal because it prevents people from placing someone other than themselves on a list.
- Include a "clear and conspicuous" unsubscribe mechanism in every email. And the unsubscribe mechanism must be simple: a link click or simple reply email.
- Have a process for handling unsubscribes within the ten-day limit mandated by the CAN-SPAM Act. Ensure unsubscribe handling is in place electronically, as well as for unsubscribes received via postal mail (and any other contact information you include in the email, such as phone and fax).
- Offer recipients a way to receive some types of email from you while blocking others, along with a "global unsubscribe" option to stop all future email from your organization. All quality email marketing services offer these options as a feature of the service.
- Don't share the address of anyone who has subscribed to the list or who has unsubscribed.
- Don't harvest email addresses or use automated means to randomly generate addresses.

- Remove any sexually oriented material from your messages. The law requires such material be readily identified in the subject line as "SEXUALLY-EXPLICIT" in all caps. When "initially viewed," the message body should include only instructions on how to access the sexually oriented material, as well as your postal address, a notice the message is an advertisement or a solicitation, and a working unsubscribe mechanism. You can ignore this if the message is sent to someone who opted in.

Another note, not so much on compliance as protection. Under this law, if you want to protect email addresses on your website from being harvested, add a privacy policy notice saying you don't "give, sell, or otherwise transfer" these addresses to "any other party for the purpose of initiating, or enabling others to initiate," email messages.

To download the complete text of the CAN-SPAM Act of 2003, visit: https://www.ftc.gov/sites/default/files/documents/cases/2007/11/canspam.pdf.

Special Restrictions for Emails Sent to Wireless Devices

Some email addresses cannot legally be sent unsolicited commercial emails at all according to the CAN-SPAM Act. These include email addresses given by wireless carriers to customers specifically for the purpose of mobile messaging. Because these messages in many cases would cost the recipient money, you must first have the recipients' affirmative consent to send them commercial messages. That means they must opt in to your list or otherwise give permission to be emailed.

Also, you must gain this affirmative consent in a way that doesn't cost them anything, as well as inform them that they:

- Are consenting to receive commercial emails on their mobile device.
- May receive charges for these messages (depending on their carrier and plan).
- Can opt out at any time.

A list of the domains to which unsolicited emails are prohibited can be found at https://www.fcc.gov/consumer-governmental-affairs/domain -name-downloads (this list is continually updated).

These are a small minority of email addresses, however. You are *not* prohibited from sending unsolicited emails to most email addresses as long as they do not have a domain extension (e.g., joeblow@abc.com is from the domain abc) on the domain name list found when you click on the link in the paragraph above.

Best Email Practices

While not a requirement by law, getting permission (affirmative consent) to email your recipients commercial emails is an industry best practice. That means getting the opt-in to your list before sending commercial messages at all.

However, that is not always feasible. Email prospecting can be a cost-effective way to get your message out. Just make sure you follow the law. In some cases, getting affirmative consent is impossible, such as when inquiring about a job or when you have no inbound lead strategy in place.

Another industry best practice is to make sure you're monitoring the effectiveness of your opt-out mechanism on a regular basis. Test it regularly to make sure it's working. Sending emails to those who have already opted out (particularly after the ten-day window) is a recipe for disaster in your email campaigns.

Penalties for Noncompliance

The Federal Trade Commission (FTC) and Federal Communications Commission (FCC) have laws and rules that regulate the CAN-SPAM Act and interpret and enforce it. These entities also have the right to bring suit against offenders. Other agencies, ISPs, and states have the right to bring suit as well. Civil penalties can consist of up to $16,000 for each noncompliant email. So, if you are mass distributing a spam email, *the fines can be in the hundreds of thousands of dollars.*

Aggravated violations are especially subject to damages. These include:[17]

* Address harvesting—automatically capturing email addresses posted to websites.
* Spoofing—sending emails through another computer accessed without permission.
* Dictionary attacks—trying many different combinations of possible email addresses to "hit" a valid one.
* Automating the creation of many email accounts to send commercial email.

Violations regarding sexually oriented material are particularly serious and can lead to a prison sentence of up to five years.

Always follow the law in your commercial emails. If you have any specific questions about the law in your own situation, refer to the full text of the CAN-SPAM Act or consult a good attorney.

---

17 "E-mail Marketing: CAN-SPAM Act Compliance," David J. Ervin and Christopher M. Loeffler, Kelley Drye and Warren LLP, http://us.practicallaw.com/0-503-5278.

Deliverability Basics

In my business as a copywriter, I know that the greatest copy in the world means nothing if that copy doesn't reach my intended audience. Often it's not the message that's the issue—it's getting the message delivered to your target audience. There may be an amazing offer, stellar copy, and a targeted list. But if it doesn't get *delivered,* it's worth nothing.

I'll use an analogy to direct mail. Earlier in the chapter we discussed the CAN-SPAM Act. When sending direct mail, we have strict limits on the envelope size, weight, what is contained in the envelope or package, and so on. We also have limits on the types of items we can send through the mail. Just as the law prohibits us from sending particular items through the mail—poisons, certain types of goods, etc.—so too does the law prohibit us from sending certain types of emails. Similarly, while gatekeepers (such as secretaries) may keep certain mail messages away from the decision maker's desk, in the email world, spam filters, junk folders, and ISPs can also prevent our messages from reaching the intended inbox.

The rest of this chapter will show you how to better your odds of getting your email message delivered.

Issues in Email Deliverability

If we examine the process of sending an email, whether a personal message to a friend or a relative, or an email marketing campaign to hundreds or thousands of recipients, it would look like this:

author ⟶ sender ⟶ (Internet) ⟶ receiver ⟶ recipient

You, of course, are the author, while the sender is your email program: Outlook, Gmail, Hotmail, or other email service linked to your

ISP (Internet Service Provider). The Internet is that network of connections through which your message travels to get to the receiver ISP, which then delivers the message (hopefully intact and as you anticipate it to look and read) to your recipient.

Globally, average deliverability is only 79 percent. One out of every five emails are not being delivered to the inbox. In the United States, deliverability is only 73 percent. More than a quarter of sent emails aren't even being delivered. Canadian marketers fare better, with 89 percent average inbox placement.[18]

For their 2016 report, GetResponse and Smart Insights surveyed a group of 1,831 customers, mostly senior managers responsible for digital marketing, asking, "How do you monitor and improve deliverability?" On average, across all types of industries, 28 percent of marketers are not managing or testing deliverability. By far the highest incidence of lacking testing of deliverability is the vacations, hotels, and leisure marketers, with 42 percent not testing deliverability before sending the email marketing messages. On the other hand, only 16 percent of travel and transportation marketers fail to test deliverability before sending.[19]

As you can see, deliverability is a big problem for many marketers. With 21 percent of all emails not even getting delivered to the inbox—and 28 percent of marketers not managing or testing deliverability—your care in these matters will put you ahead of much of your competition if you own a business or operate marketing campaigns. Even for personal messages, you can increase your chances of having your email delivered.

---

18 "2016 Deliverability Benchmark Report: Analysis of Worldwide Inbox Placement Rates," Return Path, https://returnpath.com/wp-content/uploads/2016/07/2016-Deliverability-Benchmark.pdf.
19 "The State of Email Marketing By Industry," GetResponse, http://www.Getresponse.com/resources/reports/state-of-email-marketing-by-industry-2016.html.

Factors That Affect Whether
Your Email Gets Delivered

So where are these undelivered emails going? In many cases, they are intercepted by spam filters and landing in the junk folder. Junk, or spam, folders are ways email servers segment incoming emails. Emails deemed to be "junk" based on complex algorithms will be diverted into the junk folder, and you may never actually see them. You may very well have hundreds of emails sitting in your junk folder right now. Some of them may be emails that weren't junk at all but got diverted to that folder anyway because of server policies.

Sender Reputation

The single biggest issue that affects whether your email gets delivered or is sent to the junk folder is your sender reputation. Sender reputation is a computation made by ISPs and email providers about the trustworthiness of your IP address. With all the spam and phishing emails being sent every day, your sender reputation is a measure of how trusted you can be not to engage in such practices.

The fact is that 83 percent of the time that emails aren't delivered, it is because of poor sender reputation.[20] Sender reputation is typically affected by spam filtering intercepting your emails, as well as spam complaints made by recipients. In every email program, there is the opportunity to label a message as spam. Get enough spam complaints or forwards of your messages to the FCC, and your sender reputation will suffer drastically—another reason why it's important to avoid spamming recipients. You may even be blacklisted.

A blacklist is an access control mechanism that means, "Allow everybody, except email addresses on the blacklist." An email spam filter may keep a blacklist of addresses, any mail from which would be prevented

---

20 "Reputation Monitor," Return Path, https://returnpath.com/solutions/email-deliv erability-optimization/reputation-monitor/.

from reaching its intended destination. There are also a number of online blacklist websites intended to weed out spammers.

You can check out your own sender reputation for free at a number of different websites, such as senderscore.org.

Subscriber Engagement

In addition to sender reputation, subscriber engagement is a major factor in getting your email delivered. Your subscriber engagement is a measure of how involved, or "engaged," your audience is with your emails. Are they being opened? Are the links being clicked?

In other words, your subscriber engagement will be poor to the extent that your emails are being ignored and left unopened, or links aren't being clicked. Your subscriber engagement will be strong to the extent that your emails are being opened and links clicked. When your subscriber engagement is poor, your emails are more likely to be intercepted by a junk filter or land in the spam folder.

Since subscriber engagement is such a big factor in whether your email gets delivered (and it has been more so recently than it used to be), then it makes good sense to regularly clear your list of those who are not engaging. You may want to send an email informing them that they are about to be taken off your list unless they say otherwise. This process can dramatically help the subscriber engagement of your list. Even though you're losing subscribers, your list as a whole is a better one, and you're rendering your emails more likely to be delivered to the inbox. The quality of the list is just as important as, if not more important than, its quantity.

Bounce Rate

In email vernacular, a failed delivery is commonly called a *bounce*, because the undeliverable message literally rebounds back to the sender, often within seconds of being sent. There are, however, two types of bouncing going on.

Remember those large, underfilled pinkish rubber balls used in the lower grades of elementary school? Those things were rather annoying—they didn't really *rebound* back to the thrower, but more or less came back without much velocity or energy. This could be seen as a *soft* bounce—and in the email marketing world, is typically due to a *transitory* problem. This could be where the recipient's mailbox is full, or the recipient mail server is too busy.

Unfortunately, just because a bounce is *soft* doesn't mean that repeated attempts to send to the address will be successful. Even if the address is legitimate, the recipient may have abandoned the email account so that the mailbox is perpetually full.

So, a "soft" bounce may be the result of the receiving mail server refusing the connection, either because it's in general too busy or because the connecting mail server is considered to be spamming.

These refusals look something like this:

Server XISP.com is not accepting connections
Connection refused by: XISP.com

Sometimes, if your server is being "temporarily" blocked, the message will be categorized as a "soft" bounce, too:

Anti-spam YISP.com has refused your connection as your mail server has been temporarily blacklisted.

Then you've got those little, hard polymer "super balls," available in those vending machines in pizza parlors and arcades—our local discount store has a rack of them at the exit—in the attempt to capture just a few more cents from the parents of small children. You know what I'm talking about—these super balls rebound so hard, and so fast they could put your eye out if you're not careful! This image is a *hard* bounce. In email marketing, it's generally the result of a *permanent problem*, such as when the recipient address just doesn't exist. In that case, you'll see an error like this one:

Requested action not taken: mailbox unavailable
JOHNB@EXAMPLE.COM is not a valid user

Basically, hard bounces tell your mail server to *stop trying to send to this address.*

Many ISPs use "hard" bounces to reject messages they consider to be spam. Spam is a scourge not only because it wastes *your* time to delete it from your inbox, but because it wastes your ISP's network resources. A mail server that is busy processing spam has less capacity to handle email people want to receive.

The usual strategy ISPs and organizations have taken to combat spam is to block suspect messages or senders as soon as possible so as to keep their resources free for legitimate mail. In accordance with the rules of the Internet, they are supposed to inform the sender the reason why the mail was refused.

Here's an example of that kind of message:

Message blocked for abuse. Please contact the administrator of your ISP or sending mail service.

Spam Trigger Words

While the bounce rate, sender reputation, and subscriber engagement are important factors in the deliverability of emails, avoiding spam trigger words still plays a role—especially considering the fact that sender reputation is affected by spam filtering.

Years ago, putting the word "Free" in your subject line would likely have automatically triggered a spam filter. Now, that's not necessarily the case, as long as your sender reputation and subscriber engagement are strong.

Nonetheless, you're still taking a chance at nondelivery if you use spam trigger words in your subject lines (or even in some cases in the body of the email). You've certainly seen these kinds of words and phrases in emails you've received. Here's a small sampling of these kinds of terms:[21]

$$$	Affordable
Price	Profits
Cash	Save $
Discount	Credit
Eliminate debt	Lower interest rate
Increase sales	Click below
Visit our website	No fees
Fast cash	100% satisfied

You can find a larger list online at https://blog.hubspot.com/blog /tabid/6307/bid/30684/The-Ultimate-List-of-Email-SPAM-Trigger -Words.aspx.

Be sure to test delivery with good email tracking software or by using a service that tracks delivery for you such as Constant Contact. In some cases, you may find that even though a larger percentage of your emails are going to the spam folder, it's still worth it in terms of response rates and sales to use the spam trigger word. After all, spammers use these terms for a reason: they work.

Recipient's Whitelist or Address Book

Getting the "From" address used in your emails added to your recipients' address book or personal whitelist is a *crucial* step in getting your emails into the inbox, instead of going into the spam folder. You need to remind people to take the step of adding your "From" address to their address

---

21 "The Ultimate List of Email SPAM Trigger Words," Hubspot, https://blog.hub-spot.com/blog/tabid/6307/bid/30684/The-Ultimate-List-of-Email-SPAM-Trigger -Words.aspx.

book/whitelist. Consider adding a single sentence at the top of *each* of your emails.

Here are three examples of effective reminder statements:

> *To ensure our email is delivered to your inbox, please add the email address messages@ourcompany.com to your Address Book or junk filter settings.*
>
> *To ensure regular delivery of our emails, please add us (youwanthis@mycompany.net) to your Address Book. Thank you!*
>
> *To guarantee delivery of this newsletter, please add ournewsletters@finecompany.com to your email Address Book.*

You may wish to go so far as to explain to the reader *how* to set the junk filter settings in a special section of an email message, or devote an entire emailing to this issue. Review the process for the major email applications and Internet Service Providers, and write up a step-by-step instructional email message.

Some companies offer phone support to any reader who may need a "walk-through." Do what it takes to ensure your messages don't get diverted into the bulk or trash folder—never to be opened or read.

10 Ways to Increase Deliverability

Here are 10 ways to help increase the likelihood your email messages will be delivered by the receiving ISP and avoid future deliverability problems:

1. **Understand content filtering basics:** Ignorance of filtering mechanisms is no excuse for not getting messages delivered. Read any bounce messages received, track which messages had high bounce rates and low open rates, and see if you can reverse-engineer offending content.

2. **Monitor delivery and bounce rates by ISP/domain:** Periodically, or better yet after *every* delivery, run reports by major domain and ISP on your messages. Look for unusual bounce, unsubscribe, spam complaint, and open rates at specific domains.

3. **Monitor spam complaints:** Even the best permission marketers receive spam complaints. Monitor the number of spam complaints for each mailing, and establish a benchmark average. Look for mailings with spam complaint percentages that vary from the norm.

4. **Make only one connection per email message:** When connecting to an email server, send only one message per connection. Some systems still try to shovel as many messages through one connection as possible, which can be likened to throwing five hundred email addresses into the BCC field. Generally speaking, however, using a good email marketing program will circumvent this issue.

5. **Limit the sending rate:** Though the ideal send volume depends on the list's nature, make sure to follow the special provisions of your email-sending application. Send bulk emails not all at once but in several different distributions. Keep in mind you will also need to accept feedback in the form of bounced messages—your outgoing speed shouldn't affect your ability to receive bounces.

6. **Always accept bounces:** Some email systems (especially older ones) have a habit of rejecting bounce messages. These "bounced bounces" arrive at the receiving ISP and can raise red flags. Nothing irks an ISP more than sending a response that a recipient doesn't exist, only to have the notification rejected and the mailings continue.

7. **Validate your HTML content:** One of the dirtiest tricks in a spammer's arsenal is invalid, broken, and malicious HTML

code. If you use HTML in your messages, make sure your code is error-free and follows W3C HTML guidelines.

8. **Avoid scripting:** Security risks due to script vulnerabilities in email browsers have increased over the years (scripting is the use of commands within email messages: keywords, buttons, or menu choices, for example). For greatest delivery success, avoid using any scripts in messages. Instead, drive your readers to your website, where use of dynamic scripting can be fully implemented.

9. **Create a reverse Domain Name System (DNS):** A DNS is what translates alphabetic domain names into numeric IP addresses. Make sure your outgoing mailing IPs have valid RDNS (reverse DNS) entries set up. This ensures when a receiving email server checks who owns the IP trying to connect to it, you'll come up as the result, passing one of the many basic checks ISPs do to deter spammers. What is a reverse DNS? Reverse DNS is the process of using DNS to translate IP addresses to hostnames, and is nothing more than the opposite of forward DNS, which is used to translate hostnames to IP addresses.

   Remember these two things: Internet hostnames are the names which we use to refer to domains on the Internet, such as *www.gothere.com* or *www.freewill.org*. IP addresses are the numbers which Internet routers use to move traffic across the Internet, such as 216.17.138.115 and 216.136.204.117.

   I know this sounds complicated, and your eyes are glazing over, so **contact your web hosting provider for assistance.** This is exactly the right situation to contact technical support; they'll make it seem easy.

10. **Set up an SPF:** A *Sender Policy Framework* (SPF) is an additional step to verify an email sender's identity. The protocol is fairly easy to set up; your network administrator should be able to do it in less than five minutes.

In a nutshell, SPF is just a single line within your DNS entry that identifies which IP addresses are approved to send email for your domain. Taking the single step of checking the existence and/or accuracy of your SPF record can have positive effects on your delivery rates.

The recommended steps are as follows:

a. Determine the IP address or addresses of your email marketing server(s) by contacting the responsible IT representative within your organization or your hosting service.

b. Make sure that those IP addresses of your email marketing server are a published part of your public SPF record. Many senders publish the IP addresses of their own company's internal email server in their SPF record, but neglect to list the IP addresses of their email marketing server in that record. For maximum deliverability, your organization's SPF record should contain both sets of IP addresses.

c. If you haven't already published a full SPF record for your organization, do so as soon as possible. The publishing process is relatively easy, and there are several free tools available to help you do so, listed in the resources section.

SPF adds another layer of authentication to your outgoing email and protects against "phishing" attacks on your brand. You should know that some ISPs, such as AOL, *require* SPF to be implemented to be considered for their whitelists.

Today, nearly all abusive email messages carry fake sender addresses. The victims whose addresses are being abused often suffer from the consequences, because their reputation gets diminished and they have to disclaim liability for the abuse, or waste their time sorting out misdirected bounce messages.

You probably have experienced one kind of abuse or another of your email address yourself in the past, for example when you received an error message saying that a message allegedly sent by you could not be delivered to the recipient, although you never sent a message to that address.

Sender address forgery is a threat to users and companies alike, and it even undermines the *email* medium as a whole because it erodes people's confidence in its reliability.

See if you can determine what may have caused the problem. It could be the subject line, or perhaps you've sent too many messages in too short a time. Remember, a high number of spam complaints may result in an ISP blocking current *and* future messages. Some resources you can use to monitor complaints are located in the resources section.

Avoiding the "Promotions" Folder

It's not just the spam folder we have to be vigilant about. You may have noticed that your incoming emails are automatically segmented into different folders. If you have a Gmail account, for instance, your emails are segmented into "Primary," "Social," and "Promotions." Other email providers divide folders into "Inbox" and "Clutter" or similar terms in addition to the junk folder; 90 percent of commercial email lands in the Promotions folder.[22]

Why should we try to avoid having our emails land in the Promotions folder? Because it is less likely your recipient will read them. Not everyone reads emails that are in the Social and Promotions folder. It takes extra effort to click on those tabs—and it's reasonable to assume that many people *never* check those folders at all (or even know they exist).

This has been shifting lately, however. More people are indeed checking their Promotions folder and reading the content, according to Return Path.

---

22 "Happy Holidays, Marketers: Gmail Teaches Consumers to Shop from the Inbox," Return Path, https://blog.returnpath.com/happy-holidays-marketers-gmail-teaches-consumers-to-shop-from-the-inbox/.

Nonetheless, how do we better our chances of getting our emails read and get them in "Primary" or "Inbox" instead? Thankfully, it's relatively simple.

Here are a few methods to help keep your email out of the Promotions folder and in the Primary folder instead:

- *Personalize.* Address the person by name if you can. Yet personalization is not always possible or feasible. For instance, since email opt-in boxes convert better with fewer fields, you may not include "Name" in your email signup, in which case you will not be able to collect names and personalize your emails. Personalizing your emails does, however, tend to lead to higher rates of engagement by your subscribers, which can help your emails get delivered. Test to see what works for you.

- *Limit images and design.* Use plain text or properly formatted HTML. Fancy graphics or too many images can trigger the Promotions folder. Think about a personal email you would send to a friend. In most cases, you would send a plain email with no design whatsoever. This is not to say that design is out of the question, but in many instances it does make delivery more challenging. *If* you use design in your emails, this is all the more reason to make sure your HTML is flawless. The more design, the more opportunity for HTML tags to be unclosed or otherwise defective. Make sure you use an online HTML validator, which analyzes and cleans up email HTML. You can validate your email's HTML by visiting https://www.htmlemailcheck.com and copying and pasting your code into the box.

- *Limit links.* An abundance of links can land your email in the Promotions folder, especially if the links are to different websites. Then again, if you are linking to a website, it makes sense to provide a link "above the fold," near the top of your email, to increase your conversion rates. Just limit these links as much as is feasible for your own promotion.

Will these guidelines ensure that your emails stay out of the Junk and Promotions folders? No. But taking these steps will significantly increase your chances of getting your email to the inbox and place you far ahead of much of your competition—many of whom do not test deliverability at all. Always remember: "First, get it delivered."

The "Inner Circle" Secret for Increasing Email Open Rates

In email, a click-through rate (CTR) is the percentage of email recipients who click on any hyperlink within the email. So, if you send an email to your list of ten thousand prospects offering them a free white paper, and two hundred click on the hyperlink, your CTR is 2 percent.

Today, the explosion of spam and the widespread use of email filtering software have depressed click-through rates to new lows. So how can you get more clicks from your email marketing?

According to an article in *The Marketing Report*, a survey by Nielsen/NetRatings found that most people regularly open and read a maximum of sixteen permission-based emails. The only way to break into the inner circle is to displace someone, the survey said.

And an article in *DM News* reports, "Marketers will have to enter that emerging inner circle of trusted companies from whom people are willing to keep reading e-mails."

Okay, but how do you break into this inner circle of email senders whose messages your prospects will open and read?

It's not easy, but there are at least six options that seem to work with some level of success:

1. **Free e-zine.** Write and publish a truly valuable e-zine and offer it free to folks who give you their email address. If you publish regularly (at least once a month) and provide content of genuine worth, readers will come to value your publication and establish a relationship with you. You will have entered their "inner email circle," because they will view anything with your name in the "From" line as being from a trusted adviser and worth their time to at least read and open. A great example of such an e-zine is Agora's *Daily Reckoning* (www.dailyreckoning.com).

2. **News and updates**. Similar to an e-zine, some publishers send short news bulletins to their subscribers on a regular basis. *ComputerWorld* sends a daily online update with short items from the magazine. You can purchase a short online ad in these updates, thereby buying your way into the reader's inner email circle. CMP, a trade publisher, emails a monthly update, *Business Technology Advisor (BTA),* to the subscribers of all its publications. For $200 per thousand, you can sponsor *BTA*, having the entire issue devoted to your firm and products. Since CMP subscribers know and look forward to *BTA*, your message gets a higher readership and response than it would if you send it under your own banner.

3. **Service and upgrade notices**. Software users will read and open emails from the software publisher that contain news about upgrades, technical information, or service policies. If your customers regularly need to receive service and product news from you, get in the habit of delivering it via email. Then they will be "trained" to read your emails, so when you send a promotion, it too will get opened and read.

4. **Transaction emails**. A survey from www.quris.com shows that customers do value and read two specific types of emails: (a) transaction confirmations and (b) account status updates.

You can get your promotional message read by embedding it into routine emails that contain transactional or account status information. A good example is Amazon, whose customers open and read the emails amazon.com sends because they might contain news about their order.

5. **Alert services.** Consumer newsletters, especially investment advisories, have pioneered this approach. When you pay for your monthly subscription, the publisher offers you a bonus: additional content, sent periodically via email, to keep you updated on the topic between regular issues. The catch: You have to give the publisher your email address to receive this free online bonus. The publisher quickly builds an e-list of subscribers who eagerly anticipate and read the emails, because they are viewed as valuable information they pay for as part of their subscription. The most successful publishers keep the information content of the emails high, but also liberally promote products and services to these email alert recipients.

6. **Club or membership.** Your prospects will read emails from clubs, associations, online communities of interest, subscription websites, and other organizations of which they are members. Therefore, if you can create a club or have your email distributed by one of these membership organizations, you can enter the prospect's email inner circle.

As a rule of thumb, whenever you can send email to your prospect using one of the above methods, your chances of getting opened and read increase exponentially vs. sending a typical promotional email.

CHAPTER 3.

Anatomy of an Email Message

In this chapter, we're going to review ways to create and optimize each part of an email message. Starting with the "From" line, we'll work our way through the "Subject" line to the headline, lead, body copy, close, signature lines, and postscript. We'll also review the use of bullet points, images, calls-to-action, hyperlinks, and other email copywriting techniques and direct response mechanisms.

Two Main Parts: The Head and the Body

Email messages have two main parts: the header and the body, which is the message itself. The header contains the name and email address of both the sender and recipient, the name and email address of anyone who is being copied, the date of the message, and the subject of the message. The exact content of mail headers can vary depending on the email system that generated the message.

First, let's look at what some online marketers say is a most important part of the header: the "From" line.

The "From" Line

The "From" line details the sender's Internet email address (which is presumed to be the same as the Reply-to address, unless a different one is provided). The "From" line is what your addressee sees right next to the subject line—even before they open the email. Statistics show this one line can have an amazing impact on the receiver:[23]

- 68 percent of Americans say they base their decision to open an email on the "From" name.
- 43 percent of email recipients click the Spam button based on the email "From" name or email address.

If you search online for examples of "From" line mistakes, you'll find any such errors are overshadowed by "Subject" line errors. Yet, if close to 70 percent of Americans use the contents of the "From" line as criteria for opening the message, you've got to make sure your "From" line sounds legitimate and correct.

Your subject line

This is the second most important part of the email header. The subject line is a short description of the topic of the email message. To underscore the importance of a well-written subject line, two more statistics:[24]

- 69 percent of email recipients report email as spam based solely on the subject line.
- 35 percent of email recipients open email based on the subject line alone

---

23 See: "15 Emails Stats that are Shaping the Future," http://www.convinceandconvert .com/convince-convert/15-email-statistics-that-are-shaping-the-future/.

24 See: "19 Eye-Opening Statistics About Sales Email Subject Lines That Affect Open Rates [SlideShare]," https://blog.hubspot.com/sales/subject-line-stats-open-rates -slideshare.

But here's a thought-provoking statistic which begs the question about the importance of your subject line: emails with no subject all together were opened 8 percent more than those with a subject line.[25] In the pursuit of professionalism, I can't recommend you deliberately leave an email subject line empty. Not only do you risk having your message seen as spam, leaving the subject line blank may immediately irritate the reader, who—by your omission—is forced to open the email to see what it's about.[26] In chapter 4, I'll give you proven alternatives that routinely outperform blank subject lines, getting better reception from recipients while boosting click rates.

One way to get someone interested in what you have to say is to personalize subject lines. In fact, in the first quarter of 2015, personalized subject lines provided a lift in open rates of as much as 41.8 percent.[27] Here are a few examples of personalized subject lines:

- Brand new: Wealth and Spirituality for Mike
- "Here's to more abundance for Rosemary in 2014 [VIDEO]"
- "Sharon's 7 energetic allies"

The Headline

Plain-text messages don't have headlines; in effect, the subject line is the headline. But if you're sending HTML marketing messages, you have

---

25 See: "19 Eye-Opening Statistics About Sales Email Subject Lines That Affect Open Rates [SlideShare]," https://blog.hubspot.com/sales/subject-line-stats-open-rates-slideshare.
26 See: "The 9 Worst Mistakes People Make in Email Subject Lines," http://www.businessinsider.com/worst-mistakes-in-email-subject-lines-2015-1.
27 See: "Email Marketing Chart: Personalized subject lines," https://www.marketingsherpa.com/article/chart/personal-subject-lines.

the option of using a headline in large, bold type above the body of the email. Examples:

- Daily Deal
- Stop the Wealth Killers Before It's Too Late
- 15% Off Christmas Items & Calendars
- Pure silk blouses . . . 30% off
- The Ultimate Tax Shelter
- FREE subscription to Copy Mastery
- How to make money working from home
- Gotten a speeding ticket lately? Read this.
- Become a bestselling author in 60 days.

"The direct headline should be used far more often than it is," says copywriter Dean Rieck. "No cleverness. No jokes. No wordplay. The direct headline gets right to the point."[28]

When writing your email headline, make sure it follows the "4 U's" principle. It needs to be *useful* to the reader, give the reader a feeling of *urgency*, convey the idea the main benefit is *unique* and do all of the above in an *ultra-specific* way.

Don't rush the process. Brainstorm dozens of headlines before deciding on the best, most powerful headline. Don't neglect the A/B testing mentioned earlier; it a fantastic method for testing not only subject lines but virtually anything in your marketing materials, including headlines.

The Salutation

How you start an email sets the tone and may shape the recipient's perception of you. It can also determine whether they keep reading.

---

28 See: "9 Proven Headline Formulas That Sell Like Crazy," http://www.copyblogger.com/proven-headline-formulas/.

The salutation is the opening line of your email where you address the recipient directly, usually by name. What salutation you use will depend on the tone of the relationship you have—or want to cultivate—with the receiver.

If you're sending an automated series of messages to a list, your salutation will depend on the kind of information you requested on the sign-up page. (If you've asked only for the visitor's email address, personalizing the message with a first or full name of course isn't possible.) Instead you're left with: "Dear Subscriber" or a one-word greeting like "Hello" or "Hey!" if you're going for a casual, friendly tone.

"Dear" is the one of the most appropriate salutations you can use. "Greetings," "Good Morning/Afternoon," or "Good Day" followed by the name of your recipient (if you know it) are also acceptable email openers. "Hello, [name]" is acceptable and 'Hi [name]' is a less formal option.

The Body Copy

The body is the main part of an email message. It contains the message's text (lead and supporting paragraphs), images, the close, signature lines, and (if applicable) the postscript. For the body of the email, use fonts that are sans serif, the most popular of which include Verdana, Arial, Arial Black, Tahoma, and Trebuchet MS.

How big can an email be? The Internet email standard does not limit the size of an email's body text, but mail servers do have limits on how big a message can be.

Commonly, the maximum message size, including attachments, ranges from 10 to 25 MB. (The minimum size that must be allowed for an email's body and header lines combined is 64 KB.)[29]

---

29 See: "Learn the Difference Between the Email Body and Its Header," https://www
.lifewire.com/what-is-the-difference-between-email-body-and-header-1171115.

With personal emails, which for most of us are text messages, size limitations are simply not a concern; the size of even the longest text email is minimal. The size limitation comes into play when you attach PDF, PowerPoint, or even very large Word files.

When you attempt to send files larger than the limit your email services provider allows, you will get an immediate notice on your screen that the file is too big to send. So you have three choices. One is to send a URL link to a web page where the same content or document is posted. The size limitation from your ESP applies only to attached files, not the size of files reached by hyperlinks included in the body of your email.

The second option is simply to split the attachment into several smaller files, each of which is below the size limit, and email them one at time.

The third option is to use a service such as www.dropbox.com. With Dropbox, you can hold the document on the Dropbox server, and your recipients, provided they get a Dropbox account, can go to the server and pick up the files you want them to have.

Your leading paragraph

People often begin emails with an ice-breaker like, "I hope this finds you well." Unless it's an email sent to someone in your network you know well, this is a weak start. Instead, your opener should say something more about you and the reason you're writing. Here are some real-life examples of email openers:

- Here's your daily roundup of our latest and greatest marketing posts. Enjoy!

- Don't stress if you don't know where to start. We've got you covered with great tools to make getting online easy, no matter how much (or little) experience you have.

- The Rain Dancer Playbook is coming off the market this Friday at 5:00 p.m. Pacific Time. To get the current pricing, you must start your free trial before the deadline.
- Get the brands you love and the savings you want. Add these offers to your Account and see how easy it is to save big.

Experts argue your opening paragraph should be no longer than three or four lines. **To get the focus you need when writing the opening paragraph, answer the following questions:**

- Why are you writing this email?
- What do you want to tell your recipient(s)?
- What do you want them to do as a result of your email?

If you hit a roadblock in writing the initial paragraph, here are a few starters to get you going:[30]

"If you're like me . . ."	"What if . . . ?"	"You are invited . . ."
"I need your help."	You have a free gift waiting . . ."	"You're important to us."
"If you are a _____, then you can _____."	Give a warning. "According to _____, two-thirds of _____ will lose their jobs in the next 12 months."	Ask a question. "Do you make these 5 mistakes when you're shopping for groceries?"
"For the first time, you can . . ."	"This is your last chance."	"I'll get right to the point."

---

30 See: "Message & Media: 48 Copy Starters for Letter and Email Openers," http://www.targetmarketingmag.com/article/48-idea-starters-direct-mail-letter-email-openers/all.

"If you like _____, you'll love _____."	"You have ___ days left to pick up the phone or go online to . . ."	"They didn't think I could _____, but I did. And you can, too. Here's how."
"Our records show it's time to _____ your _____."	"You're in trouble. And so am I. Here's why."	"Are you paying too much?"
Lead with your offer; e.g. "Click here now to get my full investment recommendations on my favorite utility stock."	"Did you know that you can now . . ."	"Because of your loyalty . . ."
Tell a story. ("It's late at night and . . .	"Believe it or not . . ."	"Good news!"

When writing your body copy, a smart rule of thumb is to use subheadings to tell the reader you've started a new topic. Subheadings also enable the reader to pick and choose what topics to read and divide the information into small units, so the reader isn't overwhelmed by too much information. Another way to make your messages more readable is to use bullet points.

Using bullet points

"The essence of a great bullet," wrote *Copyblogger* contributor Robert Bruce, "is brevity and promise."[31]Bullets break up the text into bite-size pieces without writing new topic sentences. Bullets also give you an easy way to list ideas instead of embedding the lists in complex paragraphs. Bullets effectively create structure in white space, making a message easier to read—and easier for recipients to respond to (if necessary).

---

31 See: "8 Quick Tips for Writing Bullet Points People Actually Want to Read," http://www.copyblogger.com/writing-bullet-points/.

Brian Clark, of *Copyblogger* wrote a definitive guide to using bullets in body content. Here are his 5 cardinal rules for bullet points that convey your points clearly: [32]

- Express a clear benefit and promise to the reader.
- Keep your bullet points symmetrical (one line each, two lines each). It's easy on the eyes.
- Work to avoid bullet clutter. Don't present a jumble of subtitles, bullets, and sub-bullets. Just use a simple bullet list.
- Keep your bullet groups thematically related, begin each bullet with the same part of speech, and maintain the same grammatical form.
- Recognize bullets aren't necessarily proper sentences.

---

32 See: "Little Known Ways to Write Fascinating Bullet Points," http://www.copyblogger.com/little-known-ways-to-write-fascinating-bullet-points/.

Here are some additional recommendations for using bullet points in your emails:

- Use bold, italics, or underlines for the first word or two of a bulleted list as a way to emphasize a key term or point.
- Make your bullet points consistent in structure and style. You can structure your bullets as a list of items, lists of questions, sentence fragments, or even complete sentences. But don't mix and match these different types within one set of a bulleted list.

- Avoid very long, multiple-sentence bullet points. Bullet points should be just a line or two. You don't want them to be an entire paragraph, or they lose their benefit.
- Avoid nested or multilevel bullet points: Although nested bullet points can be helpful for communicating complex ideas, they don't display well in emails.

Consistency in punctuation is desirable, including punctuation at the end of your bulleted items. Follow these rules for the use of punctuation in bulleted items:

- If the bullets are full sentence, then end each one with a period.
- If the bullets are questions, then end each one with a question mark.
- If the bullets are phrases or sentence fragments, then do not end with any punctuation.
- Avoid ending bullet points with semicolons (";"). This was once a common practice, but is no longer used much these days.

How to insert bullets into your email

To make a bullet list if your email program or service lets you send messages formatted using HTML, most typically:

- Make sure the message you are composing is set to use formatting.
- Click the Insert bulleted list button in the composition toolbar.
- To add a new bulleted point: hit Enter.
- To end the list, hit Enter twice.
- To make a sublist: hit Enter, and then hit Tab.

In plain text email messages, you'll use a special character to emphasize the beginning of the bullet point. You can use characters like ✓✳✱☞•◦ >>—but you want to keep in mind that the recipient's computer might not display these correctly. When creating bulleted lists, you need to:

- Make bullet points consistent in structure.
- Punctuate bullets consistently.
- Avoid ending bullet points with semicolons.

To make a bulleted list using just plain text in an email:

- Start the list on a paragraph of its own, separated from the paragraph before by an empty line.
- Use "*" (a star character with a whitespace character before and following it) to denote a new point.
- Start each point on a line of its own.

Email images

Pictures have the power to make a lasting impression on your reader. Despite this power, there can be problems with including images in your HTML email messages. The first: recently Google indicated that image blocking affects 43 percent of emails caused by a combination of corporate firewalls, outlook settings, and reading offline on mobiles.[33]

Yet, people like visuals in their emails. In fact, 65 percent of users like emails that are mostly made up of images, while only 35 percent prefer their emails to be text heavy.[34] Fortunately, there are some very simple ways to handle image blocking: adding "alt text" to your images is one of the easiest.

---

33 See: "Email marketing best practice guidelines—40% of viewers probably not seeingimages,"http://www.netimperative.com/2016/07/email-marketing-best-practice-guidelines-40-viewers-probably-not-seeing-images/.
34 See: "The Ultimate List of Marketing Statistics," https://www.hubspot.com/marketing-statistics,

Alt text is the text that is displayed by the email client instead of your image when images are blocked. This way, you tell your reader what the image is, giving them context.

The second way you can combat blocked images is to ask your subscribers to whitelist your emails or add you to their list of safe senders. Send instructions in your welcome email so your subscribers will get your emails from the start and also see all supportive images.

What types of image files should you use? Here's a chart of file types detailing the best application and the pros and cons of each image file type:[35]

Image Type	Works Best With	Pros	Cons
PNG	All Images	Best quality, regardless of content Supports full transparency Great for text Can fix some distortions caused by other file types Doesn't compress when uploaded	Larger file size
JPEG/ JPG	Photos	Small file size	Distorts image to reduce file size Doesn't work well with text Doesn't support transparency Compresses when uploaded
GIF	Logos Simple Graphics Low Resolution Images	Small file size Supports basic transparency Doesn't compress when uploaded	Limited to 256 colors Images can appear grainy if they use web-unsafe colors Not good for photographs

---

35 See: "Prepare Images for Upload," http://knowledgebase.constantcontact.com /articles/KnowledgeBase/5558-prepare-images-for-upload.

While JPGs are often great for smaller images, they don't work as well with images that include text. PNG files support text well and can fix some distortions that are caused by other file types. You should always keep in mind that very large images may cause scrolling and some clients, like Outlook, may crop images that are more than 1,728 pixels in height.

Here's something to remember: emails with three or fewer images and approximately twenty lines of text result in the highest click-through rates.[36]

Hyperlinks

A hyperlink refers to data that the reader can directly follow either by clicking, tapping, or hovering. It points to a whole document or to a specific element within a document. "Hypertext" is text with hyperlinks and the text that is linked from is called "anchor text."

On the target site with the content you want to share, right-click with your mouse on the address bar (URL) in the browser to capture the full address. Now go to the body of the email you are composing. Then right-click to paste the URL into the body of the email. Hit enter. It will turn blue with an underline, meaning it is now a hyperlink. When your recipient clicks on the link, the content you want them to see at that address pops up on their screen in a separate window.

There are guidelines for including hyperlinks in an email:[37]

- A link should be identifiable to the email reader by the color (traditionally, "Hyperlink Blue") and because it is underlined.
- A link should go where it's intended to go. Make sure it does by checking all links prior to sending.

---

36 See: "New Data: How the Amount of Text and Images Impact Email Click-Through Rates," https://blogs.constantcontact.com/email-images/.
37 See: "10 Best Practices for Using Links in Emails," http://blog.marketo.com/2009/12/10-best-practices-for-using-links-in-emails.html.

- A hyperlink should be added to key phrases that identify what the link is going to render.
- Links should be structured throughout your email.

There are *contextual links*, those highly relevant to the content, with the most important and relevant links at the top of the email. By top-loading in this way, these links are likely to increase click-through versus those hidden lower in the message.

In addition to contextual links there are *bonus content* links, placed outside the contextual body content, often in the postscript. You'll want to mark these links with the value of the offer clearly stated.

Let's not forget about *permalinks*: those are links which are always the same and always available in your communications, like "forward to a friend," social network links, and the unsubscribe link. Your permalinks should be located in the same place in each email so email recipients don't have to spend time searching.

Your links allow your reader to save time when reading an email, select which offer or detail they want to understand better, or read more about—all without distracting them with information that may not be useful. Adding links to your emails helps engage your audience and drive visitors to your website.

Calls-to-action

"The only way on earth to influence other people," wrote Dale Carnegie, "is to talk about what they want and show them how to get it."[38] This is the basic idea behind one of the most important components of the call-to-action, or CTA. A call to action not only grabs a subscriber's attention, it encourages him or her to act.

One easy trick for writing a call-to-action that amplifies the value of proceeding is by using the fill-in-the-blank technique. First, think of

---

38 See: "Dale Carnegie's 29 Principles on How to Win Friends and Influence People," https://paulcarl.com/dale-carnegies-29-principles-win-friends-influence-people/.

an upcoming promotion you'll be running through email. Next, trade places with your subscriber and, within the context of this promotion, finish the following sentence: "I want/need to _____." This is a fine start to creating calls-to-action which resonate with your audience. Your calls-to-action in HTML emails should be:

- Visually striking with copy that compels you to click the offer.
- Brief: A couple of words is best, no more than five is ideal.
- Action-oriented: Begin with a verb like "Download" or "Register."
- Located in an easy-to-find spot that follows organically from the flow of the email
- In a contrasting color from the rest of the email, while still fitting in with the overall design.
- Large enough to stand out—but don't detract attention from the main content on the page.
- Easy to understand and clear. State exactly what the visitor will get if they click on the CTA and go to the landing page.

Here are a few real-life examples of email calls-to-action:

Reserve your seat	Book Your Tickets	I'm coming!
Register now	I'll be there!	Count me in!
Find out how	Sign me up	Save me a spot
Download my free e-book now	Learn more	Start your free trial
Make an appointment	Book Your Free Consultation	Find out how
Start today	Start now. Get results.	I'm ready to see a change
Let us know how we did	Give us your feedback	Keep reading

Your Email Close

The close is the last thing the recipient reads, so it's smart to think of it as the "cherry on top": done right, it can do a lot to give you a professional appearance and nurture a relationship.

There are eight popular closings, all ones you've probably used at some point in time: thanks, regards, cheers, best regards, thanks in advance, thank you, best, and kind regards. Out of those eight, those that expressed gratitude were far more likely to receive a response than others. "Thanks in advance" was the most effective closing, receiving a response rate that was almost 14 percent higher than the least effective closing, "best."[39]

If you're stumped as to a close for an email message, here are a few closers to try:[40]

All the best	Goodbye and good luck	Thanks for your help
Sincerely,	Yours Truly	Sincerely yours
Regards	Great job!	Thank you
Be well and keep in touch	Your help is greatly appreciated	Thank you for your quick response
Best wishes	Hope this helps	Very truly yours
Best regards	Cordially	Yours respectfully
Cheers	In anticipation of your valued response	Until next time
Cordially	I thank you for your time	Wishing you continued success
Enjoy the weekend	Looking forward to your reply	With appreciation
Fare thee well	Stay tuned	With many thanks
Warm regards	With appreciation	In appreciation

39 See: "If You Want To Hear Back About A Job, Add This To Your Email," http://www.refinery29.com/how-to-close-an-email.
40 See: "39 Ways to Close Your Emails," https://www.prdaily.com/Main/Articles/39_ways_to_close_your_emails_16167.aspx.

Sig Files

What are the things you should include in your email signature lines, also called sig files? The sig file contains information the reader needs to get in touch with you: your full name, title, company, address, phone number, fax number, email address, and website URL. Here's an example:

Bob Bly
Copywriter / Consultant
31 Cheyenne Dr.
Montville, NJ 07045
Phone 973-263-0562
Fax 973-263-0613
www.bly.com

When preparing your email signature lines, don't overdo it. All you really need is what you see above. Don't include your email address or inspirational quotes. But you can include one or two hyperlinks to valuable content showcasing your expertise—it could be a link to a blog post or white paper of interest, or a link to an online video.

It's popular today to include your picture or company logo in your email signature line and some folks even recommend varying font size and color to create visual interest. But, it's not essential.

Two things you really don't want to do is to include your email address (it's redundant) or inspirational quotes. Many people include links to their social media pages in their signature lines. It's also possible to include a call-to-action ("Get your free guide to Facebook Marketing"), but one thing you don't want to do is to *overstuff* your email signature!

The Postscript

A postscript is an additional remark at the end of a letter or email, after the signature and introduced by "P.S." The postscript is a standard direct mail copywriting tactic; it has the ability to effectively reinforce your core message while—at the same time—a well-written postscript can create urgency. Here are two real-life examples of email marketing postscripts:

> P.S. Order now and you get a free Bonus Gift (retail price: $29)—yours to keep even if you return our "Creativity" course for refund:
>
> www.creativityoutsidethebox.com

> P.S. Order now! Call 1-800-TEACH-12 (1-800-832-2412) to speak to our highly educated, friendly, and engaging Customer Care Team. Knowledgeable about all of The Great Courses, our representatives are standing by to help select the best courses for you!

How should you use the postscript? You can use it as bait, emphasizing the main selling point from your email one more time, but from a different angle. It can be your final plea, where you create an emotional response and provide a sense of urgency. By highlighting a testimonial, a postscript can be a built-in cheerleader.

Here are some simple guidelines to writing postscripts:

- Remind your reader of the deal or special offer.
- Introduce another benefit, one which you never mentioned in the copy.
- Quote the price of your product in a postscript.

- Add urgency with a time limit or reminder about limited supplies.
- Add multiple postscripts (P.S., P.P.S., etc.) to call more attention to the postscript area.
- Instead of P.S., try "NOTE," "By the way," or "One last thing . . ." after the signature.
- Keep the P.S. to two or three lines maximum: it's intended to be an afterthought.

Email Attachments

When attaching files to your emails, make sure you do not attach files that are too big, as free email services have limitations on size of attachments that can be sent. Ten megabytes (10 MBs) is usually allowed, sometimes higher, but you should check first with your provider. Right-click your mouse, while hovering over your file to be sent, and you will see the size of your file, along with other properties. That way you can be sure that your file will get through, or that you need to compress it first.

In some cases, you can right-click on the file as you are attaching it, and also select compress, which packs it up into a smaller package. If you have the Dropbox service, for example, you can put the file into the Dropbox. Then insert a link to the Dropbox in the body of your email. Another option is to use a file compression program such as WinZip to make the file small enough to send via email.

Closing Thoughts

There's no question emails are fast and easy to use. And email marketing is a vibrant and powerful way to connect with people. Still, they need to be constructed and used thoughtfully. After all, your email messages are, whether invited or not, an intrusion into the life of your recipients. It's important to treat them with care. Protect their privacy, protect their sensibilities and follow the Golden Rule: "write to your reader as you would wish to be written to."

CHAPTER 4.

Optimizing the All-Important "From" Lines and Subject Lines

In chapter 3, we looked at all the various parts that go into an email message. In this chapter, we focus on and explore in greater depth the two most important parts of your email: the "From" line and subject lines. Campaign Monitor reports that 68 percent of Americans base their decision to open an email on the sender name.

When readers open their email accounts, the first thing they view are all the emails that have arrived since the last time they checked it. They may be busy, so they will scan, select, and delete emails they do not want to waste time on, and read those they do.

It is important, therefore, that you capture readers' interest by first using your name or another familiar send (e.g., your company, your e-newsletter) in the "From" line and, that your subject line shows a compelling reason for why you sent your email to these readers and why they should open and read it. Those are the first two things readers see as they scroll down the inbox list, and if they are not interested, based on either the "From" name or subject line statement, they will delete the email.

"From" Line Fundamentals

Here are some examples of a clean, professional approach to creating a "From" line, where the sender's full name is followed by a domain name–driven email address:

- Robert Bly <rwbly@bly.com>
- Kim Stacey <kim@thefuneralcopywriter.com>
- H. Clay Atchison III <clay@mcadamsfloral.net>
- William Savino (bill@socialfuneralfunding.com)
- Robert Varich <rvarich@allstate.com>
- Peter Bajorek <peter@bajoreklaw.com>
- Paul Jarvis <paul@pjrvs.com>

In each case, the sender owned a domain name; lending credibility to the "From" line. Compare those to the additional real-life examples:

- Roger Dexter/VP <cca4dmcopy@gmail.com>
- Nick Usborne <nickusborne@gmail.com>
- Shangrila Hospice <shangrila.hospice@gmail.com>
- <judy.marshall258@aol.com>
- Savings.com <customercare@email2.savings.com>

It's fairly obvious which addresses would leave the best impression: those linked to a privately-owned domain. If you don't have your own domain name, you'll certainly want to avoid using nicknames and numbers in the email address shown in the "From" line. Some sales trainers say that an email from America Online or Gmail means you do not have a serious prospect, but with an email from a company domain name, you do.

Should you use both your first and last name in your "From" line? Some people say yes, because (especially if the reader knows you) it instantly gives them assurance the message is worth an "open."

And when should you use the business name? That depends on the subject, the body, and the purpose of your message. The goal in writing your "From" line is to have readers recognize you as a professional, let them recognize you as an individual (not a business entity), let them feel safe and treat you seriously.

Here are my some guidelines for the "From" line:

- If you're sending the email to an existing customer or someone else familiar with your company, use the company name in the "From" line.
- If the recipient knows you, use your first and last name.
- If the recipient knows both you and the company, use both in the "From" line.
- If the recipient knows you but not your company, consider using just your name.
- If the recipient knows neither you nor your company, use only your name but also the company or department name if it sounds important or official in some way; for example, Consumer Affairs Division.

How to Maximize Your "From" Line in Emails

There are three kinds of "From" lines you can use in business email: the business name, the business name, but with a direct contact name in front, and the name of a person who is recognized as the business and brand. Three fictitious examples are:

- ABC Industrial Holdings <info@ABCIndustrial.com>
- Carol Layland, Public Relations Manager, ABC Industrial Holdings <clayland@ABCIndustrial.com>
- Benjamin Tonyson <bst@tonyson.com>

The first "From" name represents the company when it is sending out emails to customers, or when the company is a well-known brand name the reader is familiar with. The second "From" name, includes a person and company title, along with the company name, giving the emails a more personal tone, or if the recipient knows the sender by name and title. As a public relations manager, this person gives the latest news about events, upcoming product launches, and newly hired people taking over key positions in the company. Readers and news journalists, who want to know more, can contact her directly at her email address to get more information about questions they have.

The first two business emails share information on multiple levels, such as marketing, sales, customer relationship management (CRM), current news, and transactional emails (e.g., order status). Who sends that email, the company as the brand, or the public relations contact, decides the type of content given in the email. The "From" line never changes, and the content is always presented in the same style, but includes new events of interest as they occur.

The third fictitious "From" example is the sender's name, used in both personal and business emails, and is very well-known to the recipient. Benjamin Tonyson runs his own business at Tonyson.com, building websites for clients. His emails will be less formal than those from the brand enterprise, ABC Industrial Holdings. Readers already know him as offering website design consultation and implementation. He may send out an email once or twice a week, giving information about web design that readers find interesting. Or, he can be an individual sending direct emails to other individuals, and to businesses.

On occasion, he will also send out discount offers to readers who may be interested in having him build their websites, while the price is lower. A strategic move for Benjamin would be to add the title of website designer or consultant after his name, so readers scanning their email lists would remember at once who he is. If he is already well-known, then he may not need that extension added on.

Another way to optimize the "From" line, is to add a contact phone number after the name. There may be times when a reader or client wants to reach you directly, and remembers that if he looks for your email, your phone number is right there by your name. It is convenient for readers and clients to contact you at a moment's notice, because the phone number is attached to your email name in the "From" line and easy to find. This is particularly important when you and a client are conversing back and forth on a project, and the client wants to pick up the phone and call, instead of using email.

Once the "From" line name is decided on, the name chosen should remain the same whenever any emails are sent, such as between you and clients during a project, or in sending out to your readership list. There are occasions when you can adjust it, however.

My name, Robert Bly, or Bob Bly, along with my email address, is on all my "From" lines for my emails, whether I am sending to my readership list, my clients, or my external vendors. I also have a readership list for my Direct Response Letter, which I put out once a week, and the letter's name is added to my name on the "From" line, differentiating this email from all others.

As a business marketing writer, rather than just selling products to my readers, I also like to engage with readers through my Direct Response Letter e-newsletter, by presenting topics of interest, relevant to today's news. The letter is conversational and readers get to know me better as a person, particularly when I give opinions about various topics. An example of my Direct Response Letter e-newsletter is shown below. The email address tag after my name remains the same in all my emails, and where everyone can contact me, such as clients, vendors, subscribers, and those who have comments or questions.

Subject: Writers: avoid boredom and burnout forever

From: Bob Bly's Direct Response Letter <rwbly@bly.com>

To: (recipient's email address)

You are getting this email because you subscribed to it on www.bly.com or because you are one of Bob's clients, prospects, seminar attendees, or book buyers.

You may unsubscribe if you no longer wish to receive our emails.

Dear Direct Response Letter Subscriber:

My primary driver for becoming a freelance writer was to avoid boredom— a challenge for me because I am easily bored, most 9 to 5 jobs put me into a coma, and writing is one of the few things I can do to earn a living that doesn't.

In fact, just like my writing hero Isaac Asimov, I love to write.

But today I think there is a danger of more writers getting bored with their work . . . and that danger is niching.

Now, specializing in a writing niche makes good business sense, because specialists are more in demand than generalists.

The problem is that if all you do is write in your specialty, and your niche is very narrow, you may be in great demand and make a lot of money . . . but you might also get bored and burned out by writing essentially the same thing over and over again.

One writer I read, TB, has been, so far as I can tell, writing about nothing but the silver market for decades.

As a result of this laser-like focus in a narrow niche, he is considered one of the top experts in silver.

But when I read his newsletter, I can't help but feel he is repeating the same few articles over and over again.

And I can't imagine that he isn't a little sick and tired of writing about the same narrow subject every day of his life.

I would not want to be TB or have his career, as good as he is.

My writing hero, Isaac Asimov, had multiple niches: humor, history, words, Shakespeare, the Bible, science, science fiction, detective stories, and a few others.

He once stated in an article that he was never, ever bored. The reason? He had multiple projects going in multiple niches simultaneously.

Asimov would start the day working on project A and keep going as long as he stayed interested and enthusiastic.

When his attention began to wane on project A, he would put it aside and turn to project B—and instantly be re-energized and revived.

I do likewise, and as a result, I am virtually never bored with my work as a writer.

In fact, I am usually having so much fun that I agree with what Noel Coward said: "Work is more fun than work."

Also, some writers I know handle only one big project at a time.

If they get bored or run out of steam on project A, there is no project B to turn to—and so they quit for the day.

Like Asimov, I always have multiple projects going, and they vary in size: big, medium, and small—ranging from Google pay-per-click ads and landing pages, to white papers and video sales letters, to courses and books.

If I put in a hard, long morning on a big project, and feel my energy running low, I turn to a smaller, easier piece of writing to change up the pace and get my steam back.

I am not saying the method used by me and Asimov is the best approach to freelance writing for every writer, or even for you.

It was just the best for him, and it is for me.

You do what works for you.

Sincerely,
Bob Bly

P.S. For simple productivity-boosting secrets that can quickly and easily help you become a $100 to $400 an hour writer, watch this short video and check out my e-book "Super Productivity for Writers":

www.superproductivity4writers.com

The "From" line in this email shows that this is from me, but as my Direct Response Letter, instead of other emails that use only my name and email address. When readers see this in their email line-up in their account, they know they are receiving a different email that is more personal, sometimes comic, hopefully entertaining, and thought-provoking.

How to Change or Adjust Your Name for the "From" Line

With most email providers, to change your "From" line, it will be a simple procedure of going into the settings function, found on the top function bar of your email account. There, you can view how your current settings presents your name and email address. If you wish to create different content emails, then you can add/create a second email address in that same account, using your name with an extension on it, denoting that this is where different content is sent from. Remember that readers receiving emails from one name and email address, must easily recognize the second email "From" name as being from you too.

What Works Best in Subject Lines?

The goal of the subject line is that once readers have recognized that you sent them an email, they will look at what your email is about. That information is put on the subject line, the second most important opportunity for you to get your readers to open the email. The reality is that this part of your email may be the hardest part of crafting an excellent email, as opposed to the content body. While there is no guarantee of getting a high percent open rate on your email, you will want to create the very best subject line possible to entice readers to open it.

When email marketers talk about open rates, it is not just calculating when readers open the email. Readers must also engage in some manner within the content body, by clicking on links and images, according to Steven MacDonald at SuperOffice.com. In order to calculate open rates against the total amount of emails sent, those that bounced (failed to deliver to the inbox), are first removed from the tally of total emails, and then calculated by percentage. If your rate of opened emails is 25 percent or higher, then you are doing well. If less, determine first if the campaign is delivering results, and if so, then you are not underperforming, says MacDonald. It also depends on the industry your emails fall into (i.e., insurance, medical, manufacturing, and so on).

Now that you know more about open rates, here are some helpful tips to get yours opened more.

- *Keep your subject sentence at fifty words or under.*

Use enough words that get the message across, but keep it brief. That is just long enough for the reader's quick scanning eye to see the message, stop, and open the email. One point to consider is what open rates you have when emails are opened on mobile phones. As there are less words visible on the screen, you can test best ways to create a subject line that has engaging words right in the beginning of the line, that readers can see on the mobile screen. In fact, there is no one current size that fits for every screen, per CampaignMonitor.com in 2015, who also said that 53 percent of all emails were opened on mobile devices that same year. Best practice: be concise and keep it short and direct.

- *Use words that arouse curiosity.*

Leave no doubt about what the reader is going to find in the email content. If you are having a hard time coming up with a good subject line, then write the content body of the email first, which will help you find the right words to convey the message. Here are some sample subject line topics that are short and to the point.

Subject: How to create legendary promotions
Subject: How to pick and work with only the best clients
Subject: Start your own business at age 50+

Each of these titles has something of interest to readers from every level of their career, whether in a business, or working as a freelancer. The first subject title attracts marketers and copywriters, who are always looking for better tips on creating the best promotion.

The second subject title addresses how we all want to work with great clients and would love to know more about how to find and recognize whether potential clients will be a good fit for us. Such tips can also help with deciding whether potential joint ventures with other people will work or not before getting too far along in the partnership.

The last subject title recognizes that there is an older generation of people, the baby boomers, who understand that their upcoming retirement is not going to be what their parents had to live on comfortably in their retirement. So, looking at how to build a new business to help supplement retirement funds is important to many mature people in that category. Astute younger people, who understand the concept of having multiple streams of income rather than just one, will also jump on this information. The information for all three subject lines are short, concise, and tell you everything you need to know about what is in the email.

* *Use a call to action (CTA) subject line.*
  In this case, you can use a time frame for readers to quickly grab the information before an end date, or lose out. The opportunity is lost unless they act now. Give the subject line message a sense of urgency, such as the following fictitious samples:

Subject: Sign up now before our doors close forever!
Subject: Our 50% discounts end tonight at midnight! Shop now!

Subject: Only 3 more copies of my book are available! Hurry, before they are gone!

If you decide that there are people still interested in signing up, or making a purchase, then send out a notice saying you are extending the deadline just a little longer.

Subject: Deadline extended! Ends 9 a.m. (Central) tomorrow, so hurry to get yours!!

Another pointer about time-based CTAs is that you should give a reasonable amount of time for readers to act. Sending out a one-time email only four hours before the deadline occurs, can be an irritant because some readers may need to wait until payday to get money back in their banking accounts to pay for your product. Instead, send two earlier non-urgent emails before the deadline, letting them know when the deadline is so they can prepare to buy. Then send out the final urgent message that time is short and they need to act now.

- *Use a question in the subject line from time to time—shake things up.*
  Invite readers to think about the question you posed, and they will want to open the email to find out more, or find out what the answer is. For example, here is one question recently asked in the Direct Response Letter subject line.

Subject: Should you ever give up?

In fact, this can be a loaded question that many people want to know the answer to, and it can cover just about any aspect of our lives. It can be in business, marriage, or taking the right classes in college to achieve a certain outcome. The question is thought-provoking and there may be no true answer, except that which we find individually within ourselves, based on our own set of life circumstances. Most likely, you will get many comments back from readers, with some who say that persistence is key to success, or others who say they just finally burned out and went on to something else. For them, the dream cost far too much in time, energy, and money.

The point is that the question gets readers to open the email and read about the different ways one can interpret or answer this question. Another excellent question that generated many comments was the following:

Subject: Should you always charge the most you can get?

This is another engaging loaded question because many people feel they are not successful unless they charge high prices, even if they do not have the experience to back them up. This can also be applied to selling products, medical devices, new drugs that propose to cure or relieve medical symptoms of one or more illnesses, or a new way to work more efficiently using a cloud service. Consequently, you are hitting readers on an emotional or controversial level.

You are engaging your readers to think about your subject message and how it might relate to them in their own businesses, their clients, and their customers. Or, they may have questions to ask you, which might lead to another subject of interest for the readers in the next email.

The important "From" and subject lines of your emails have been presented to show how to best create the most attractive, engaging emails that will get readers to open your emails. But there is another side to how these two most important points of your emails are created. One is the ability to track emails, based on the "From" line, which as shown from my lists, offers two different types of content.

The second pointer is the ability to track and analyze how subject lines are received, such as how many emails were opened, based on the subject matter. From there, you also track how many readers went a step further and clicked on the CTAs. Numerical analysis of click-through rates is a very important statistic you need to know, that helps you with deciding how to strategically build future emails. The final point would be how many sales you made, from those emails offering products and services. For non-selling emails, you can analyze how many readers made comments about the email content sent out, also of use to your marketing strategy. This leads to the next section on how to test subject lines for best results.

More Ways to Write Stronger Subject Lines

"The first thing that your email recipient sees," wrote Kabir Sehgal, "is your name and subject line, so it's critical that the subject clearly states the purpose of the email, and specifically, what you want them to do with your note."[41] His active duty service taught him how to structure emails to maximize a mission's chances for success. Kabir advocates the use of keywords that characterize the nature of the email in the subject. Some of these keywords include:[42]

- ACTION—Compulsory for the recipient to take some action
- SIGN—Requires the signature of the recipient
- INFO—For informational purposes only, and there is no response or action required
- DECISION—Requires a decision by the recipient
- REQUEST—Seeks permission or approval by the recipient.

---

41 See: "How to Write an Email with Military Precision," https://hbr.org/2016/11/how
    -to-write-email-with-military-precision.
42 See: "How to Write an Email with Military Precision," https://hbr.org/2016/11
    /how-to-write-email-with-military-precision.

Here's something you may have noticed about all of these examples: the subject lines range in length from 17 characters/spaces to 55 characters—which leads to the issue of subject line length.

The ideal length of your subject line largely depends on what devices and email clients your messages are read on. And today 54 percent of email is opened on a mobile device.[43] This means, when writing subject lines, you need to keep display line length in mind. Here are the facts:[44]

Email Client	Maximum Subject Line Length
Outlook 2010 preview	54 characters
Outlook 2010 compact	73 characters
Outlook.com	60 characters
Gmail	70 characters
Thunderbird	66 characters
Yahoo! Mail	46 characters
Android (480x320 px): portrait orientation	27 characters
Android (480x320 px): landscape orientation	46 characters
Android (800x480 px): portrait orientation	30 characters
Android (800x480 px): landscape orientation	62 characters
iPhone: portrait orientation	41 characters
iPhone: landscape orientation	64 characters
Windows Phone: portrait orientation	42 characters
Windows Phone: landscape orientation	61 characters

43 See: "Mobile Email Usage Statistics," http://www.emailmonday.com/mobile-email -usage-statistics.
44 See: "How to Determine the Best Length for Your Email Subject Lines," https:// www.campaignmonitor.com/blog/email-marketing/2015/12/best-email-subject -line-length/.

What's the recipe for a good subject line? It needs to be direct, self-explanatory, and engaging, like these:

- 5 steps to Internet marketing success
- Marketing with postcards
- Get paid to talk
- Blog topics for your review

Many marketers do A/B split tests by sending the same email, one with subject line A and one with B, each to half of the list. In subject line split tests, I have seen the winner generate as much as 25 percent greater click-through rates than the loser.

But the subject line also needs to fit the line length accepted by the devices most often used by your target audience. If they are among the 54 percent using mobile devices, you'll need to keep subject line length in mind.

On a typical desktop computer, laptop or tablet, the inbox will display approximately sixty characters of an email's subject line. Pinpoint, a major email service provider, has found that subject lines of forty-five characters or less get higher open and click-through rates than longer subject lines as a rule.[45]

How to A/B Split Test Subject Lines for Maximum Results

As mentioned earlier, subject lines can be the hardest part of writing an email. You always want to create the most effective grab line that gets readers attention, and prompts them to open the email. From there, the content body does the rest of the work.

---

45 See: "The Ideal Email Subject Line Length," https://www.pinpointe.com/blog/what-is-an-ideal-email-subject-line-length.

Both the "From" line, but more importantly, the subject line, are part of what attracts readers to open emails. Once they see in the "From" line that the email is from you, then the subject line is what completes their interest in wanting to know more about what you are offering, or what you say about a certain subject.

Major software packages, such as 1shoppingcart.com and Infusionsoft .com, have built-in ad trackers for A/B split testing. Additionally, if working with a commercial bulk email provider, such as MailChimp, most will have capabilities for helping you track A/B testing campaigns that can be set up in your account dashboard. This is more effective than having to set up your own list manually to put into the different A/B or C groups, if doing more than two.

Subjects lines also give a way for you to test and analyze what is working best with your group of readers. Do they always open your emails when you ask a question in the subject line? Or you may want to know if your group is interested in building a business after the age of 50+. You can find out these answers in your email dashboard, which presents the number of click-throughs on opening the email first, and then seeing how many readers went a step further and clicked on links, such as CTAs, within the email.

You can also test subject lines by changing them up, saying the same thing but in a different construction of the sentence. It is always important to know first what you want to achieve when you conduct this research.

For example, you may want to test one subject line with using a number in it instead of just text. When offering "10 ways to design better emails" is used, as opposed to "Ten ways to design better emails," and you get a high rate of return (ROR) on the number version, then you know numbers work well as an incentive. It is all in how you use a number in the subject line. Additionally, you may want to know if asking a question is better than making it a statement instead.

You can also test to see how readers respond to negative versus positive subject line statements, such as "Read this now, or lose your Social

Security benefits tomorrow!" Now that would scare you into reading it at once, especially if you are on the verge of applying for your benefits. The key point about negative subject lines, is that they must be believable, not hyped up beyond belief, or readers will catch on quickly.

How do you find out these numbers? You can do what is known as A/B testing of your subject lines to see which prompt larger open rates. The best way to understand the numbers that come in from such testing is to create a spread sheet, putting each subject line to be used, inserted in the left column. Then fill out the columns to the right with the variable information you want answers to, connected to the subject line test. For the following sample of a mock A/B test, the table shows a subject line sent out recently, which was first a statement, and then recreated as a question. The key variable here is the open rate.

Table keys: Inbox = successful send to inbox; Open = reader opened email; CT = click-throughs on links, CTAs; TOD = time of day; BUY = percentage of click responders who purchased product.

Subject Line	Inbox	Open	CT	TOD	BUY
Earn top dollar writing landing pages. (A)	100%	75%	49%	7:30 am	12%
Do you want to earn top dollar writing landing pages? (B)	100%	55%	38%	7:30 am	5%

In this sample mock A/B test re-creation, these two emails were sent out to two thousand East coast subscribers early in the morning on a Monday at 6 a.m. Eastern U.S. time. One thousand subscribers received the A version (control), while the other thousand received the B version. Both sets received 100 percent success in reaching subscribers' inboxes. A time limit of six hours was used as the cutoff point for collecting data on each version. Reporting data was shown in percentages.

For version A, open rates were at 75 percent, while version B had 55 percent. Click-throughs on links were: version A at 49 percent, and version B at 38 percent. Time of day was put through Microsoft Excel's pivot table tool, showing that the highest average time for email opens was at 7:30 a.m., Eastern, leading to an assumption that most emails were opened before going to work. Finally, the A version showed that 12 percent of those who clicked through to the landing page, made a purchase. The B version showed 5 percent of those who clicked through to the landing page, also made a purchase.

You can also use a subject line tester, of which there are several of note. The Touchstone Subject Line tool at www.touchstonetests.io/#all -signup allows you to sign up for a free trial, and you can see how their proprietary algorithm works to give you results on your subject line submission. When doing a live A/B split test, they use 10 percent of your database, which must be uploaded first, and the results can figure out lost revenue and conversion. You can set up the test to complete within hours or over a period of days.

The Adestra Email Subject Line Keyword Checker has you input single key words in the test box, and then you select the target category to see how well it does. You can find the tool at http://subject-line-checker .adestra.com/.

SubjectLine.com also has a subject tester, which allows you to try one out for free, before having to sign up to use it further. Any of these subject line testers can be useful in helping you develop a better subject line, although they are not absolute.

The best way is to use your account with the bulk email provider of choice in helping you with A/B testing, particularly when testing subject lines. Most providers now have analytic capabilities for testing with each part of your email to see which works best. The most important point is to make sure your email does not end up in the spam box.

When testing your subject lines, be sure to note any variables, such as a modified "From" line, time of day when people might (or might not) be more active in checking emails, or even what day of the week worked better than others. Other variables include who you are sending the email to, such as a segmented group of readers, between the age of 25 and 45, depending on your readership focus. Even which month you are testing in is a variable, because of what might be happening during that month for most people, such as December and Christmas, or Hanukkah. People are either buying more, depending on the economy, or they have less time to view emails. These are all factors (or variables) to take into consideration when analyzing your research data.

Other Things to Consider About Subject Lines in Emails

With the advent of mobile phone emails, consider the length of your subject line and how it comes across on the mobile phone screen. Test different lengths of subject lines, and see which gets opened more often on mobile phones, as well as in browser accounts. You can also test subject line opens across different devices.

What you might also want to know is if the length of the subject line, when longer on a mobile phone screen and partially hidden, affects your open rates or not. About thirty characters is a reasonable length to fully view the subject line on the mobile phone screen in its entirety. So, if your subject line is typically longer than that, and you see that mobile phone users do not open emails as much as those on laptop or desktop browsers, then you may want to reduce the characters in the subject line, or choose more impactful words to show at the beginning of the line. Then test again to see if more mobile phone users begin opening your emails after that change. Remember to keep it short and concise.

Be constantly aware of your click-through rates and analyze them constantly, first with opening your emails based on the subject line, and then click-throughs on links within the content, to know how well your emails are working. You will gain a wealth of information about how your emails are coming across to readers and, when there are problems, you will be able to quickly resolve the issue, based on your ongoing analyses.

CHAPTER 5.

Rules for Writing Clear, Compelling Emails

Effectively communicating with other people, whether it be in business or in your personal life, will require getting your message across by providing all the details needed for the reader to clearly understand and think through the topic. Based on the information provided, a decision is made, and action taken, if needed. Writing business communications, such as emails, requires a clear, but not dry, approach to addressing the reader, then laying out the topic in a concise method of using the least amount of words to effectively convey the message.

Concise and brief are not the same thing. Brief means simply that something is short. Concise means that it conveys all necessary information but does so in the fewest words possible. People often get this confused, and in the belief that brevity is supreme, omit important information from their writing. The result is incomplete coverage of the topic with lack of communication and clarity.

Emails are the most vital tool for businesses to use today. A recent report from *ClickZ* (6/14/17) notes that emails continue to have the highest ROI of any digital marketing channel. Staying in touch with customers, vendors, and employees is important in focusing on excellent communication daily.

When there is a problem, it must be solved quickly and efficiently, particularly when it applies to system or logistic operations, or customer concerns. Consequently, emails must be written clearly when dealing with issues and solutions and have a pleasant tone of voice, no matter what type of email it is. Even a refusal must still be pleasantly constructed, keeping the customer or an employee accepting of the outcome. Constructing any email should incorporate the following points.

Check Spelling and Grammar

While you can be conversational and pleasant, business communications must keep an upper level of professional decorum. Business communications, such as a hard copy letter or an email, should not overuse slang words or terms. And I advise you to avoid profanity in business writing.

Spelling and grammar must also be correct and convey the message exactly as proposed from the company to the customer, vendor, or employee. Always remember while composing any letter that there is a human at the other end, much like you, if you were the one to receive the email. You must check the copy for details that could be construed the wrong way, possibly landing you in trouble with your boss or with the legal department.

In the United States, having a large multicultural society means thinking through every communication before sending it out and understanding who the reader is. The reader must be foremost in the mind of the writer while composing the communication. Never discuss issues of race, politics, or religion, unless you are responding to such a situation that has occurred between an employee and a customer, that could be detrimental to the company. Apply finesse and make sure the legal team has oversight on the situation and with every communication.

Your communications must always present you or your company in the best light possible. How you create your messages must reinforce your personal or company brand. Misspelled words can rankle the reader because it upsets the flow of reading when a word is not spelled correctly, rather like having a sudden hiccup while drinking a glass of water.

An astute reader comes across a misspelled word and stops to double-check what is being read, just to be sure that he saw what he saw. This causes a break in the reading flow and is irritating. It also reflects badly on you or the brand, leaving a less professional impression of who the reader is dealing with.

A spelling (or grammar) mistake makes the writer look lazy and unprofessional. In the reader's mind, he or she might decide that it is a waste of time to read further, because the writer did not take the time to proof the letter well enough, showing the writer's lack of respect for the reader. If you, as the writer, did not care enough to check spelling and grammar, then why should the reader care about your message?

Even if you are writing less formal emails to friends and family members, this is not the time to get sloppy about grammar or spelling. Take advantage of automated spell check in your word processor or your email program system. It is there for a good reason. But that is only the first step of editing. Grammar, the composition of words in a sentence, along with punctuation, are also essential to delivering the message correctly and effectively. While spell check helps, there are times when a correctly spelled word is used but it is not the right one to convey the message, like "to" versus "too." Do not just rely on spell check to get you through.

Tip: Think of writing to your friends and family members as a time to also practice your grammar, and make a conscious effort to go back and correct misspelled words.

When you have written your letter or your email, go back over it and decide if you have said everything the way it should be said, along with offering all the information needed to help your readers understand the message.

Applying the use of good grammar is also important because where you put words or punctuation in a sentence can change what the sentence means. For example, look at the following simple sentences:

Tonight, we will have Janice, Thomas, and Sally for dinner.

Potentially, this looks like we are getting ready to commit cannibalistic murder. Bad news. The better way to say this is:

Tonight, we will have Janice, Thomas, and Sally over for dinner.

Now, we know there are people coming over to eat dinner with us—a much better outcome. As you have seen, one missing word changes the whole statement completely. One will bring the police to your doorstep; the other version shows there will be pleasant company coming over for dinner. What you said or wrote can mean two different things. Therefore, how you construct your email or letter must say exactly what you mean, with no chance for it to be misinterpreted in any other way. With technical writing, for example, accuracy is paramount in building product educational pieces, instructions, and reports, especially when it comes to safety issues, exact measurements, or procedures on repairing a computer.

How to Plan Your Email: the 5 Ws

Journalistic news composition is based on the five Ws of the inverted pyramid: who, what, where, when, and why. Add on "how" and you have the complete framework of delivering news effectively in compiling all the necessary information people want to know about. What is left is deciding which word is necessary to lead the news with.

"Inverted pyramid" means the most important information is at the top, called the lead. Everything below the lead supports the lead in regression of importance. This becomes the first W (what) in building your communication.

What is the reason for the email?

Using an upcoming customer service email sample, there is a problem that a customer has with a company's product, so a customer service associate finds out how to solve the problem first for the customer, and then writes back to the customer with the solution to the problem. Almost all responses of this nature are done through email in business today, unless a customer does not have email. It is quick, efficient, and can be responded to easily by the customer.

The subject box shows what the email will be about: "Your request for product replacement." The first paragraph gives recognition to the issue (a complaint) for why the email is written. The rest of the email offers an answer or solution to the request. It shows how the problem is being solved and when it will be solved. All the information needed is laid out completely, and ends with the writer's signature and contact information.

Who will receive the email?

The one who receives the email is the customer who made a complaint about the product bought at a store or online. Included in this sample communication is a carbon copy (CC) to the department manager overseeing the problem, so that a line of communication includes more than just one person at the company to handle the situation.

(The term "carbon copy" originated back in the day when letters were written on typewriters and photocopiers were not widely available. Behind the sheet of paper you typed on, you placed a sheet of carbon paper, and behind that, another sheet of blank paper, called the "second sheet." The impact of the keys transferred the carbon black to the second sheet, giving you a copy.)

Why was it necessary to send the email?

There was an initial complaint made by an unhappy customer, and a solution had to be devised so that the customer could be compensated for her troubles and aggravation. The company, in the form of customer service, is writing her back by email to tell her what the company will do for her.

In this case, what, who, and why, were the main reasons for writing the email to the customer. We look at the other Ws which should be included within the email, as part of the solution for the customer.

When will the replacement be sent?

The email states when the new product replacement will be sent out (within 24 hours), including instructions on how to send back the damaged product, free of charge. The instructions for sending it back will be included in the new product box.

Where will the product be sent to?

The email should clearly state that the product will be delivered directly to the customer's home or to the customer's place of business. It should also say whether the customer must be present to receive and sign for the package. The customer should also be informed exactly how the package will arrive: by registered mail, United Parcel Service (UPS), or FedEx. If coming from Amazon, the company also has its own delivery service besides using the regular services listed.

Here is the final sample composition of a customer service response, using false names.

Subject: Your request for product replacement

From: ABC BoundCo (ABCinfo@ABConline.com)

To: (recipient's email address)

CC: Jane Doe (jdoe@ABConline.com)

Date: Tuesday, April 5, 2015 9:35 AM

Dear Ms. Betty Johnson,

I received your complaint about the defective product recently sent to you, and offer our apologies that this happened to one of our loyal customers.

I reviewed the situation and will be sending a new replacement product to you at once. The package is set to leave our warehouse by special courier in one day.

Once the tracking number is generated, I will send that on to you so you know where your package is. We will deliver this to your home address on record, as per your latest request. You just need to be present to sign for the package.

I have also included shipping instructions on how to send back the defective product in the same box that your new replacement product will arrive in. Return shipping is free of charge, and all you need to do is call us to come and get the package when you are ready.

I hope this will help you with the issue that occurred and if you have any further problems, please feel free to contact me directly at my phone number listed below. I will be happy to help you further if you need it.

Thank you very much for your patience, and for letting me know there was a problem with the product we sent you originally. I do apologize again for the inconvenience you experienced.

Let me know how the new replacement works for you, and whether you have any other questions.

Sincerely,

Justina Smith
Customer Service Specialist
ABC BoundCo
123-456-7890
jsmith@ABConline.com

In the above customer service email, the "How" of solving this issue runs throughout the solution provided, along with Why, When, and Where. This simple email is constructed with the customer in mind, at every step of the way. How the company plans to restore the customer's faith in the company is shown through the willingness to send a new replacement of the product, free of charge, including how to send back the original faulty product, also free of charge. The only thing left for her to do is sign to receive the package, and then call the company to come get the boxed faulty product once she is ready.

Clarity and detail, as shown in the earlier email, also apply in many other types of business communications. The exact same earlier sample letter can also be sent by standard snail (with a stamp) mail letter sent by the president of a business, responding back to the same unhappy customer if she did not have email.

Writing the Effective Complaint Email

There are times when you will want to write a letter to a specific person at a business and then send it through either the email system or by snail mail. One such occasion would be to officially log a complaint about a product or service, and you have not received any useful help from multiple contacts with the company's customer service. You would send this letter by registered or certified mail so that you can track it and know it was received. If you write this letter in a professional, courteous manner, then you are more likely to receive a response back.

You can write this as a customer of a company that recently billed you twice in one month for a monthly service, for example. In this case, you are on the other side of the situation from what was presented in the earlier sample customer service email. You need to lodge a complaint that your subscription has been charged twice, and you want to know how they will make it right for you. You either want to get your money back, or else have one month free of charges. To ensure that customer service and billing will be willing to work with you, adopt the same polite tone while detailing exactly what happened, and when, including how much was charged.

Your completed complaint letter would look like the following sample below.

Subject: Need help with overbilling on my account

From: Betty Johnson (bjohnson@internetservice.com)

To: CSbilling@subscription.com

Date: Tuesday, January 15, 2015 12:35 PM

Dear Associate at CSbilling Department,

I received notice from my credit card account today that I had been charged twice for my subscription this month. Normally, I am charged every month on the 5th, so I am writing to inquire if there is a problem occurring with my subscription account.

I have never had this happen before, so I am assuming it is just a temporary glitch. But, I do need to bring it to your attention at once so it can be resolved.

Please review this issue and let me know why I was charged twice. I have included a copy below of the last transaction made today on the 15th, as well as a copy of the charges normally made on the 5th every month.

Subscript-XWZBA457 $25.00 Jan 15, 2015 (second charge made today)

Subcrt-EWVXW229 $25.00 Jan 5, 2014 (this is the normal monthly charge)

As you can see, the identification number for the charge today is a little different from the regular charge. This may be an attempt from an outside source to hack your system as well. I do hope you will be able to figure out how this happened.

Please let me know if you will send one of the charges back to my card, or if you will give me one month free of charges in compensation for the system error.

Thank you very much for taking on my issue and please respond as soon as you can. Also, send me a notice that you have received this email, so I know you have it. I would be happy to answer any question you have for me.

Sincerely,

Betty Johnson
123-456-7890
bjohnson@internetservice.com
(provide address here if you need to do that)

While this sample email shows a customer complaint email to a business, businesses must also, from time to time, complain to third-party vendors, when something goes wrong, or products are not delivered on time. When third-party vendors do not deliver products or materials on time to a manufacturing facility, this affects the manufacturing company's supply chain of daily production, for example, creating a backup or stoppage.

The company now loses time and money, waiting for supplies to show up. Hence, a manager must be prepared to construct an urgent email message quickly and effectively, and get it sent to the third-party vendor. In some cases, this email also backs up an urgent phone call already made to the vendor. The issue of financial loss in time and money must be concisely presented and recorded.

Five Principles of Email Composition

Here are some simple guidelines that can help you routinely compose emails quickly and easily, resulting in messages that are clear, concise, and compelling to your readers:

Get your facts straight

Before you write the email, you should have all the facts gathered in one place, so you can outline by order of importance to the issue. The five Ws, already mentioned, plus How, can help with deciding what points must be included in the content, first. The next step is to layer the body composition, from the most important topic at the top, to finally closing the email.

Be concise

Avoid unnecessary words. Emails should be concise, containing the fewest words needed to convey the message. Topics that need accuracy in numbers, or any scientific, medical, or legal issues, must be correctly presented. If a scientific formula, conveyed in an email, is found to be incorrect, the first time someone knows about it is when the formula fails. Hopefully, it is not something that blows up a laboratory, or worse. Create the first draft, then go through it, asking what words are needed, and where you can cut out unneeded words.

Write for the reader

Keep the reader as the focus of your composition from beginning to end. The reader's issue, or the need to know something, is the reason why you are writing an email (or a hard-copy letter). Ask yourself if each sentence is relatable to the reader and the issue. Will it say something of importance to the reader and help him decide what to do? You can view this as if the reader were sitting across the desk from you as you deliver the facts to him. Picture that reader, rather than a nameless and faceless person at the other end. This would be based on what you know about this reader, or group of readers, such as a department of employees.

Know your goal

You must know exactly what you want to communicate and achieve by writing an email. Your objective might be making a customer happy because you helped him (or her) with a problem and got it solved. Or you are persuading readers to sign up for the company's credit card, including the great benefits that come with it. The goal must align with all the persuasive content that came before.

Close on a positive note

There is nothing better than a happy ending, especially when it comes to solving complaint issues. The customer is happy, and the company gives a sigh of relief because disaster is avoided by offering a timely fix to the problem. Plus, it is always nice to help someone, especially when it is your (the company's) fault to begin with.

Use a positive tone in business emails, but do not go overboard with it. Excessive emotions used in emails can sometimes be viewed as more of a turnoff, rather than attracting a customer to do something. Avoid excessive flattery, as it may come off as a desperate ploy. Unless you know the reader well, then how would you know how great, pretty, or smart they are.

Choosing the Right Messaging

There are many types of business emails, such as the customer service responses, which are direct and based on solving problems to keep a customer. Other emails may cover instructions for employees to carry out a task using a new computerized method, sending delivery instructions to third-party vendors, or notifying customers of new payment capabilities, guaranteed to make their lives easier. There are emails to attract new customers, and those written to regain old customers who have melted away into the mist.

Your tone of voice changes with each type of email you create, based mainly on why you are writing it, and who the reader is. Those two components decide how you construct any email. Use a touch of humor, if in alignment with the message and the reader. If you are in doubt about how to create the tone of an email, consider yourself in the reader's viewpoint, and how you would react to the tone and the message.

Writing for Online Readers

When creating any online content, including emails, always choose to write simply, unless the readership is in a technical genre that needs the use of scientific or medical words to convey the message. However, even a technically based readership would like a break from reading scientific research reports, so keep it easy to read, even while giving accuracy where needed. Avoid being too formal.

For the public and for your customers, use words that are compelling and persuasive to keep them interested in your message. Keep the message entertaining, and remember to keep sentences short, use simple words, and use one to two sentences in a paragraph. Make it easy for the readers to understand your message and have no doubt at the end of the email, about what you intended to say to them.

CHAPTER 6.

Email Design Options: Text, HTML, Text in an HTML Shell

There are several aspects to consider when deciding whether you want to design a straightforward text email or one with Hypertext Markup Language (HTML), which also includes graphic call-to-action (CTA) buttons, social media icon graphics, and product or service pictures.

In the early years of email, straightforward text emails were the regular format as received over browser email applications, with the reader's choice to receive HTML emails with pictures and graphics. Then came tablets and iPads, and now mobile phones, changing how a designer can create emails that everyone can read on any device or platform (see chapter 15).

Today you have three options: straight text, "text in an HTML shell," or full HTML with text, formatting, photos, and color. Let's take a quick look at each and then drill down into the design techniques for each.

Text Emails

The biggest positive point for plain text emails is that the focus is on the content, appearing more like a conversation rather than a sales pitch, even if there is one. Personalized emails, with the reader's name included, typically receive higher responses than form emails to the reader's email address. These emails, to the readers, are much like receiving an email from a friend, coworker, or business colleague. A text mail is also more likely to make it past spam filters, which can be triggered by overuse of images in HTML emails.

Another key point for a plain text mail is that there are no images or graphics included. Any links given within the email are written out in text, rather than using a call-to-action (CTA) button graphic, and are clicked on to get to a web page.

Before the advent of the mobile phone and email applications (apps) that now allow you to receive your email on the go, an email designer did not have to worry much about how text would align itself on an email web page when read on a browser. A popular rule is to add line breaks after every sixty characters for display on desktop PCs, but mobile phone screens have changed that concept.

iPhone and Android screens deal with sentence breaks poorly, chopping up text midsentence. The best practice is to use word wrap within each paragraph. Try using a larger font size too, such as 16-point, to see how that comes out on the screen. Never use more than two sentences in a paragraph, and consider using just one sentence in a paragraph, with a space afterwards.

An alternative is that email designers could use a container column to ensure the proper flow and alignment of text, particularly when it comes to mobile phone screens and the varied apps used to open emails. When using a container column, be sure to set the largest width at no greater than 600 pixels (px), although less is even better. Containing the width for text and images to 600 px, allows the same email to adjust to all screen widths, such as laptop, desktop, and tablets screens as well.

When designing simple plain text emails with no graphics or images of any sort, you can insert your text into the body of the email template in the container column from Windows Notepad or any other generic plain text software program. What is very important here is that content is set to flush left (no justified), and that paragraphs have one to two sentences at most, set with word wrap. Use the Sans Serif typeface Arial font between 14 pts for regular content up to 22 pts for headers.

You need enough white space between paragraphs, including between any text links so that it is easy to use a finger to tap on it. You can create borders within the body by using one set of keyboard characters that run across the page or container box.

A design example is to set your email headlines in capital letters with the border running across, above, and below the headline. The first row below is called the masthead. An example is shown below with a line spacing of 1.0 and the equal (=) sign used to make the first border, and a hyphen (-) to make the secondary border. The borders should extend to the last letter of the headline to keep it tidy. To avoid all caps, if you feel strongly that it is "shouting" online, you can use just initial caps.

Graphics in a true text email are limited to what you can make using the keys on your keyboard and your text editor. Horizontal double lines, single lines, dashed lines, dotted lines, and asterisks are some of the top options:

===

YOUR DAILY EMAIL FOR A BETTER LIFE
January 1, 2017

===

Thought for the Day: Keep a Smile on Your Face as You Greet
Your Employees

....

A headline is added underneath the masthead with a theme statement separated by a colon, and the message included after that. Then the borderline thickness underneath is reduced from the ones above to show that it is the first headline. Underneath that, the body of the email is displayed in several paragraphs, along with any links, starting with a personal salutation to the reader.

When entering in a website address (URL) within the body of content, type it in and then hit the enter key so that it becomes active. A blue line will show up underneath the URL text. On a mobile phone, this is important as it is too difficult for a reader to try to copy-paste a text URL and then go paste it into a browser's URL box, although it can be done.

Add in a double space, or line space of 2.0, to show enough white space between the text copy and the links. Make it easy for readers to use their fingertip to click on a link for more information. If you are on a computer with a mouse, you move the mouse onto the hyperlink and click.

You can also go to bit.ly.com to shorten a long website address so it fits nicely across the screen without wrapping two to three times. Other URL shortening services are ow.ly, tinyurl, buff.ly, and goo.gl. These are excellent for using, particularly if you want to use straight text in your email, as the short URL generated by the service is recorded and allows you to track how many activations were made with that link.

End your email with your sig file which should include your contact information at the bottom. Do not forget to add in any disclaimers to the information you are providing, as well as an unsubscribe link, all of which is mandatory in every email.

Text in an HTML Shell

"Text in an HTML shell" refers to emails that look like text but are in fact coded in HTML. This is done because the HTML language, consisting of tags and snippets, gives the designer the look and feel of text, while adding capabilities for font variety, boldface, and italics. In addition, open rates cannot be tracked in pure text emails, but can be measured precisely in both text in an HTML shell or conventional HTML emails (those with color and images).

The advantages of using an HTML shell for text email is that your email will be easier to read, is still contained within the set parameters, and is less likely to be kicked over to the spam folder. Let us look at how to set up a basic shell in HTML using Windows Notepad or Notepad++ (free) for Windows. If you are on a Mac or Unix-based system (i.e. Linux), the TextEdit plain text version is the equivalent software to use. For presentation purposes in this chapter, we put the HTML shell with its tags inside a table column.

The Basic HTML Shell

```
<html>
<head>
<title>Name for your page</title>
</head>
<body>
The main content of your email goes here. When done, close the body
section with the tag below. Then close the shell with the HTML tag.
</body>
</html>
```

If you want to add a header in the body of text, put in <h1> to show the first header, which is the larger size of font used on the page, up to 22 px (pixel). Type in the header name and then close the line with this tag </h1>. If you want to center that header on the page, then before the header line, insert the tag <div align="center">, insert the header tags, then close the section with </div>, as shown below. When you open a tag (<html>), you must remember to close the tag at the end (</html>).

The HTML Extended Shell

```
<html>
<head>
<title>Name for your page</title>
</head>
<body>
<div align="center">
<h1>Your Subject Header</h1>
</div>
The content of your email goes here. Add your image anywhere in the body using the following tag. If you want to center the image, repeat the tags for centering the header above.
You can add more text in the body after this, until you are done. Now, the tags are closed in reverse order from the opening of the shell tags.
</body>
</html>
```

If you are using HTML5, the font size attribute is not supported, and you will need to use a CSS snippet instead. For now, we are using basic HTML with common tags. Font size here is decided by using <h1>, <h2>, or <h3>. This is like the Styles section on the Home tab in MS Word documents, where headers reduce in size from Heading 1 to Heading 2. In HTML5, this is represented by <h1> down to <h6>.

Free snippets and libraries can be found on the Internet and it is important to look for the latest resources available to you for building and developing your design in HTML and CSS, along with programming codes. You can also get help from your commercial bulk email service provider, who is most likely to be up on the latest advances in HTML and CSS, as well as other tools available.

The use of HTML also allows for a method of tracking when readers open the emails. From there, clicks on links can be tracked, returning valuable information back to you about how your readers are responding to the message. When using a commercial email service provider, such information is presented in reports that you can easily access from the administrative panel of your account.

Full HTML

Full HTML email includes pictures and other images that enhance the message, especially if the product needs the inclusion of a visual reproduction so that customers can decide to buy it or not. This is especially important when selling clothes, electronic products, books, movies, and art pieces. HTML is the language that sets the page to look a certain way on a browser, such as three side-by-side columns of text, with a row of images above those columns.

When using visuals in HTML emails, using the responsive approach is always best, along with modifications, such as the hybrid approach to get around problem issues with those apps that do not work with the media query. It is important to remember to not use too many images in the email, as they can be interpreted as spam by some email applications. Images are also vulnerable to acquiring viruses and, therefore, should use an alt-tag that provides text indicating what the image is.

Alt-tags are also important to use in situations where a reader does not want to see images, or if there is some technical issue, such as slow connections, or a problem in the src attribute. The alt-tag provides a text version of what the image is, even though the image is not shown. Here is an example of an alternate text connected to an image, written in Notepad++.

<img src="images/blackcat.jpg" alt="Beautiful Black Cat" width="80" height="80"/>

The beginning of the tag is img for image. Then, src identifies the path for where to get the image, such as on the web, or in this case, a folder called images. The name of the image in the folder is blackcat.jpg, always saved with lowercase letters, and written in HTML as lowercase too. The alt tag gives the name you decide you want to see on the screen when the picture is not shown—Beautiful Black Cat. Finally, the width and height can be included, if necessary, to constrain the image size. You can also change the width and height of the image (80x80) by changing the numbers to be higher (larger) or lower (smaller).

It helps to first plan how your design is going to look, based on what you want to include in it. You can do a simple layout by drawing a template on a piece of paper so you can see where there may be issues with too many visuals, or not enough, to balance the space. Here is how a simple design may look on paper with the browser view on the left, and phone view on the right.

Browser View (left) and Phone View (right)

Title of Page on Browser			Title of Page on Mobile Phone	
	Picture			Picture
				Picture
Aenean eu leo quam. Pellentesque ornare semlacinia quam venenatis vestibulum. Donec sed odio dui.	Aenean eu leo quam. Pellentesque ornare semlacinia quam venenatis vestibulum. Donec sed odio dui.	Aenean eu leo quam. Pellentesque ornare semlacinia quam venenatis vestibulum. Donec sed odio dui.	Aenean eu leo quam. Pellentesque ornare semlacinia quam venenatis	
			Aenean eu leo quam. Pellentesque ornare semlacinia quam venenatis	
			Aenean eu leo quam. Pellentesque ornare semlacinia quam venenatis	
Footer: Contact Information, Disclaimer, Unsubscribe Link,			Contact Information, Disclaimer, Unsubscribe Link,	

Remember that the simpler your emails are to read or look on any platform, is what you should design for when putting together a layout. It should be easy to read, especially with readers who are on the go, and want to quickly scan through your message. If the text is too small to be easily read, the reader may move on to another email that is easy to read.

Aside from using the design services of your commercial bulk email provider, there are HTML editors on the Internet that you can use to play with design options, even if you are an HTML novice. Some are free and others you may need to pay for to get more editing options. These editors help with adding in preset snippets and if you want to see what the email is going to look like, you can switch to the visual or preview side of the editor to view it. Some of these editors are MailStyler, TinyMCE, Trellian WebPage, CoffeeCup HTML Editor, and KompoZer, among others. An example of what an email template looks like is shown below.

From:

Subject:

Date

Image/Logo here
Size = between 380 to 600 wide, height as needed

Connect with us here on social media!

Put Your Headline Here

If using a single column, start your text here, flush left to the page or column border. Make sure your first paragraph gives the reason why you are sending this email. After you have added one to two sentences, add a link or CTA button to an external landing page where people can sign up, or purchase something.

Then you can add more text about what you are offering, including features that grab your readers' attention. After one to two paragraphs of one to two sentences each, add another link or CTA button to close the message.

Add your signature, and a postscript here if you want to add a bonus incentive. Then underneath that, you will add in all your contact information.

Add a disclaimer in this section, if you need it. Add your unsubscribe link here.

Once you have come up with your own special design, particularly if you want to identify as a brand to your readers, then you can upload your email design to your template on the email provider's website. A template allows you to add in your content in all the right places. The template for the phone version would reduce the size of the top image to fit the screen, with the right-side image (260 x any height) and text column to flow down underneath the left image column. This makes it very easy to read on the mobile phone.

Cascading Style Sheets (CSS)

Email designers also use Cascading Style Sheets (CSS) language in conjunction with HTML, a necessary step for creating responsive emails that will open properly on mobile phones and other platforms, dependent on a screen size. CSS describes how the elements of HTML should be displayed on any screen.

If you had three side-by-side columns of text with a row of images running across the top of all three columns, the CSS language prompts behind the scene how such a layout must reset itself to fit on a mobile phone screen. Typically, it is set up to take that row of images and have them slot down into one column, one image above the other, so this fits on the mobile screen. The same is true for the three columns of text, which now folds into one column. That is what we call responsive to the screen.

The use of a simple HTML shell is essential to keep the text organized on the page, in alignment with the logo or social media graphics. Even with one image, such as a logo, you will still need to use HTML. You can add in text links to the content and the email will come out fine. But if you add any type of graphic into your letter, then you must use some HTML language to keep the text formatted properly.

How your email appears on the screen can also depend on which email application is being used to open the mail. The solution is usually for the reader to click on the message asking if the reader wants to see images. Once clicked, then all the text sentences line up again and will not split in midsentence. This is particularly true of mobile phone apps. Therefore, it is vital that every email design be tested by sending it to a variety of devices first before a full client list send out is done. The most effective manner of designing emails to date is to use a hybrid-responsive approach to laying out the design, and is explained a bit later on in this chapter.

How a general text email opens on one email app on mobile phones will change when opened in another email app. This becomes clear if one reader has subscribed to a company's offerings through two different email clients. The following screen shots from a Samsung Galaxy J7 Android phone, show how one account from a Yahoo! email app shows up first as text, and then is adjusted manually by the reader to show images, such as social media icon graphics.

Text email in Yahoo! email phone app–before tapping on the Show images

Text email in Yahoo! phone email app–after tapping on the Show images

Note that the left image above has sentence breaks before tapping on the box to show images. On the right side, when images are selected, then the sentences line up again, but the text is a bit smaller within the same screen viewing space.

The Gmail app presents its own conundrum when opening emails that are basically text, but might have social media icon graphics that can be clicked on. If HTML is not used to control the design, then unplanned changes can occur. When the reader opens the email, the icons are already visible, as set up by this viewer, and the text is skewed, as shown in the example below on the left. This is a different problem from the Yahoo! app that showed broken sentences before the email was changed to show images after being opened.

Text mail in Gmail phone app with images already set to show

Text mail in Gmail phone app with the choice for "revert auto-sizing" selected

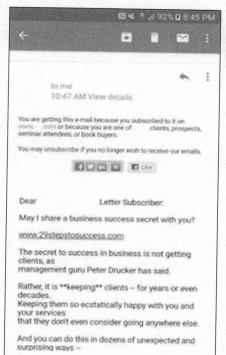

Both email versions were opened and read through a browser on the Internet first, without any issues. The changes occurred in the transition over to mobile phones.

Scalable, Fluid, Responsive Design

Scalable design entails building a single column format, using a large font (14 and above) for the main body of text, and offering easy to access call-to-action (CTA) links. It is the most simplistic design of all, and is regularly used by marketers for shorter messages. All information and content should be flush-left on the page, ensuring the best optimization of screen scale over most platforms.

Under a fluid design, percentage shows sizing parameters within the language, and content fills space across the screen at a width setting of 100 percent, rather than just a fixed width at 600 px or less. In this case, such text on larger screens can flow too far across the web page unless constrained in some manner. Therefore, fluid design relies on both percentages and fixed width properties.

The use of an HTML shell becomes important to hold text within a defined fixed width. While the 100 percent is still included to accommodate the larger screens, the border width is confined to 500 px, or less when the email is opened on a mobile screen. The content of the email can be contained in a stated table with a fixed width.

A CSS media query is added within a fixed width-fluid design layout which prompts the script to change to whatever platform screen the email is being opened on. However, with a desktop application, the emails appear in a separate screen from the ISP or email service provider, such as Outlook, which I use. Yet, Outlook does not recognize media queries. More on the issue of Outlook in the hybrid section and how that issue is solved.

The origin of responsive email comes from responsive web design, and is explained as a process of using fluid tables and images, in conjunction with media queries. It is a combination of the scalable and fluid elements, along with the media query, but a step further. The distinction is that CSS media queries can change the fixed width of tables and images, seen on desktops, into fluid widths on smaller screens, such as mobile phones.

This controls how layouts reset themselves, adjusts the size of text, CTA buttons, and images, dependent on the device the design is opened on. Some content can be hidden on one platform, and then brought back in on another platform, such as in a desktop browser.

Responsive design allows the email designer more control over the content display on multiple devices. This is particularly important when using graphics and images within the content that need resizing on multiple screens. When a responsive design is opened on a mobile screen, the content adjusts a three-column design into a singular column, based on the screen properties. A CSS media query set within the body of the email also controls text sizing and how links appear on the screen, including any graphics and images, based on certain conditions.

Most of the commercial bulk email providers now have these responsive templates ready to use, so that you do not have to learn all the HTML and CSS language elements that need to go into these layouts. But should you want to create original designs in the future, then learning the foundations of HTML and CSS will be helpful to you in understanding the way layouts are created.

Hybrid Language

There are email apps, such as Gmail and Outlook, which do not recognize media query and responsive design, but will recognize Microsoft conditional comments (codes) to overcome these problems. While the hybrid method of design is still a new approach to writing HTML and CSS language for emails, designers are finding new ways to create designs that fit all platforms and devices by using the hybrid method.

The hybrid approach, a combination of both fluid and responsive design, as explained previously, is considered the most effective application of designing emails that respond to any screen. The principle of the design is that it uses fluid tables and images by default. While media queries are still used, the hybrid approach is to also use Microsoft's conditional comments, which can be read by those applications that do not recognize media queries and the CSS max-width element, such as Outlook and Gmail. Fixed-width ghost tables can be applied within the regular elements of responsive design, so that Outlook will pick it up when emails are opened.

It can also be more difficult to use when using a complex design, such as a three-column layout, along with images. This requires a designer to be very knowledgeable with HTML and CSS, including MS conditional comments, to know how to set this up, but, ultimately, is the most effective process of getting emails to open properly on nearly every platform.

If you are working with a commercial bulk email provider, find out if any of their designs use the hybrid method. If not, ask if you can upload any hybrid template you find, to your account. Litmus.com offers free hybrid templates for download and can be used with many commercial bulk email providers today. You just need to create an account to join if you wish to use any of these from the community.

Tracking Emails

Tracking emails was briefly mentioned earlier, but it is important to take advantage of any tracking and data reporting services your commercial bulk email provider offers. At the least, you can see how many readers are opening your emails, and whether they click on links within the email, or on images, such as pictures and CTA button graphics. This offers insight into how effective your design is in getting readers to do something other than read your email.

You can also use a transparent 1 x 1 image pixel within HTML emails, although readers who open the email must select the choice to show images for it to activate. Alternatively, if not using images, the pixel can be attached to an active link in the email. Many of the commercial bulk email providers already have this installed in their templates.

There are also companies who specialize in just offering scheduling and tracking tags that are set into your email and will return data back to your server for further review. This is independent from what your commercial bulk email provides, in case their offering is not enough for what you need. Companies that offer this service are Bananatag, Yesware, ToutApp, Contact Monkey, Mailtrack, Sidekick, SalesLoft, Cirrus Insight, ClearSlide, Velocify Pulse, and others. Some of these services provide apps, while others provide plug-ins.

The ability to track emails gives you information that helps with validating emails, an analysis of what time of day was better for sending out emails that would be opened, and also giving information about where customers were located. You would also want to know what percentage of your readers opened their emails on browsers, tablets, or mobile phones.

You can also analyze the information to see what images were clicked on, including any CTA buttons and social media images. Your data report will also show whether pictures and buttons at the top of the email were clicked on more than those at the middle or bottom. This will tell you what you might need to eliminate in future emails.

Essentially, you cannot track an email unless there is a link, an image, or some other element with HTML in the email. Even if you only add one link or one image, such as social media images, you can track that email.

Businesses today, with astute marketing research managers, are also integrating customer relationship management (CRM) information with returns from email reports about what customers click on while reading emails. This is adding to the gold mine of understanding their customers, what they like, what they are not interested in, and how to give the customers a better personalized service.

Follow-up emails can be sent to customers who show an interest in something they read, but they did not buy yet. Another email can be sent a week later, that reminds the readers they were interested then, and asks if they would like to know more about the product to make a purchasing decision.

The more you know about the readers you are sending emails to, the more effective you can make your marketing strategy to hook your readers into finally making a purchase, or signing up for your service or product. It all starts first with designing your emails, using HTML.

CHAPTER 7.

Rich Media and Embedded Video

Video presentations have become very popular in marketing campaigns, and more businesses are now engaging in creating videos for their products. Posting a short video on a landing page or website home page, for instance, can boost conversion rates up to 15 percent or more. While text content is still essential and should be used to balance images and videos and to avoid the spam box, busy people may prefer to see a product or service in action, rather than only reading about it.

But the main reason to consider incorporating video into your email communication is as follows. There are four primary modes people have of absorbing information: reading, watching, hearing, and experiencing. An email that is only text or HTML conveys content primarily through the written word. When you add video to the mix, you engage reading, watching, and hearing. Add a webinar, and you may also add experiencing, provided the event is interactive.

And increasingly, we are becoming a nation of video watchers. Video is one of the hottest trends in Internet marketing today. Every month,

1.5 billion users log onto YouTube worldwide and watch on average an hour a day of video on their mobile devices.[46] Incredible as it sounds, more than three hundred hours of video are uploaded to YouTube every minute of every day.[47]

Television trains us to love video from an early age: Kids and teens ages eight to eighteen watch TV nearly four hours a day and spend almost two additional hours on the computer outside of school and playing video games.[48] As boomers, my generation was too, watching everything from *The Rockford Files* and *Star Trek* to *All in the Family* and *M*A*S*H*.

Video engages your digital prospects and customers in a way ordinary text communications simply do not: 100 million Internet users watch online video every day. Video emails have a 44 percent higher engagement rate than ordinary text or HTML emails—and nearly double the click-through rate. What's more, prospects are 85 percent more likely to buy your product after viewing your video.

Steven Tulman of Business2Community.com (B2C) recently stated that 70 percent of businesses using video in their marketing are pleased with the results. Nearly a third of overall Internet users (one billion+) are watching YouTube videos, a video platform where you can find a video on just about anything you want to know more about. For example, if you need an overview on how to write HTML and CSS, you can find it there for free.

Approximately 75 percent of Fortune 500 executives—and nine out of ten consumers—watch video online. And roughly two out of three of these executives go to the company's website after viewing the video.[49] On the other hand, only 20 percent read all of the text of your emails.

---

46 https://www.mediapost.com/publications/article/303338/youtube-introduces-new-immersive-virtual-reality-f.html.
47 Ragan's PR Daily, 6/23/17, "8 changes to make your content more engaging," Josh Althuser.
48 https://www.rchsd.org/health-articles/how-tv-affects-your-child/.
49 http://www.brafton.com/blog/video-marketing/generate-b2b-leads-with-your-video-content-our-3-best-practices/.

By adding video to your emails, you can:

- Demonstrate your product.
- Get prospects' attention and interest.
- Boost open and click-through rates.
- Tell your story in words *and* pictures.
- Make your email the one they read.

Video marketing has steadily increased in strategic implementation, with roughly 91 percent of businesses now engaged in video creation of some type. Like technology and software, advances are made every day in further developing techniques in implementing videos in marketing campaigns, including emails, which are a major distribution point.

How long should an email video be? Two minutes at the most— long enough to quickly grab the attention of the viewer. An added link can be given to send viewers to a longer video on a website or even YouTube. Longer videos embedded directly in the email, however, can get your email thrown into the spam box.

How to Develop Your Email Video Campaign

1. Decide on what your goal is—make a sale, get downloads— and how you will capture those who do not buy at once, but show interest in buying later. This is called segmenting your readership. You will know who is interested after your first send out of the email.
2. Plan what your email content will say, and work up a script for the video. Remember, no longer than two minutes.

Assuming a narration rate of 120 words per minute maximum, your video script should not exceed approximately 250 words for the audio portion; your narrator can always speak a little slower or faster—but not much.

3. Design a storyboard, if you need to, so that you can time your speech with the video frames. The better you have this part laid out, the easier it will be to film the piece.

4. Choose what video host you want to use, such as YouTube, Viddler, or Vimeo. Both are very popular and work on most email platforms. YouTube does have an issue with playing videos, however, with another video in a playlist off to the right side, which auto plays right after your video plays. There are two ways you can avoid this: either change the auto play setting from the button in your video, or at the top of the playlist on the right, toggle the blue checked auto play to off, which now shows grey. On my pages, we prefer Vimeo or Viddler.

5. Select what video shooting tools you want to use: camera (with video capabilities), video cam, your laptop or desktop video recorder, smart phone, or using a whiteboard software package.

6. Select your background venue for the video, based on the product you are offering, such as in your home office or at your worksite. You may choose to use your office bookcases behind your office desk as background, or you can choose an off-site background relevant to your product or service. If you are doing a video about a new car, for example, be on-site at the dealership, with the car in place by you. Make sure there is little to no noise around you so you can record your speech without distraction. One video on how to get rich showed the creator of the program walking on a ninety-acre spread, which he explained he just bought as an investment, giving the impression that he was wealthy and successful.

You should also know that while you can embed a video in an email using HTML5, for example, not all email platforms will allow the reader to watch the video directly in the email. Instead, plan to also include a linked thumbnail of one frame from the video that has a play button image pasted within that thumbnail. There are tags you can add to your embedded link in the HTML script, that allow a YouTube video to auto play when the reader gets to your landing page, without clicking a second time. One sample example from using a YouTube video is:

http://www.youtube.com/embed/JX4yoKfz2fY

where JX4yoKfz2fY is the video ID generated by YouTube for your video. While you can use the ampersand (&), some have found it better to change the ampersand to the question mark (?) in the tag. Note that new ways of writing scripts change often, so you may need to ask your video host what they are successfully using. The final version is the following sample term:

http://www.youtube.com/embed/JX4yoKfz2fY?autoplay=1

You can alternatively use a graphics interchange format (GIF) image which runs for three or four seconds, that can be clicked on to go to the video on a website. Or the GIF can activate when the reader gets to the site, where three or four frames are used to create a mini presentation of the product. Both videos and GIF are considered rich media, which is addressed further on.

Decide on the Email and Video's Goal

One example of your email marketing goal is to promote a new product (book or online course), which you discount for a short time, to gain your first buyers. Readers always love getting products and services at a cheaper rate. Giving a limited time to buy before the product moves up to full price is an added urgent incentive. I rarely sell a product online without giving a ten-dollar or higher discount off the list price for low-priced items.

A short two-minute video that gives information about the book or the new course is a great teaser for them to want to know more, or to go buy it off your sales page as soon as possible. Your email should be solely about the product or service being offered, with concise content that gives a brief explanation of benefits and features, leading up to the viewer activating the email video to watch for more information. Having the discount for a limited time only gives the customer an incentive to buy now instead of later.

Videos used online today range from thirty seconds, called "explainer videos," to a half hour or more, called "video sales letters." For email, running time is typically 120 seconds or less.

If you think on a strategic level, then consider sending out the first video email on a Wednesday or Thursday with the notice that the price will go up in three to four days. Why? People get paid, typically, on a Friday, and can choose ahead of time to put aside some of their paycheck to buy what you are selling. When you create the email, put the word "video" in the subject line, as Talman states that open rates typically increase by 20 percent over text emails, with click-through rates up to 65 percent higher.

Design and Plan the Email Text Content and Video Script

When you are including a video, give enough preliminary content in the email in the fewest words on what is being sold. The video reinforces that message, but also gives more information and the incentive to buy. Put a call to action (CTA) button underneath the video block, just in case the reader wants to go buy the product right away. Put one in the video as well.

Make your video script conversational and engaging. Decide what information is best presented visually in the video, rather than by text. The email text covers what is not in the video, but compliments it.

If you are selling a product, such as a book, online course, a tractor, blender, or lawn mower, for example, then videos are great for visually showing off the product in use. An online course that shows how to paint landscapes with a new method or approach can present the highlights of how a picture will look, after using that method. As the expert with this new method of painting landscapes, you will give out just enough to tease readers into buying the new book or online course, so they can do that new method themselves.

As painting is very visual, you can do a voice-over with your script and show painting samples in the video, while speaking about them. If you are talking about the course itself, then use media images to back up what you are saying.

Do not just talk into the camera. One production technique is to have some visual imagery running on a split screen while the other half of the screen shows you talking. If you are presenting interesting highlight points of the course to your viewers, then visually show on the split screen those same points, using interesting images with diagrams. Your viewers will remember the images much better than the spoken-only version of the highlights. Or you can just do the voice-over to the video and just show images on the screen while talking.

Do's and Don'ts of Video Hosting

Never try to host your videos from your website host's server, as all kinds of things can go wrong. For example, uploading your video to your WordPress website in the Media Library, will take a long time to get there, because video files are typically huge, measured in megabytes (MB), such as 100 MBs. Then when you install it on your site, it may not run properly. If enough people click on the video at roughly the same time, your server will likely crash. You are now dead in the water, and viewers have moved on to something else more interesting than a blank screen.

Always use a third-party video host, which will do all the necessary background tweaks to the video so that it is ready to play nearly everywhere on the Internet. Once you add the embedded code the video host company generates for your video, then an image of the video pops up on your site as a fallback video frame image and your readers can just click on it to see the video. The same is true when embedding a video in your email. Let the third-party companies do all the hard work for you.

Check with the video host company to be sure that they also convert the video into the different file formats that cover any browser or device on the market. These formats include H.264 (MP4), WebM, and Ogg. Google Chrome plays all video file formats, while Internet Explorer (IE) and Safari only play MP4 formats, and Firefox only plays .ogg, or .webm extension files. Make sure the video host company formats for all devices as well, such as mobile phones.

Choosing the Right Video Hosting Service

You can check through your business emails to see which video hosts are currently being used most often. Determine how clear the film resolution is as well as the audio, although that can be due to the equipment used to create it. You will also need to decide what audio background you want included, such as a musical piece. Observe copyright rules for music and make sure the music you want is free to use.

Vimeo, Viddler, and Google's YouTube are three conversion host sites, meaning that you create your videos first with your own tools, such as a camera, videocam, GoPro, Camtasia, or whatever you choose. You can even use your mobile phone to do it if you are on the go and find something you want to capture quickly that reflects your goal. Then you can either edit the video using your own editing programs or upload them to Vimeo, Viddler, or YouTube to edit them there. Check further on in this chapter for more information about video editing programs and tools you can use.

Once you have the video you want, you can upload the video, so long as you have an account. YouTube requires a Google account, and if you have a mobile phone which uses Google accounts (Android) to personalize your phone, then you already have the YouTube app and account.

Both Vimeo and YouTube have online video editors which you can use once you have uploaded your video to your account. If you have your own video editor, such as Adobe Premier Pro, then you can do that on the computer and then upload it. If using a video shot on your mobile phone, both Vimeo and YouTube have mobile phone video editing apps too. But if you want a more professional-styled video, however short, just upload the videos to the accounts and save them there, unpublished, for editing later.

Vimeo and YouTube are primarily mentioned because they are both the most successful hosts on the Internet in showing videos across most platforms without any glitches, including emails. Viddler is also popular and works well. Remember, though, that some platforms do not show videos, only the fallback image. While you can use free or trial accounts with nearly any video host company, consider paid accounts to get more perks added on. You will need to check if advertising by any hosting company is put on the same page as your video.

Other video hosting companies to look at are Wistia, Sprout Video, Vzaar, Brightcove, Viewbix, Vidyard, Cincopa, and many more. Look over as many as you can to see what their offerings are. Each will have some original specialty features. Use your goal as a guideline to find just the right partner to help you get your message across.

Amazon also has video hosting on its cloud service (AWS), an excellent option if you are already using AWS to distribute published content, such as e-books and other media through your email system. Its most positive feature is the capability to access videos on demand, 24/7, avoiding bottlenecks in streaming, thus eliminating the need for a dedicated server, and it reduces expenditures. Additionally, live events can also be captured in real time, while simultaneously creating video on demand (VOD) for future use. This provides a function that other hosting companies are less likely to offer.

Computer Software Programs for Editing Videos

You have shot the video(s) and now want to edit it. There are many software programs available—some for free, others for a price. Adobe has Premiere Pro, a video production and editing program, which also integrates with Adobe Audition for high-quality audio effects and fidelity. Both come in the Adobe Creative Cloud subscription package for a monthly fee.

Other programs you can use are AVS Video Editor, Final Cut Pro (MAC), Sony Vegas Movie Studio and the Pro version, Lightworks, Cinelerra, Pinnacle Studio, Corel VideoStudio, Camtasia, and CyberLink PowerDirector. These are just a few that are available for video editing.

Your goal is to edit the video so that the resolution is clear, the colors are vibrant, and the sound is of high quality. Some programs mentioned above will provide online help, including training videos, to help you maximize using the tools offered in the programs.

Camtasia, by TechSmith, is one of the most popular video editing programs and is available for both Windows and Mac systems. There is a free version, but the professional version is preferred, especially if you will be doing more videos in the future. It is an easy-to-learn program and is excellent for capturing near-perfect video and audio outputs from your laptop or desktop, including recording VoIP calls through programs, such as Skype. Export files with the extensions of MP4, WMV, MOV, AVI, and M4V. A mobile app is also available. You can find the download for the program at www.techsmith.com/store to get the latest version.

Using Mobile Phones, Videocams, or Cameras with Recording Capabilities

There are many options for tools to create your video with. Most laptops and desktop monitors have installed video cameras that you can use to create the video. Figure out if you need a plug-in microphone, so that your voice is clear without any static. You will need to do a test run with your audio and video system to decide if you need different tools. If you do not like how you look, or how your voice sounds when recorded, you might want to hire someone professional to do the video at your location. They do the talking and you record it.

Alternatively, look at online companies who have remote voice-over talent listed, such as Fiverr. You can send your talent the script, and they can record it themselves and send it back to you. You can also hire someone else to create two minutes of original music for your audio background if you want to have that in the video, such as with a whiteboard presentation video. Ask if your musical talent will also mesh the vocal recording with the music background. Finally, you can hire someone to mesh the finished audio recording with the video, and your project is complete. It is also a lot less work for you, at a reasonable price.

Your mobile phone can also create videos from nearly anywhere you decide to do this if you do not own a video cam or camera with recording capabilities. Most mobile phones now have extended functions available to take advantage of lighting situations, meaning you can shoot the video at nearly any time of day. Make sure you are in a place that is not too noisy or your voice will be hard to hear over the racket behind and around you. You might also want to invest in a mobile phone tripod so that you can stand in front of the phone to do your video without worrying about any shaking.

If neither the desktop or mobile phone option is desired, use a digital single-lens reflex (DSLR) camera (14 to 24 megapixels) that also records video, or a video cam, and decide if you want to bring a laptop so you can tether the camera or video cam to it. That way you can quickly download the video to the laptop and look at it to determine quality of the video, and whether to do another recording.

I recommend you bring an assistant or friend along who can help you get set up, and position you in the video screen for maximum effect. Draw a barely visible X mark with chalk on the ground, if you need it, so you know where you should be placed, in case you need to step away for a minute. You can also mark the screen width guides, so that if you move around a bit, you know how far you have for side-to-side movement before you are offscreen.

When you are going out into the field (anywhere outside your home or business) to make a video, create a photographer's bag (or use a rolling suitcase with an extending handle) that holds everything you need. Build a list ahead of time of tools and accessories that will go in it, so you can double-check the bag before you leave.

Make sure camera (and laptop) batteries are fully charged, and have extras on hand. Use a tripod to ensure a steady shot. If you think you will need it, bring a lamp stand or two, to help with focused lighting for the scene. You can also bring a portable charger, just in case you need it.

When I speak at an online or live conference that is being videotaped, I put in my agreement that I get a copy of the MP4 file and permission to use it however I wish. If the sponsor is not videotaping, I hire a local videographer to tape it for me.

As a final thought, consider doing the short two-minute video for the email and a longer one with more information in it that can be used on your website later, or in your online course. Make sure also that wherever you are creating your video, that it must align fully with whatever you are offering, such as a product, service, or online course.

How to Embed a Video into Your Email

When using a commercial bulk email provider, you can simply drag the video content block right into the email section where you want it to be seen. Then you link it with the URL of your video, so that it activates when clicked. Check with your bulk email provider as to how videos show up in their email templates. Add in your alternative screen frame from the video, just in case the video does not play.

The other way is to create a spot in your HTML shell, using the HTML5 <div><video></video></div> snippets. In between the video snippet goes a host of information about the video, how it should be displayed if approved by the platform, including width and height. When not accepted, then the next section after the closing tag </div>, known as the fallback section, would show how to present the static video frame image in the email with an embedded link to a website.

Be sure to always include the width and height of images, along with the alt attributes (see chapter 6), so that if your video does not show up, the substitute image or text link will, and readers can click on it to get to the video.

You can also create a table of contents at the top of the email, so that readers can go to the video there, for example, or add a link to the video underneath the video block as another way to get to the video. Most important, do not forget your CTAs at the end of the video and in your email.

Whiteboards or Sketch Versus Live Footage

Whiteboard animation videos are seen online and look like the old-time whiteboards or chalkboards, normally seen in school or business meetings. The software or service draws illustrations that go with the narrative on a white background.

The animated version online is like this older concept of presentation doodling, but is more artistically and quickly done, while providing entertainment in the process. There are many providers online that now offer these services and programs. You can see one example of such a whiteboard animation at: www.myveryfirstebook.com.

Easy Sketch Pro v3 is one software that helps you create a whiteboard presentation. It starts with uploading your images, and then simply dragging the images onto the board on the screen. Each board screen receives the placed images you want to see in the drawing/sketching process.

You can also add in a music track as a background. Then you can select the hand (and arm) that will be doing the sketching of the images you selected for that page. You can then make it interactive by using a hotspot clickable image and, finally, export it into an MP4 format file on your computer. Add on a voice-over script and you are ready to publish. While these are more informally styled videos, they still come across as professionally made. Another fun trick is to upload a video and set it so the first frame is made as a sketch for the opening section. Then it seamlessly transitions into the live video with people talking.

Whiteboard videos have gained in popularity over the last few years, particularly as software capabilities have progressed to add in new features and tools. Many viewers find such presentations engaging and entertaining as well.

Aside from marketing purposes, some schools are turning to this type of presentation, so that children are more engaged in learning their lessons, rather than sitting through boring slideshows. Seeing something being "drawn" on the screen is far more entertaining visually than old picture slideshows.

Other available whiteboard programs are GoAnimate, where you create your whiteboard video on the Internet site with your browser. Video Scribe, a downloadable program, is another drag-and-drop method, using images provided in the library. You also can choose between using a pen or pencil or a hand with either one. You have the option to create your own drawings in another program, then covert the file into a scalable vector graphics (svg) format, saved with the .svg extension, to import it into Video Scribe.

Other programs to look at are PowToon, Explaindio Video Creator software, TTS Sketch Maker Text to Speech Whiteboard Video Maker, and Video Maker FX. It is preferable to buy software packages for a one-time fee, starting with a trial to see if you like the program.

Whiteboard videos are also preferred over live videos where you use a whiteboard on a stand, and drawing everything while you are giving your speech. If you have limited artistic talent in drawing, you may find it uncomfortable, aside from anything else that might go wrong, such as the board falling over to the ground.

Using Other Rich Media

While videos fall under the term of rich media, there are other types of rich media to be used in emails, such as short animations, graphic interchange format (GIF) images, floating banners, and CTA buttons. A GIF image is a compressed file that downloads to a viewer's screen in a very short amount of time. It is, accordingly, most suitable for use on the web (and emails) and can be a static image or created as an animation, using several picture or video frames that repeat continuously. For instance, on a product involving nutrition for cells, the sales page had a banner displaying a continuous loop GIF that showed cells moving within a fluid.

You can buy packages online from companies that offer premade rich media mentioned above; one is https://giphy.com/search/premade. Be sure if you are professionally or commercially publishing your images, that you have the proper rights to do so. Better yet, you can create your own, if you are willing to spend the time to learn how to do so. The biggest learning curve will be in learning the software you choose, so you know its fullest capabilities.

Media tips to remember

- Make sure that your bulk email provider allows you to send short videos in your emails. Check first on any possible restrictions and best practices for alternatives.
- Note that many recipient platforms may not show videos within the email, but will allow for a fallback image from the video to be placed in the email that links out to the video on a website.
- Using a third-party video host is far preferable to hosting videos yourself. Avoid the potential headaches inherent with self-hosted videos.
- Weigh the pros and cons of embedding your video in your email. One advantage to using the image of the video instead, is that the viewer goes to your website to see the video and may hang around to look at products and services. They might find something else they want to buy, or sign up for. With an embedded video, they just stay on that page and do not engage with you as well. On your website, after the video is over, they may want to ask questions or make comments. Make sure someone is assigned to answer those questions and comments quickly and efficiently.

CHAPTER 8.

Hyperlinks, CTAs, and Landing Pages

Both hyperlinks (also called links) and calls to action (CTA) image buttons play important roles in emails, websites, and landing pages. It is the way that viewers can get other pieces of information from across the Internet, or within websites. Without links, online commerce, social media, and subscriptions to online courses, among other items of interest, become difficult for consumers to access. Think of a massive spider web, then consider that web strands are the pathways to intersecting nodes, at which an Internet address is found. The hyperlink, also at the base of any CTA button, is what gets you there to that address so you can apply an action, such as buying a book or signing up for a course.

Hyperlinks are the foundation of the Internet, allowing us to view a document (webpage), or series of documents (websites). If you want to see a specific website, you can type the address, known as the uniform resource locator (URL), into your browser. Then hit Enter on the keyboard to get it. This action will bring up the home, or index page of a website and, from there, you can click on internal hyperlinks to see other pages in that website infrastructure.

The hypertext transfer protocol (HTTP), seen in front of a website address, is the foundation of connectivity to content on the World Wide Web (WWW), and defines the formatting of messages, and how they should be transmitted. This allows browsers and servers to respond to the protocol commands. Rather than thinking that you are going to a website, the HTTP command is bringing the website documents to your browser for you to read and interact with.

You often see the other version of HTTP, which is HTTPS, used for security and encryption of data, such as a commerce site where financial transactions take place. You can also find it in URLs when you visit your bank online to get your statements and account balance.

These components, plus the use of the hypertext markup language (HTML) that describes the content and format of any webpage, make up the pillars of the WWW's foundation, per documentation from Mozilla's Developer Network (MDN). HTML allows for the use of both internal website, newsletter, or document hyperlinks, as well as those that call for external websites (home page), a specific webpage on a website, and one-page landing sites.

Hyperlinks

Hyperlinks, simply known as links, are always used in an HTML format, even if most of the surrounding content is text-based without using any images. Links found in emails are constructed to have a reader click on it for more information available on an external page, where the reader can sign up for something, or make a purchase.

Links are URLs of website addresses or specific pages given in text format which, when the writer clicks on the Enter key after the address is typed, becomes active with an underline beneath the text. The whole website address link then turns blue, making the link stand out from all the other plain text. All the reader need do is click on it to activate the command to bring in the requested information onto the browser screen.

Hyperlinks, as activated blue formatted links, stand out from the rest of the text content in an email, as the place to click when the reader desires to take an action of one sort or another. Hyperlinks in emails take up less space, especially if the content body is also basically text. Links can also point to images, videos, audio files, and anything else that can conceivably live at an address on the Internet. A good rule to follow is to have the link open on a separate browser tab, rather than replacing the email page, simply because readers can easily return to the email after they are done reading the other page.

When using these links in emails, use the same destination link two to three times at the most, such as one after the introductory paragraph, one after the last paragraph, and maybe one after your signature, or a postscript (P.S.) message. You can figure out the amount of times to use them, based on how long your email content is. Too many links will make you look desperate to make a sale.

In ordinary postal direct mail, we have the call to action and response mechanism (mail a reply card, call this toll-free number) usually at the end of the letter. In email marketing, we have the response hyperlink typically three times: at the end of the email as with a postal letter, but also in the P.S. and in the lead of the email.

Why in the lead? Because that way, someone who knows they are interested immediately is not forced to scroll through the email to reach the hyperlink at the end, and forcing prospects to do this is proven to lower click-through rates. It's not a problem in paper direct mail, because you can quickly glance at the last page of the letter to find the response instructions, and also, they are on a separate reply element within the envelope, making them even easier to find.

Why in the P.S.? Because long experience shows that the P.S. gets high readership in letters, whether in print or online. For this reason, many snail mail copywriters also repeat the offer and call to action in the P.S.

When a hyperlink is created to sell a product or service, in most cases, the link's name will stand for that product or service, and leads straight to a landing page where that product or service can be bought. For example, I recently sent an email out on how to become a published novelist. The landing page URL where interested readers can learn more about the product and buy it is www.getyournovelpublished.com.

Another way to create a link is by highlighting a string of text and adding the website URL on to that highlight. This is created behind the scenes in HTML, using an <a> tag along with an href attribute, which must be used within the string for any URL to be an active hyperlink. The link is followed by the text that is seen on the page. The section of text with the HTML and URL added behind it is highlighted in blue, showing it as an active link, even though there is no underline used. An example would be:

You can go here to find out more about **publishing your novel**.

The HTML behind the blue text looks like this:

```
<p>You can go here to find out more about
<a href="https://www.getyournovelpublished.com">
    publishing your novel</a></p>
```

The <p></p> snippet is a paragraph element, and allows the line text to be separated from other surrounding text as an enclosed block with an actionable link.

You can also create an HTML-defined line of text, called a title which, when you hover your mouse over the blue linked text, shows more supplementary information before you click to get the destination page. However, as many readers today are opening emails on mobile phones, this title line may not be a helpful tool for you to use in emails, or on websites, as mobile readers typically have no access to a mouse for hovering over text and links. Therefore, the alt-tag text becomes your most important element to have in your content.

Create supporting command links, which tell a reader to get a certain software, like Adobe Acrobat Reader, if they are going to download one of your PDF (portable document format) documents. For example, just after describing to readers what your PDF-formatted report is about, you can let them know that they need to download the Acrobat Reader, if they do not already have it, before downloading the PDF report. You can put the link to download the Adobe Acrobat Reader just before offering the link to get the PDF report.

```
<p><a href="https://get.adobe.com/reader/">
Download Adobe Acrobat Reader
</a></p>
```

A word of caution: always make sure that text links specifically name what they are for, such as the above link for getting the Acrobat Reader. If you just say that **you can click here**, and you say that several times in one page, it can be confusing for the reader if each link is activated for different target points. Be sure to state what the link is.

Relative vs. Absolute Hyperlinks

An absolute link will define the URL of a website and may also include a specific page on that website as well. An example of this is the link shared with you previously:

www.getyournovelpublished.com

In fact, behind the scenes in HTML, the full address is <http://www

.getyournovelpublished.com>. This is an absolute address that is always there and never changes, unless you move that page.

A relative link is commonly used within a website or an e-newsletter. If you want your readers to click on the link to read a report (Best Practices), found in a subdirectory (reports) on your website, you would simply use www.mainsiteURL.reports/BestPractices.pdf. You could present the link like this:

Read the **Best Practices** report here.

Readers know to click on the blue text link which, then opens the Best Practices.pdf from the reports subdirectory. These two types of URL hyperlinks are vital to know whenever working within your own website, or if linking to external websites and landing pages. Also, remember to use a website address shortening tool, such as bit.ly.com and tiny URL, to reduce excessively long addresses. Keep text links short in appearance so it is easy to see and act on.

While the focus here has been on text links, you can also use images, pictures, and videos to act as hyperlinks, using the same HTML URL formats behind the scenes to make these actionable. Chapter 6 gave information about using the alt attribute in regards to the use of images and videos, and having the fallback image, when images or videos do not display or play inside an email. Remember that videos are best presented when hosted by a third party instead of yourself.

Whether using images, pictures, or videos as links, they should all relate to your message. Do not just put up an image of a beach, when it has nothing to do with linking to your website or landing page, unless your message is about travel opportunities, or a theme you are presenting, such as relaxing at the beach in December while writing your life story.

CTAs (Calls to Action)

Calls to action (CTAs) are generally a linked image or a graphic button. Words on the button (e.g., Order Now) tell the reader to click and take a certain action. By the time the reader has moved down the first section of the content body, and sees the first CTA button, the content has prepared the reader to take an action (click on the button) if he or she wants to know more, or is ready to buy. The content before the CTA presents the first step in a motivating sequence to persuade a reader that what you offer them is something they want or need, either to satisfy a need, solve a problem, or accommodate a desire.

CTAs should be visible and placed in the center of an email or landing page, with a space before and after the button, thus highlighting it from surrounding content. Using a color, particularly one that stands out from the page background, ensures the reader cannot miss it. Examples of two CTA buttons are shown below, along with the CTA message.

While a bit large on this page, these CTAs are very easy to see, and to click and act on when found on a landing page, for example, or in emails. Be sure the CTA image does not overwhelm the surrounding text by being too large, as shown below. Nor should you make it too small, to the point where the text message inside is barely readable. If too small, the impact is lost.

Be sure to make your images as interesting as possible. If using rectangular or square shapes, then round off or bevel the edges, and fill the image with a gradient color. Never use an image that is flat, one-dimensional, and boring in appearance. Most image editors have plenty of options to give your buttons a 3-D look, or to add transparency to one of the two colors included in the gradient application.

The text message should be in a contrast color to the button's fill color, so the message is clear to see. You can use different background button shapes, such as circular, but do not go overboard with crazy designs that detract from the message. Make sure the message is short and direct.

In Chapter 4, conducting A/B testing on email "From" and subject lines was discussed, and you can do the same testing with your email CTA buttons too, especially if you want to try out a new shape for a CTA button. Consider sending one color background and styled text to the A group, and another different colored (and shaped) CTA button to the B group. Alternatively, you can also do the B group with text-based hyperlinks, just to see how they measure up against each other. In one landing page, we tested red, yellow, green, and ochre CTA buttons. The ochre won. That does not mean all CTA buttons should be ochre; it means color can affect response rates and you have to test everything, including color!

It is important to remember when testing CTA buttons, that you keep everything else about the email the same, such as the "From" line, the subject line, headers, and content body. Only the CTA buttons are measured against each other, or against text hyperlinks. Do not forget to also test your CTA button first to make sure the link is working properly, and that readers who click on it will reach the target the way you want them to.

Alt-Tags and Search Engines

In Chapter 6, alt-tags were discussed for images, like the Beautiful Black Cat, along with width and height for the images. In the case of the CTA button, the inserted CTA text for the button becomes the alt-tag text, or can be expanded on, if images are blocked in emails, for example.

Alt-tag attributes, given within the image tags, also offer opportunities to increase your rankings with search engines. To do this, use text in the alt-tags that states exactly why the button is there, even if readers cannot see it. Avoid using more than 125 characters (including spaces), and use only a few relevant keywords. For those people who are visually impaired, and who use screen readers, the alt-tag text becomes important as the text is read out loud to them, so they know what is there.

Title attribute text can also be used but, generally, is not considered necessary, so long as the alt-tag text, with a relevant keyword or two, is there. Search bots pick up keywords in alt-tags of images included in emails, websites, and landing pages. Surrounding content should also align with alt-tag keywords to enhance search results.

Therefore, as Google points out when talking about best practices with images and search engines, if your photo still has an image number on it, rather than a name that states what it is, then Google will pass it by. Change the name of the image before you place it into the web page so that search engine optimization is fully functional and search engine bots can find the image (and surrounding text content) anytime someone searches for something similar.

Hyperlinks and CTAs, including all the behind-the-scenes alt-tags and SEO information given, become crucial to the success of how your landing page for your product or service will be found on the worldwide web. You can tie in a CTA button color scheme used in the email to also appear in the landing page message, providing a certain continuity in branding the message and product, or service.

Aside from your website, if you have one, the landing page is the place where you conduct sales, which is the lifeline of your business. Once you have designed and sent out the highly effective email to readers, that gets them to your landing page, then you must follow through with effective and persuasive content and design to get your readers to act.

Email vs. Landing Page Copy

We need to remember that the copy for email marketing campaigns is not wholly contained within the email itself. It is really in two parts.

The first half of the message is in the actual email. The email contains a link to a page on the web. When you click on that link, you jump to the page, where the remainder of the message is presented, along with the online order mechanism.

In a traditional direct mail package, the message is unevenly split. Consistently, 98 percent of the copy is in the letter and brochure, with the remaining 2 percent on the order form.

In email marketing campaigns, the division is less balanced and more varied. As shown in Fig. 8-1, there are four basic ways to divide the sales copy between the email and the response page:

1. *Short email, landing page*—Many marketers with simple lead-generating offers use short emails (the traditional three to four paragraphs) with a link to a "landing page." A landing page is a short web-based form, usually with a headline, a couple of paragraphs explaining the offer, and a mechanism for the recipient to fill in his information and submit his response. This format is similar in length and style to the traditional one-page sales letter and business reply card used in lead-generating paper direct mail.

2. *Long email, landing page*—This is similar to #1 above, except the email, by Internet marketing standards, is "long." For convenience, I define a short email as any email that, when printed out, takes half a page or less. By comparison, any email that takes more than a page when printed out is "long." This format is similar in length and style to a direct mail package with a four-page letter and a simple four-by-nine-inch order card.

3. *Long email, micro site*—This format has a long email and a long landing page, known as a "micro site." The micro site is a custom

URL designed specifically for the offer. Unlike a landing page, which is usually a single screen, the micro site's lengthier copy requires many screens. The micro site can be broken into distinct pages (see www.hypnoticwriting.com) or it can be one continuous document through which the reader must scroll (see www.surefirecustomerservicetechniques.com). This long email / micro site format allows for maximum copy, and is ideal for translating lengthy promotions to the web.

4. *Short email, micro site*—This format combines a short email up front with a long-copy micro site on the back end. It is ideal for offers that require a lot of copy but are being transmitted to prospects who might not read a lengthy email.

Marketing emails are typically sent to one or more of the following types of e-lists:

- *House files.* As with traditional direct mail, email marketing works best when sent to your house list of customers and prospects. If your house files don't have email addresses, there are several ways to obtain them. You can run your file through an email address appending service, and expect to find email addresses for between 10 percent and 30 percent of the records. You can also make email address collection part of your ongoing marketing and customer service records. For instance, one of my vendors that awards gifts based on bonus points offered to add three hundred bonus points to my account in exchange for my email address.

- *E-zine subscribers.* Theoretically you will get high response rates mailing to people who have signed up for your free e-zine. However, these folks are often freebie seekers, and may not be qualified prospects. Therefore, results vary. Some e-zine lists are pure gold. Others generate less sterling results.

- *Rented opt-in e-lists.* You can rent e-lists for email marketing campaigns at costs ranging from $100 to $300 per thousand. As with traditional direct mail, test lists in small quantities before rolling out to any.

Another option, as previously discussed, is to run classified ads in other people's e-zines with a link to your landing page or micro site. This lets you get your message to people at a far lower cost per thousand than solo emails. However, the circulations of many e-zines are unqualified and unaudited; therefore the quality of the audience you reach can be questionable. Again, you have to test.

The bottom line: Email marketing can work without having emails competing with *War and Peace* in word count. By strategically splitting your copy between the front-end email and back-end response page, you can get your message across without having time-pressured Internet users fleeing in terror.

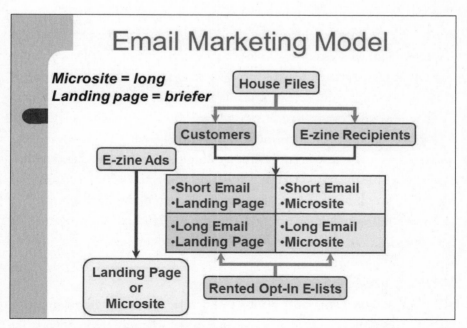

Fig. 8-1. Email length guidelines and list sources.

Landing Pages

A landing page is a one-page site on the Internet, where people come to learn more about your product or service, and to take an action, such as buying your product. Once they take an action, they are redirected to the proper form to fill out, whether it be signing up for a subscription or to buy your product. Getting your readers to do what you want them to do requires extensive planning, and development, to achieve that goal you set in place. If you want to know what a landing page looks like, which may help you with coming up with your first design, see Fig. 8-2 for an example. When driving traffic to this page by sending a sales email to my opt-in list, the conversion rate—percentage of prospecting clicking onto the landing page who buy the product—is 32 percent:

www.myveryfirstebook.com

This long-column approach is one of many designs on the web marketplace, but has worked very well for the books I have written over the decades. Depending on what product or service you are selling online, look at other marketing pieces related to your product category, and look at the design of those landing pages to see how it might work for you and your product.

For lead generation, landing pages are shorter, because you are not asking someone to give you money, but rather giving them something for free. Fig. 8–2 shows a successful landing page for my lead magnet on business-to-business marketing. This landing page, with accompanying fill-out form, generates leads for my freelance copywriting services. It also gives more customer information, which can help with readership list segmentation, should it be wanted in future marketing campaigns.

Writing your landing page

Start out by reviewing your product or service, such as what it does for buyers, how does it help them (make a list), why should they buy it from

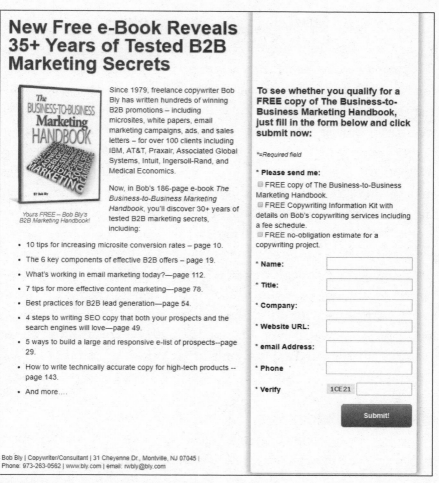

Fig. 8-2. Lead magnet landing page.

you, and why should they get it now. Make a list of tips that might be helpful, especially if you wrote a book about gardening in the southern United States, for example. For each tip, tell them what page they will find that answer on, for that tip. Tell them what page they can find the best design for a green house. It will take you some time to come up with such a list, but it will be invaluable, once you begin planning and writing the content for your landing page.

As you begin writing your content for your page and product, use a persuasive and motivating approach from the outset. Mine is simply called The Motivating Sequence. There are five steps in the motivating sequence: attention, problem identification, solution offer, proof, and call to action. They are described below as a guideline for writing any persuasive document, whether a landing page or an email marketing messaging page.

Attention

Start your copy with attention-grabbing persuasive and alluring headlines that focus on your readers' needs and desires, as relates to your product offering. Readers arriving on your landing site have already given you their attention, and now you need to keep their attention. If you had written a gardening book that specialized on developing British gardens in the southern United States, you can grab readers' attention by telling how readers can design and grow their own British garden too. If they buy your new gardening book, then they will find out the secrets of building and supporting a lovely British garden on their own property.

Identify your readers' problem or need

Those readers in southern United States may want to know how such a garden will fare in a warmer climate than found in Britain. Address climate problems, and then show how the way you have developed the soil sets a better foundation for planting trees, bushes, and flowers typically found in British gardens. You can mention various plants and note what page the answer to successfully grow each plant will be found on. If you have come up with your own recipe for feeding certain types of plants, then say what pages those recipes can be found on.

Tell stories about how companion gardening also worked well, when some plants needed a certain flower planted next to it to thrive. You can tell readers that companion gardening solutions can be found on specific pages. Give those page numbers. Features can also include best watering systems that can be built for each part of the garden. Tell readers what page that is on.

You can highlight some of the features by using small colored squares, triangles, stars, or circles, to replace standard bullet points found in regular text documents. They should not be an overwhelming size, but complement the size of the text you are using. See samples below.

Intersperse content with a headline statement in a slightly larger font size, and change the color from black to a more interesting color that stands out. If you are using a color scheme for your design, then work out what colors work well within that scheme, but present a contrast.

Position your product, service, idea, or suggestion as the solution

By telling your readers that you have a solution for nearly every problem that might occur when growing British garden plants, then you have set yourself and your book as an expert in the field of British gardening, at least in the southern part of the United States. For example, show which plants need a full day's worth of sunlight, while others need mostly shade. Say what page that is on if they want to know more.

If you have statistics on how well your own garden grew in your development trial, then offer those numbers, such as in a before and after situation, rather like a case study. Show how you overcame some of the problems that came up, although do not give too much away. Just tell them what page they can find the answer to some of the problems you had when first starting out.

Offer proof

Now prove that your idea, service, or product is indeed not only a good solution but in fact the best solution, superior to all other sources of action available to your reader. For our gardening example, aside from your own success with designing, building, and keeping a British garden, if others have already tried your gardening system and been successful, then show that success through customer reviews and testimonials.

Readers like to know that others have already tried the gardening system, and been successful. Show documentation, such as having invited an agricultural specialist from the state you live in and what the results were when soil was tested. There are all kinds of statistics that can be included and you can add page numbers where these can be found.

Ask for action

Now that you have given evidence that you have the knowledge to help others with your new book, ask readers to click on the link to buy it. Offer a guarantee of ninety days, if you wish to sweeten the deal. Depending on how much content you use on your landing page, strategically place your CTA buttons after the right amounts of motivating content, including the first group of listed features. Try to balance large amounts of text with CTAs and use small arrows, or other shaped graphics, to change up the content design.

Finally, you will integrate your bulk email service with the landing page links and CTAs, with forms that readers receive when they click on those links, such as registration pages, the sales / credit card information form, the invoice form, the thank you form after purchase, and any follow-up forms, such as a bonus notice sent after purchase.

Most bulk email clients have templates available which can be changed to suit your own needs. Your thank you email notes, auto-generated after a purchase, should be personalized, as readers appreciate the use of their name, as opposed to a generic thank you form.

These forms should already be designed to align with the product, and you could include a picture of the product bought, giving the whole system a more professional appearance. Each form should have the necessary boxes where readers can enter needed information, including drop-down boxes, such as for a state or a country.

Last Word on Design and Headlines in Your Copy

Use headlines that continue to capture readers' attention, which also helps to break up continuous copy. It is like taking a breath every now and then, and introducing another way of thinking about the information—interjecting a new idea that the product offers. My landing page for getting your novel published adds these headlines in the copy after a certain amount of copy, and they are in a different color.

Each headline should be relevant to the upcoming copy that the readers will see after that headline. Use emotive words, such as "secrets revealed," or tell them to wait, because there is more to come. There can be a headline, along with eight paragraphs of copy that support the headline. Then a new headline is introduced, with two paragraphs of copy, and a supporting list of features. Your headlines, CTAs, and bullet graphics go a long way in building a pleasing design to enhance your message, so that readers stay engaged in what you offer.

You can start laying out your copy in a mock-up one-column design, and consider how much content you want in place before you add in a contrast color headline or your CTA button, or even a set of colored bullets for your features. Once you have a first mock-up of your content, along with collected original images, CTA buttons, and other graphics you will be using, then you are ready to set up the physical landing page.

How to Find the Right Landing Page Service

While I have my own website at www.bly.com, I also have many land-ing pages, one for each of my products, and it is part of a package deal with my hosting provider. You should check first with your web-site hosting provider to see if they offer landing page packages. If not, there are companies on the Internet who specifically offer landing page services for a certain amount of views per month. If you are new to this side of a single domain / landing page arrangement, then look for those companies that offer a free service for five-thousand-plus views per month, or a free trial first.

What you need to ask yourself first is how many landing pages with their own domain names do you think you might need now, and in the future? Is the pricing right for how many landing pages you can build, along with how many views you can have, before the pricing begins to rise?

If you are creating multiple products that each need separate landing pages with their own product-based domain names, then here are a few companies to look at first, as a starting point. Try each first before signing up for a regular subscription, as you do not want to add costly monthly fees to your Internet commerce endeavors until you are ready for such an expansion. Look for issues such as how easy it is build a landing page, how sign-up and payment forms can be integrated from outside email and commerce vendors (MailChimp, ConstantContact, PayPal, all credit card payment capabilities, etc.), and the level of customer and technical service you get. This last one is essential if you need help fast. A plus point are those companies that include A/B testing in their landing page package.

IM Creator offers you a chance to build your first landing page with e-commerce solutions, free of charge, per their website. That is one ver-sion of their services. The other is the PRO/Whitelabel version, which may be an excellent choice for those in the website building business who want one platform from which to offer clients custom-built websites, with everything included.

Other companies on the market are **Lander**, at landerapp.com, where you can try their landing page services (among other services that they offer) first. Small businesses pay between $16 a month (paid annually) to $49 a month, with a percent reduction if paid annually. You can start with a two-week trial to see if this works for you. Pricing can change quickly on the Internet, so make sure you know what each company charges and look for available discounts first before signing up.

Other companies to review as a beginning point are Landingi.com, PageWiz.com, LeadPages.net, LandingPageMonkey.com, and Wishpond.com. You can also create your own if you are using WordPress. You would just need to buy a domain name for your page.

In this chapter, you have learned how hyperlinks and CTAs in your emails lead to your landing page for your product or service, and how persuasive copy will lead readers to buy your product. Based on the product or service you are selling, each piece ties together to make the ultimate engagement package that helps you successfully reach your goals.

CHAPTER 9.

Autoresponders

An autoresponder is software or a service that automatically sends out either a prewritten single email or a sequence of emails on a preselected date or at a time. The sequence is usually triggered by a specific user action, such as when the user returns a completed survey or downloads a free e-book or fails to renew a subscription. The carefully planned use of autoresponders can boost online sales in digital marketing 10 percent to 30 percent or more.

It's worth repeating: An email autoresponder series can boost your conversion rates 10 percent to 30 percent or higher. Canadian hockey great Wayne Gretzsy remarks, "You miss 100 percent of the shots you don't take." *Why should you risk the loss?*

Practically speaking autoresponders are a great boon because your business receives and answers requests that can be handled while you attend to other business—or sleep. In short, your workforce virtually multiplies while your payroll remains the same.

The Many Benefits of Autoresponders

The many benefits of autoresponders are not easy to prioritize. So, in no particular order of importance, consider these:

- Boost conversion rates, opt-ins, leads, and sales.
- Build relationships that bode well for consumer retention. The speedy attention you give with the help of the autoresponder makes a consumer feel important.
- Save the environment. They don't use paper and obviously don't consume trees. When communication is delivered digitally, it can be saved and filed with one or two keystroke commands. *Talk about maintaining a paperless office!* The carbon footprint of an autoresponder is almost nonexistent.
- Printing and postage costs are higher than ever and predictably rising because of the increased cost of paper and various factors involved in delivery of snail mail. Autoresponder email eliminates these costs.
- It probably costs a dollar or more to print each of your company catalogs. Yet, you will never really know if the mail is delivered to the right address. You want the best return on investment and it's easier to measure when you use autoresponders. With direct mail, you're not able to be sure who is looking at what you sent out.
- Is your current advertising technique working? That will take weeks to ascertain with direct mail, whereas the autoresponder *dashboard* calculates how well you are doing from the moment you send out the first email. (Note: the *dashboard* component of autoresponder software tells a visual "story" based upon information specific to the promotion.)

Autoresponders Form and Function

The many forms of autoresponders are panoramic and infinitely useful. While you're reading this chapter, be assured someone, somewhere is thinking up new ways to use autoresponders.

Just to give you a sense of how extensive autoresponders are, here are twenty-one popular autoresponder types:

1. Welcome
2. Abandoned Shopping Cart Reminder
3. Birthday Greeting
4. Anniversary Greeting and/or Coupon
5. Confirm a Purchase
6. Shipping Status
7. Announce a Sale
8. Campaign appeal
9. Response to Changes in a Customer's Behavior
10. Deliver a Free e-Book –or Report
11. Deliver a Course
12. Request Customer Feedback
13. Ask a Question: Give an Answer Propose a Solution
14. Offer Tips
15. Send Alerts
16. Send a Link to a Contest
17. Send a Quotation, Note of Inspiration, or Other Daily Dose of Concise Information
18. Time to Renew a Membership, Subscription, or Service
19. Make an Announcement, Send an Invitation
20. Send out your Newsletter
21. Send a Thank You Note, Automatically

Welcome messages

There will never be a better time to talk to a new subscriber than via a Welcome email. A new subscriber is a HOT lead and he or she is telling you what you offer is of interest. Get this right and it could be the highest performing email you ever send.

Shopping cart notice

Consider an autoresponder email as a reminder for a shopper who has neglected to finish working with the shopping cart. Did that individual want to complete the request to place an order? Good autoresponder companies outfit you with templates for reminding potential customers about abandoned sales. *You left an item in your cart. Get it before it's gone.*

Birthday notice

What goes with a birthday? A gift, of course. *Your special day is almost here—yes, May 17—and we are going to help you celebrate in style!* Describe the gift (e.g., 50% off the purchase price for one item in our line of luxury leather goods). Of course, you'll need the person's birth-date. Don't ask for this on the company sign-in or squeeze page because statistics show us that you will lose your opt-in. Since you're building a relationship, you have time to collect more strategic data.

Anniversary

An anniversary is another auspicious occasion that can be both appreci-ated and monetized with an autoresponder email. Physicians use anni-versary autoresponders to remind patients about important visits. School officials send out anniversary autoresponders to remind students about critical deadlines. Even religious organization personnel send out anni-versary autoresponders to remind congregants about special holy days and celebrations. Anniversaries are customizable to your business. You will be able to add photos, logos, and other features to make this autore-sponder stand-out as yours alone.

Order confirmation

We appreciate you for shopping with us! It follows that there's an autoresponder that confirms a purchase. Your customers should see something like auto-confirm@youraddress in the subject line. An example of this is auto-confirm@amazon.com.

> Hello Dr. Maria R. Jackson,
> Thank you for shopping with us. We'll send a confirmation once your item has shipped. Your order details are indicated below If you would like to view the status of your order or make any changes to it, please visit Your Orders on Amazon.com. (Proceed with details.)

Shipping Status

Autoresponders send automatic email updates once the order has shipped. It need not be long nor fancy. The shipping status update contains pertinent information for the customer about their order, and is particularly critical when multiple orders are in play. If a partial order has shipped, this information needs to be reflected in the subject line.

Sales promotion

Use autoresponder emails to notify customers of all sales. While the implementation of such an autoresponder might seem like the ultimate "no-brainer," it's useful to examine some of the basics. You generate more sales when you state specifically when the sale is taking place—dates and times—and emphasize that it is for a limited time only, and once the sale is over, it's too late to take advantage of these great savings.

Autoresponder emails triggered by customer behavior

Changes in a customer's behavior are not overlooked! Silence is a key signal that something has gone wrong with the relationship. Today's Internet consumer expects ever-increasing levels of excellence in terms of product and services. If this customer has dropped off the radar, chances are someone else has picked up where you left off. Your goal is to restart a dead or flagging conversation. Remember, there is a time and place for nonautomatic conversations. Participation in social media proves you are not a robot or a corporate drone with no time for customers. It's all about caring and engagement.

Free content offers: e-books, reports, courses

Free ebooks and reports are popular welcome gifts, especially when you are running a marketing or information service. But you may choose to make these available to your subscribers at various times, particularly if you find their attention to your purpose flagging. At times you may have difficulty distinguishing an e-book from a report. In general reports are shorter and you may want to bundle several of them to form an e-book. Ebooks have no given page length, although seventy pages that total fifteen thousand words provides a good minimum range for one. If you deliver it in chapters you're operating a *drip campaign*.

You can deliver a course or an entire university of products. You can teach simply be sending out well-researched, well-written lessons, and pass the onus of assimilation of this material to your students, or you can choose to be an interactive teacher. The writing of E-courses usually involves research; beyond this the writer should have knockout skills when it comes to organization and process analysis. Unless you are a savvy curriculum developer, enlist one to give your materials polish. Many universities, such as Yale, are providing free courses online. The value of these courses is in the thousands of dollars each, given current tuitions. There is great usefulness in employing autoresponder technology to educate, whether it is casually, or, on an Ivy League level. Your E-School amounts to someplace else where you plant your flag.

Solicit customer feedback

Requests for customer feedback are usually triggered by purchases and delivered via autoresponder email. I receive these auto responses a lot, since I do so much shopping online. Typically these will ask you to rate the product and/or service. Amazon is a good example; when you buy a used book, you are asked to rate the bookseller.

Problem/solution email marketing message

You ask a question and propose a solution, one which may require a response from the customer for her to obtain said answer. This differs from a survey, in that only one question is asked. The question may be, "(Insert Name), Do you need to learn Spanish fast?" You could explain why your product helps to achieve the goal faster and better. Next step? Provide a link to order it.

Free tips

Offer tips via email. Here's an illustration: The time to plant roses is here again. Are you ready? For the next 12 days, we're going to send you one tip each day, helping you to purchase the best roses for your area of the country. (Can a sale be far behind?)

Timely alerts

Send alerts such as weather, traffic, crime, the stock market, and news. The function of an alert is to express urgency. These are generally one-time only emails. Experience shows that emails tied in with current events and what is happening that day get higher response rates than emails that are evergreen and not related to what is on the web or news that day.

Contests

Send a link to a contest. Use the software to promote a contest of your own or an affiliate contest. You will need to embed your contest announcement with a link to enter. Contests represent a great way to draw consumer traffic to your website.

Quick notes

You can use autoresponders to send quotes, inspirational notes, or other daily doses of quick and concise content. You can prepare these as a multipart series of messages well in advance, and leave it to the autoresponder to deliver in a timely fashion according to the schedule you program into the system. Challenge yourself to assemble encouraging messages in a clever manner and recipients will associate you and/or your company with "something good."

Renewals

Renew a membership, subscription, lease or service contract via email. Autoresponders keep track of this "housekeeping" chore. Keep it simple. "We are writing to tell you that your son Jeffrey's subscription to *Toy Robot Magazine* is about to expire! There is just one issue left."

Announcements and invitations

Make an announcement or send an invitation automatically. Here again, a one-time autoresponder works well to accomplish this goal. "St. Theresa Catholic School cordially invites you to attend our Annual Dinner & Auction."

Distribute your e-newsletter

Send out your e-newsletter on a timely basis and never miss an issue! An autoresponder can take the ho-hum out of the typical missive. It's possible to add flair without the investment of much time or energy. Recipients should be more inclined to read when you're always in their email inbox on time with a relevant and entertaining issue.

Thank you notes

Send a thank you note automatically. "We are honored to be your partner and look forward to continuing our work together."

Space limitations demand that we bring this list of autoresponder ideas to a close, but only a sleepy imagination would limit your use of autoresponders to attain goals and achieve success!

Key Autoresponder Features and Functions

- *A Manage Subscribers Heading/Section* to give you an overview of the process of subscription management. You'll be able to view all current subscriptions, as well as those which have been unsubscribed. On this page, you can also track undeliverable email. You will need to segment your search by time/date. So, for example, you can view any of those fields by the current date. That will be your default field. Or you may choose another time frame. Common time frame parameters include: since yesterday, the past seven days, the past thirty days, and the past year.

- *Bulk Unsubscribe* is especially useful if you have more than one list. This tool will help you track multiple *unsubscribes* and aid you in understanding *why the exit*. By law (the CAN-SPAM Act), you must offer subscribers an easy and accessible link to unsubscribe. Penalties for non-compliance are steep. Visit the Federal Trade Commission site online for details. (Go to: https://www.ftc.gov/. As of this writing, an eight-page Compliance Guide for Business is displayed. TAGS: Advertising and Marketing—Online Advertising and Marketing—Privacy and Security.) Some unsubscribe software asks the subscriber why he or she is leaving.

- *Suppress Subscribers* in order to keep subscribers from receiving certain emails. It's usually a matter of *relevance*. If a subscriber has notified you that irrelevant messages are arriving, you won't want to irritate this party by continuing this practice.

- ***Block Subscribers*** for various reasons. You may have encountered a person who is sending unsavory communications to you or who you suspect of spying or trying to sabotage your business. I use this occasionally if a person is rude or pesky.
- ***The Messages Tab/Section of Your Autoresponder*** helps you to navigate through the critical areas of technology's functionality.
- ***Follow-Up Series*** is the bread and butter of autoresponders. This section features a prompt to begin writing a follow-up series or campaign. This can amount to a single, simple follow-up email, if that is all you need. Click on this link and expect to see three options:
  - Create a Drag and Drop email
  - Create a plain text message
  - Create your own HTML message

Expect your Drag and Drop email creator to provide you with a wealth of ready-to-use templates that you can customize for your business and other purposes. These templates range from cool and business-like to neon-bright. Many people consider this Drag and Drop feature a huge part of what they are paying for, since they are not artistic and probably don't have command of HTML, but want to send showy emails with options such as adding videos and animations. Many email services such as the one I use, Contact, has HTML email templates, which I do not use because my emails are text in an HTML shell with copy only and no graphics.

Creating plain text messages may not be as exciting, but it is a good idea to have a plain text option when you are sending an important message, since many subscribers will only be able to receive such a message on certain electronic devices, and you don't want to shut out anyone from receiving a transmission. Send out your bright and colorful email with a plain text option. You can, of course, simply send a plain text message.

On more than one occasion I've surprised listeners by saying, "Often plain text out-pulls HTML." This probably explains why most of the autoresponders I receive every day are still delivered this way. Plain text is the safer option, from the point of view of many marketers, since HTML can have "bugs" running underneath it.

While eye candy options abound, HTML will not now offer the Fort Knox security of old reliable plain text, in which case what we see is what everyone gets. From the point of view of the person sending out the email, plain text virtually shuts down hackers, SPAMMERs, and Phishers, preventing sabotage such as a distortion of your message.

It is best to track your own results with your autoresponder and weigh benefits and drawbacks on a regular basis. This issue will remain a *moving target* for some time to come.

If you have supreme confidence in your words, work only with them. Remember to run split tests to see how your audience responds to plain text emails versus those more gloriously executed and endowed. You will never know which type your audience prefers unless you go for the split test. Happily, your autoresponder gives you the tools to send as many split test emails as you require.

Those who know HTML may be the stars of the process, for they can create anything they can program.

Copywriting for Autoresponder Emails

You may hire a copywriter to write the text for your autoresponders or you may do it yourself. The software can provide structure and direction but that's all. Well, that's not quite correct—some autoresponder companies provide tips for writing effective emails and templates to deliver minimal framework to help with composition. Remember, however, it's the writing that gives life and humanity to emails.

Don't plan to write one email and call it quits because it may take at least three and as many as seven or more contacts before someone decides to buy. Generally, the pricier the item or service, the more deliberation time will be needed. If you follow up with a well-organized, well-timed, and well-written campaign that delivers value with each email—you double your chances for success.

Insert your personality into the writing and your autoresponders will shine. No one should ever think, "Hey I'm reading an autoresponder," or whatever word may be in the person's vocabulary to identify this type of communication. You'll want to be consistent, honest, and volunteer all-important information. Be honest. If the product under discussion won't be ready to deliver for three months, say so.

Let your personality shine through in your writing. The technique of "transparency"—revealing relevant personal information and stories in your writing—adds interest and engages the reader, especially in series emails such as autoresponders and e-newsletters. When you tell me that your sixty-five-year-old grandfather runs thirty miles a week, I'll want to know more about him. If you sell the brand of running shoes he wears, that should spur my interest in those shoes. If your grandfather has some tips for older athletes, go ahead—tell me. *Now, we're building a relationship.*

The Autoresponder Experience

You may not have written an autoresponder message yet, but think about how many you received. You probably know more than you think you do. I ordered some books for my nephew and Amazon.com sent a confirmation that the order was received. Soon after I got another message telling me the order was shipped. I was able to track delivery information and "see" when the gift was delivered. I feel comfortable with this vendor and I'll place another order when my sister's birthday is close.

At suppertime, I ordered a pizza online and immediately got back an autoresponder telling me that my pizza was currently being tossed, sauced, and topped per my unique instructions. Those instructions were repeated in the message. It included the time that the pizza would arrive at my door. All I had to do was put the beverages on the table and stand by to open the front door!

"After dinner, I'll be writing copy for the local Library Book Fair," writer Marilyn Pincus recently told me. "Autoresponders will be sent to library card holders to announce book fair dates and later to extend invitations and finally to solicit donations for two community college scholarships the Friends of the Library hope to fund. The Friends award at least one scholarship annually. My challenge is to write copy that will whet appetites to do more. I'll arrange for donations to be tendered on-line and I'll be sure to include clear directions for how to use this (send in your money) tool."

Proflowers sends three emails for every order: One to confirm the order, when to tell you know it has shipped, and a third to confirm delivery. As a regular customer, I find this a valuable service.

Resolving Technical Issues

Autoresponder companies sell their products with the promise that any layperson can use them. Presumably they simplify what is ultratechnical and should the need arise these vendors provide customer service to address those issues quickly and in a friendly and efficient way.

Many autoresponder users will never need to plunge into the deep seas of technology that underlie the software. The great companies run similarly great blogs and post instructional videos on YouTube with timely educational slants. Competitive companies also supply download-able issue-specific guides. Most are free, although I had to pay for a few.

If your business has a full-time webmaster or even part-time on call, as mine does, let him or her deal with the autoresponder vendors and email service providers to resolve anything technical. You have better things to do, right? And this tech stuff is no fun for laypeople, even those like me who have IT training.

Setting up Your Autoresponder Email Series

When setting up your autoresponder sequences, first click on the tab that says List Builder, which should be clearly labeled on your toolbar. When it opens, provide the company name, address, your name, and you will be given the opportunity to personalize your list with detailed, concise information about your company, too.

You can usually add some emails directly to this list, and most will allow you to transfer lists, or import subscribers. You will then see tables that elaborate on a number of options for your immediate or later use. These may include creating follow-up series messages, broadcasts, and blog posts.

To demonstrate that these programs have become a force of the twenty-first century, this area of the autoresponder should contain email parsers. Think of parsing as extracting pertinent material and forwarding it to specific locations where it is needed. These often comprise payment processors. This process will allow you to integrate your lists with any number of shopping cart options and third-party applications. And while you may be already familiar with the shopping cart applications, parsers are by no means limited to this function.

A good service will also allow you to customize and test parsers that do not appear on their basic lists. Needs for third-party integration will vary according to your business, but make sure the possibility of adding various parsers, and indeed several at a time is possible.

Double vs. Single Opt-In

Today autoresponder companies recommend the double opt-in for list building and to prevent your emails from showing up as SPAM—something that would reflect badly on you and your company. A double opt-in is a security device that decreases the likelihood of your email relationship being sucked into a black hole of deletions.

For example, for a double opt-in, Jane signs up for your newsletter or email list; she then gets another email asking for confirmation of this subscription. She responds in the affirmative and the relationship grows stronger. That way, you know it's really Jane who registered.

With a single opt-in that does not confirm the identity of the subscriber, a friend or stranger can register Jane to receive your emails. When Janes gets an email from you, it is a subscriber. She did not sign up for it. So, she may flame you, complain to your Internet Services Provider (ISP) that you are spamming, and the ISP may shut down your account.

The double opt-in ensures recipients really want your emails, demonstrating a higher level of interest. This means the person in question has taken the time to "confirm" participation. So, while the double opt-in may get fewer sign-ups than single and may build a list more slowly, it is still I believe the way to go.

The Power of List Segmentation

Your autoresponder allows you to divide your customers into ultraspecific lists to better serve them. You may sell products to women over fifty on a regular basis. The shampoo a woman uses to keep gray hair from looking dingy is popular but of little interest to a twenty-something guy. If you sell to him, you'll feature a different benefit. *Best Friend Shampoo leaves hair manageable and easy to style.* Strategic use of segmentation helps you to make more sales.

One way to segment your e-list is to communicate with your sub-scribers through surveys. Use the autoresponder's survey functions to tally data and then decide how you wish to use it. In the past, this was a laborious task. Imagine sending out surveys to a list of several thousand subscribers. Even if only ten percent respond—and we expect that auto-responder technology would yield a higher level of responses—sorting it by hand isn't feasible. *Who has the time and resources?* The threat of being left in the dust by your competition is all too real. Online services like Survey Monkey makes doing list surveys much easier and faster.

Acclaimed American basketball player, Tim Duncan remembers his mother telling him, "Good, better, best. Never let it rest. Until your good is better and your better is best." Adopt this mantra and segmentation is a no-brainer.

Drip Email Campaigns

Ultimate autoresponder success comes from the launching of and sus-taining campaigns over time. A drip campaign is when you release a series of timed autoresponder emails or postal letters to nurture prospects so they eventually become customers by placing an order, and to upsell current customers to make additional purposes.

First, decide the ultimate purpose of your campaign and set some time-based parameters. Let's take the example of a company that sells dif-ferent types of flours and baking ingredients. The winter holiday season is a great time to sell lots of flour and baking ingredients, so a campaign may deliver Christmas cookie recipes. I start to receive these after Halloween. It may begin with one email a week, but by the time the prime holidays draw closer, I may be receiving a recipe a day! These recipes always feature links to buy a product, such as specialty cake molds, or season-specific ingredients like chestnut flours (a favorite in Italian Christmas cookies).

These drip campaigns succeed because of the relentless delivery of interesting and helpful information and inherent follow-up.

Affiliate Email Marketing

Depending upon the offerings of your autoresponder company, you can begin your adventure in affiliate marketing by becoming an affiliate (i.e., associate or partner) of that very organization. Or you can use a service like Click Bank.

When possible, you enter into an affiliate agreement and are given an affiliate code. Others markets who sell your products to the lists as your affiliates use in their emails driving traffic to your sales page. That way you can track where each order came from, and for those clicks hyperlinks with affiliate code, you pay the sender an affiliate commission. This can be between 25 percent to 50 percent for information products, and 10 percent to 25 percent for merchandise.

Conversely, you can arrange to be an affiliate of other marketers whose products are relevant to your audience, place the affiliate code they give you in the hyperlinks in your emails that go to their sales pages, and collect a commission from them on every sale you make.

What's more, this opportunity should be free. If you find a fee involved, and deem it unreasonable, shop around. You can have this opportunity at no cost. You will be asked to provide your tax ID to track payments that normally are dispersed on a monthly basis. For more information on affiliate marketing, click on www.jvmagic.net.

CHAPTER 10.

Writing and Publishing an Email Newsletter

If you are in a business, association, church, or any other organization, one of the best ways to keep in touch with, inform—and yes, sell to—your members, clients, customers, prospects, or constituents is by publishing an online newsletter, also called an e-newsletter, digital newsletter, or e-zine.

I am guessing that, because you are reading this book, you either distribute emails regularly or plan to do so. The good news is the same software and services used to distribute one-shot emails and autoresponder email series can also be used to send out your e-newsletter. No separate or special "e-newsletter" distribution software or service is required.

The only change is that, as your subscriber list grows, you may have to upgrade capacity on your current software or service, or switch to a different distribution system if you outgrow the capacity of the one you now use.

Format

Although there is a wide variety in the length, style, and content of e-newsletters, they fall into two basic types: multi-topic and single topic.

As the name implies, a multi-topic e-newsletter has multiple articles, items, or stories. Typically, each item is short—only a few paragraphs each—with anywhere from five to seven or more brief articles per issue.

In a single-topic newsletter, each issue delivers only one long article. A hybrid variant is an e-newsletter that has one long lead article and then two to four additional, much shorter items. Examples of both a multi-topic and a single-topic e-newsletter are shown in appendix III.

Rules for writing multi-topic e-newsletters are summarized in Fig. 10-1. Often, the data and ideas in brief articles published in multi-topic newsletters are taken from other sources. As you can see in the figure below, you should always attribute the content to the source.

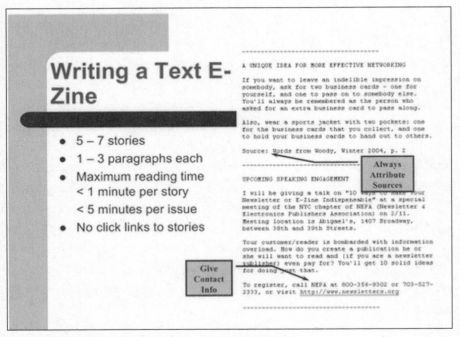

Fig. 10-1. Writing a multi-topic text e-newsletter.

Word Length

Though there is in reality no magic number for proper e-newsletter copy length, many e-newsletters are around 700 words. In a single-topic e-newsletter, the main article is a 700-word essay; mine tend to range from 300 to 850 words or so. In a multi-topic e-newsletter with seven stories, each would be around 100 words on average, for a total of 700 words. As I said, there is nothing magic about 700 words. That being said, aim for a total word count of 400 to 800 words and you'll be in good shape.

Frequency

Here are the frequency options for e-newsletters: quarterly, monthly, twice a month, weekly, two to three times a week, daily, multiple times per day, and sporadically published.

Which is right for you? There are three factors that determine frequency: your time, your information, and your audience.

The most common reason businesspeople give me for not doing an e-newsletter is that either they do not have the time, can't write, or both. So if you have no time to write your e-newsletter and no staff or freelance writer to help you, you understandably are hesitant to commit to publishing a regular digital news bulletin.

I have two solutions: First, do a multi-topic e-zine as shown in appendix III. Why? Because the articles are just a few paragraphs each. That makes them easy to write. Anyone can write a tiny article. Do seven and there's your issue. Second, you can outsource the writing to a freelance content writer. One source is www.upwork.com.

The next factor that people say inhibits them from committing to a regular e-newsletter is that they don't think they have anything to say, and so they worry about how they will fill the space.

But in fact, you have a lot to say. There is so much you can tell your prospects about you, your company, your products, their applications, your services, the problems you solve, it's dazzling. You will never run out of news, tips, and information to share. Later in the chapter is a checklist of 29 story ideas for your newsletter just to get you going.

The other reason businesspeople hesitate to send a regularly scheduled e-newsletter is fear of turning their customers and prospects off by sending too many emails. I suggest you start with monthly. If you want to reach your audience more frequently, increase to twice a month or weekly.

Then watch the opt-out rate: the number of people who unsubscribe every time you email an issue. The opt-out rate should ideally be 0.1% or less. So if you have five thousand subscribers, no more than five should unsubscribe per issue.

Whenever you increase the frequency of distribution, keep an eye on your opt-out rate. If it stays the same, you know your subscribers welcome getting more issues from you. On the other hand, if it spikes higher, they are telling you it's too much, and maybe you shut drop down to the old schedule again.

If you fear the commitment of publishing an e-newsletter on any regular schedule, say to new and current subscribers that it is "sporadically published." This way, you're under no commitment to deliver at a particular frequency, and the pressure is off.

Name Your E-Newsletter

The publication's name should "hook" a reader. The name should be relevant to the contents of the publication. Your e-newsletter should discuss Marathon Running if that is what you promised. I'm not interested in luggage or a racing bike; I'm interested in long-distance running.

Example: The newsletter title "The Fine Art of Endurance Running" gets my attention. Or, "Endurance Running" should work. Trying to be all things to all people with a title like "Moving Along" or, "In the Fast Lane" isn't likely to keep readers coming back for more. Vague titles don't help you either. They give you permission to stray and write about luggage or a racing bike!

Before you select the newsletter title, consider whether you can meet the criterion just mentioned. Do you need to expand the title? Provide a subtitle? Can you fulfill on the promise? Perhaps the publication schedule should be monthly as opposed to weekly or daily.

Catchy names are memorable. Try using alliteration and see what you can create. Consider words that rhyme and names that sound funny.

Exude authority. Words such as Digest, Report, Letter, Bulletin, Newsletter, and Reporter might help to convey the image you want. Don't hesitate to reach for a thesaurus as you search.

Short and sweet titles suggest the reader can glean information quickly. This promise appeals to readers who believe they have too much to read. Who among your potential subscribers doesn't feel that way?

Finally, you may find yourself changing the title more than once before you are satisfied. I don't write this to discourage you but to underscore the importance of the newsletter title. It's wasteful to start off with an unsatisfactory title but it's far more wasteful to hang onto it and let it become the proverbial albatross around your neck. Is the title already in use? That could be a red flag. If in doubt as to whether you can use it, check with your legal expert.

Give Readers Valuable Content

"Content is King," is a familiar slogan, but for many it is more than that—it is the mantra for a way of conducting business based on delivering useful information. Content-based businesses now actually hire journalists to write content for electronic newsletters. Articles can include links to items or services, and if you are the writer you may be wearing two hats: that of the journalist/researcher and that of the marketer.

If you decide to write the e-newsletter yourself, you should ideally be a good writer, enjoy writing, and have the time to research and write it. If you engage a writer, you should review the text and if needed give your writer your comments, so she can revise before you distribute.

Before you start writing, make sure you are providing valuable information. Consider where you obtained your data and how you shaped or, repurposed it. This is very important since a chunk of plain information that may almost be common knowledge becomes more valuable when you add details or somehow cast the information in a new light. It takes the human mind to take old information and breathe life into it, yet much of what we see is repurposed information.

Consider taking very difficult information and making it accessible to a layperson. You may want to consciously rate the value of what you are conveying using a scale from 1 through 10, with 1 representing information the reader will predictably discard, and 10 representing information so valuable that your prospect will forward it to others. Strive to always send out periodicals that rate a 6 or above, in terms of usefulness and interest. If you consistently send out newsletters of lower value, you may be dubbed a pest and sent into the junk folder.

29 Article Ideas for Your E-Newsletter

Coming up with good story ideas is one of the toughest tasks in publishing a company newsletter. Here's a checklist of story sources to stimulate editorial thinking and help identify topics with high reader interest that help to promote the company.

1. **Product stories:** New products; improvements to existing products; new models; new accessories; new options; and new applications.
2. **News:** Joint ventures; mergers and acquisitions; new divisions formed; new departments; other company news. Also, industry news and analyses of events and trends.
3. **Tips:** Tips on product selection, installation, maintenance, repair, and troubleshooting.
4. **How-To articles:** Similar to tips, but with more detailed instructions. Examples: How to use the product; how to design a system; how to select the right type or model.
5. **Previews and reports:** Write-ups of special events such as trade shows, conferences, sales meetings, seminars, presentations, and press conferences.
6. **Case histories:** Either in-depth or brief, reporting product application success stories, service successes, etc.
7. **People:** Company promotions, new hires, transfers, awards, anniversaries, employee profiles, customer profiles, human interest stories (e.g., unusual jobs, hobbies, etc.).
8. **Milestones:** e.g., "1,000th unit shipped," "Sales reach $1 million mark," "Division celebrates 10th anniversary," etc.
9. **Sales news:** New customers; bids accepted; contracts renewed; satisfied customer reports.
10. **Research and development:** New products; new technologies; new patents; technology awards; inventions; innovations; and breakthroughs.
11. **Publications:** New brochures available; new ad campaigns; technical papers presented; reprints available; new or updated manuals; announcements of other recently published literature.
12. **Explanatory articles:** How a product works; industry overviews; background information on applications and technologies.

13. **Customer stories:** Interviews with customers; photos; customer news and profiles; guest articles by customers about their industries, applications, and positive experiences with the vendor's product or service.

14. **Financial news:** Quarterly and annual report highlights; presentations to financial analysts; earnings and dividend news; etc.

15. **Photos with captions:** People; facilities; products; events.

16. **Columns:** President's letter; letters to the editor; guest columns; regular features such as "Q&A" or "Tech Talk."

17. **Excerpts, reprints, or condensed versions of:** Press releases; executive speeches; journal articles; technical papers; company seminars; etc.

18. **Quality control stories:** Quality circles; employee suggestion programs; new quality assurance methods; success rates; case histories.

19. **Productivity stories:** New programs; methods and systems to cut waste and boost efficiency.

20. **Manufacturing stories:** New techniques; equipment; raw materials; production line successes; detailed explanations of manufacturing processes; etc.

21. **Community affairs:** Fund raisers; special events; support for the arts; scholarship programs; social responsibility programs; environmental programs; employee and corporate participation in local/regional/national events.

22. **Data processing stories:** New computer hardware and software systems; improved data processing and its benefits to customers; new data processing applications; explanations of how systems serve customers.

23. **Overseas activities:** Reports on the company's international activities; profiles of facilities, people, markets, etc.

24. **Service:** Background on company service facilities; case histories of outstanding service activities; new services for customers; new hotlines; etc.

25. **History:** Articles of company, industry, product, community history.
26. **Human resources:** Company benefits programs; announcement of new benefits and training and how they improve service to customers; explanations of company policies.
27. **Interviews:** With company key employees, engineers, service personnel, etc.; with customers; with suppliers (to illustrate the quality of materials going into your company's products).
28. **Forums:** Top managers answer customer complaints and concerns; service managers discuss customer needs; customers share their favorable experiences with company products/services.
29. **Gimmicks:** Contents; quizzes; puzzles; games; cartoons.

Brainstorm with colleagues and your list of potential articles is bound to expand. It's acceptable to lift ideas from books and publications; just add your observations or a new perspective to make it your own. Keep a notebook handy (electronic or otherwise) that is dedicated to topic jottings. Don't forget to refer to it, as needed.

How to Write and Design a Text E-Newsletter

With audiences that are accustomed to getting text emails, text e-newsletters usually get the highest open rates and readership.

Audiences who are accustomed to text are probably comfortable with it and expect it. If one assumes readers are information seekers, image is (probably) not important. Therefore, the product does not need visual appeal and its okay if it arrives in plain text. The writing, however, should be captivating, clear, and concise.

When writing your text newsletter, set left margin at 20. Set right margin at 80. Use a 60-character column width. Employ a hard-carriage-return after every line. Dashed lines can separate items. Titles appear in all caps, centered, or with asterisks. Save as a text file. See Fig. 10-2 for a summary of these guidelines for formatting text e-newsletters along with a sample layout.

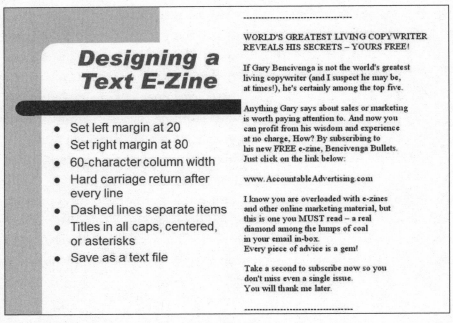

Fig. 10-2. Rules for text e-newsletter layouts.

The masthead, also called the header, is the text and layout that appears, always in the same format, at the beginning of every issue. The consistency is important. Subscribers have signed up to receive your newsletter. So when they see the familiar masthead, which includes the name of the newsletter and a from line indicating that you are sending it, they will open and read it. If you vary the header, particularly the newsletter name or "From" line, they may not recognize it, and instead delete the email as spam.

The subject line, however, should not be the same every time, but should be different for every issue. Pick the idea or subject from the issue that is most intriguing and interesting, and feature that in the subject line. You can follow the masthead setup shown in Fig. 10-3 for your e-newsletter.

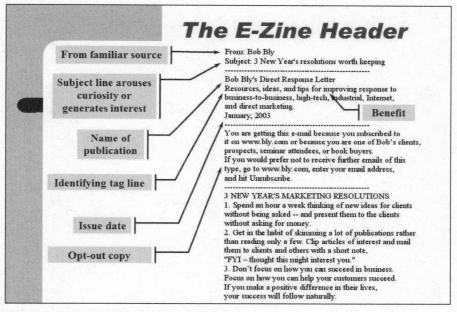

Fig. 10-3. Mastheads for text e-newsletters

Just as the masthead follows a standard format and design that is the same for every issue, each issue should also end with a standard sign-off, close, or call to action (see Fig. 10-4). While the bulk of the issue should be mostly useful information, the close is the place to tell the subscriber a little bit about who you are, what you do, and make an offer for them to find out more about your products and services. After all, you are not publishing the newsletter for your health. At the end of the day, you're using it to build a business.

But don't overdo the selling. People subscribe to e-newsletters to be educated, not to be sold. Too much selling and they will unsubscribe. An e-newsletter issue should be 80 percent content or higher and only 20 percent or less selling.

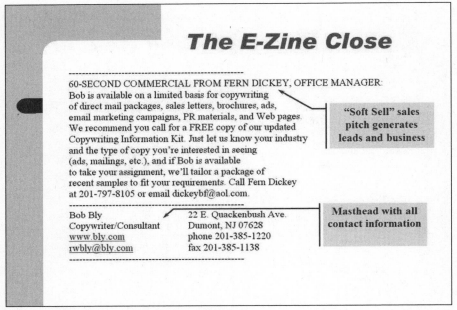

Fig. 10-4. Sign-off for text e-newsletter.

Designing an HTML E-Newsletter

HTML e-newsletters work best when audiences are accustomed to HTML. Then image (i.e., what readers see) is especially important because it's an integral part of the product and therefore, an integral part of the brand.

HTML is an abbreviation for Hypertext Markup Language. It is, as you probably guessed, the authoring language used to create documents on the World Wide Web. It uses a variety of tags and attributes.

All the time you're concentrating on writing and publishing your newsletter, there is a *truth* dancing in the background: you are putting together a segment of the company's brand. Tread lightly. Font choices and spacing as well as content work to deliver a message. Is the message in harmony with other company communications?

If the newsletter is for circus clowns, it's likely to "look" circus-y (e.g., with bold strokes and colors and unpredictable shapes). If the newsletter is for judges who preside over the lower courts, it won't look like the newsletter that is meant for clowns! Words such as somber, clean-edged, sparse or, crammed help to conjure up an appearance.

Certain products and services demand color photography that only HTML email can provide and text alone cannot. Examples include beach vacations, European travel, fashion, jewelry, flowers and plants, animals, collectibles, cigars, fine wine, cars—the list goes on and on. Also, for major national brands, they need HTML to show their corporate logo in its proper colors.

Open Rates

You send out email and then what? Do you know if was received? Was it ignored or dumped? Scrutinize your open rates to get answers. The open rate is the percentage of delivered emails opened by recipients.

My open rates range from 8 percent to 25 percent The low end is for e-newsletters going to my entire list, without segmentation. The high end is for e-newsletters going only to my clients and prospects.

When the numbers tell you that too much of the mail you send is not opened you can move quickly to determine why and make appropriate changes. Acquaint yourself with the vocabulary that is peculiar to this information. Soon you'll interpret what you learn and be able to turn it to your purposes. The key metrics are:

- Open Rates
- Hard Bounces

- Soft Bounces
- SPAM

Open rates, as you may surmise, are industry sensitive. According to a February 2017 updated Mailchimp.com report that tracked campaigns that went to at least one thousand subscribers and range from one-person startups to Fortune 500 companies, e-newsletters on hobbies had an average open rate of 28 percent. The high rate makes sense because people are extremely interested in their hobbies.

Hard bounces usually means "nobody home." Perhaps the address is no longer in use. A typo in the recipient's email address will result in a hard bounce or perhaps your message has been deflected by a spam filter. Then, too, the list could be too old.

Soft bounces suggest temporary unavailability. Are the intended recipients on vacation? Is the mailbox full? How long should you wait before you purge soft bounces from your list? One expert cleans soft bounces after five failed campaigns. I leave them on my list until they unsubscribe.

The dreaded *SPAM* designation usually means *you* are not memorable. "Originality is the key to being memorable," writes author Suzy Kassem. Are your company's email subject lines original? Let them also tell what is inside. What can I expect? What about the "From" lines? Your company name and (perhaps) your name should be there.

Physical and Mental Opt-Outs

A physical opt-out or unsubscribe means a subscriber, for whatever reason, is no longer interested in getting your online newsletter, and has actively removed his name from the list using the link and software your email service provides. You can measure your opt-out rates precisely based on reports from your email distribution service or analytics software. As previously mentioned, the opt-out rate per email or e-newsletter distribution should be 0.1% or less.

But there is another opt-out that is more difficult to measure with precision, which some call "mental opt-out." These people do not remove themselves from your subscription list; they simply stop opening and reading your publication. If your open rates are low, mental opt-out is often a big reason for that. The solution? Make your content more of it, and have a greater ration of useful information vs. selling.

CHAPTER 11.

Personal Emails for Every Occasion

Email can be an effective medium for communicating with others on a personal level as well as for business. Email makes it quick and easy to connect with those you might not otherwise connect with—friends, coworkers, family, and so on—in writing and on a regular basis.

Here are some advantages of email over postal mail for personal use:

- **It's instantaneous.** While postal mail can take from a couple of days to a couple of weeks or more to reach the person, email is instantaneous. Your recipient will receive the email within seconds of your clicking the *Send* button. If you want to thank someone for something, for instance, you can do so right away instead of making them wait to receive a letter.
- **It's free.** A postal letter costs about fifty cents for the stamp, envelope, printing, and so on. But email is absolutely free, except for the price of Internet (and you

have free Wi-Fi at your local library or coffee shop). Gmail is a free email provider, or you can purchase a personal email account with a personalized ".com"; for example, mine is rwbly@bly.com.

- **It's more convenient.** Email is easier to write than a postal letter. All it takes is a basic familiarity with computers and the email program. There's none of the hassle that can come with sending postal mail.
- **If the email bounces, you usually know right away.** If for some reason you've sent to an invalid email address, you will receive an email letting you know it has bounced and that the person hasn't received your email. With postal mail, it would take at least several days to figure out whether the address is any good—and you may never find out whether the person actually received your letter at all unless you mailed certified.
- **In some cases, it's easier to reach a personal contact through email.** This is especially the case with students. Since students tend to move around a lot into different dorm rooms, it can be difficult to retain an up-to-date address. And in many cases, students don't even check their mail. But personal email rarely changes.
- **Email allows for more back and forth than postal mail does.** If you want to actually have a conversation with your recipient, it's easy to do so with email. The reply is simple, and multiple emails can be sent back and forth in a short period. With postal mail, the conversation is much more halted. What would take weeks with postal mail can be accomplished in just a few minutes with email.

On the other hand, email has some disadvantages when it comes to personal communication:

- **Email can be viewed as less personal than postal mail.**
  Because of the easy and accessible nature of email, it
  takes less effort to write an email and can be perceived
  as less meaningful. A physical *Thank You* mailing from
  a loved one is usually perceived as more meaningful
  than an email. But this is not written in stone. Consider
  also that a personal mailing is a physical thing that is in
  the recipient's hands, whereas an email is an electronic
  communication.
- **People receive a lot of emails on a daily basis.** Their
  email inboxes are cluttered. And so they don't welcome
  more email. Many see getting through their email as a
  burdensome chore. Precisely because of email, postal letters
  are less common. So a postal letter may stand out more. It's
  possible for email to be missed, but very rarely will someone
  miss a personal letter in their mailbox.
- **People change their email addresses from time to time.**
  So it's possible the email will bounce or never be read if
  they're using a different email address.

Despite the possible negatives of using email for personal communication, email is still a great way to communicate on a personal basis. It's one of the most efficient ways to stay in touch with personal contacts.

All the same, there is an art to writing effective emails, even in personal situations. You don't want to give the impression that the email was written haphazardly or carelessly. Because of the easy and efficient nature of email, it's especially important to use care when creating them.

Here are a few general tips for writing personal emails:

1) Keep Them short

One of the rules for emails in general is to keep them short. That's because email is by nature a quick and easy medium—and the Internet competes with their attention. People often don't like to read long emails. It's not always the case, but as a general rule, you should strive to keep your emails short and thus accessible. Long emails can be intimidating and discourage a thorough read.

2) Show some personality

One of the ways personal emails differ from business emails is their informal nature. With loved ones and friends—and to a lesser extent coworkers—feel free to show a little more of your personality. Although there's etiquette to writing personal emails, you can be a little more creative than with business emails. Take into account who you're writing to. This will determine how formal you're going to be. You're naturally going to be a little more formal with a coworker than with a family member.

3) Make them pleasant to read

That means writing short sentences and short paragraphs—and generally making the email inviting by breaking up blocky passages and using interesting language.

Model Emails for Personal Usage

Here are personal emails for every occasion, which you can adapt for your own unique situations. I've also included some pointers on why each email works well for that occasion.

Note: the authors and recipients of these emails are completely fictitious.

Congratulations

For friends, family members, coworkers, and so on, who have had something major happen in their lives . . . graduation from school or college . . . a new baby . . . a new home . . . an email can be a thoughtful way to get in touch with them and let them know you're happy for them.

Here is a template you can base your email on:

Subject line: Congratulations!

Dear John,

Congratulations on your graduation!

Your mother told me recently that you graduated from the University at Buffalo with *honors*. I'm really happy for you! That's an incredible achievement. All your years of studying have paid off.

You always were a studious guy. I noticed it even when you were still in middle school.

Well done, John. You have a promising future ahead of you.

Sincerely,

Debbie

Here's what I did:

1. I got straight to the point right away, congratulating him on his achievement.
2. I mentioned where I heard about his achievement.
3. I made a couple personal comments and wrapped it up.

I was also *specific*. A generic "Congratulations" means little. In this age of social networking, "Congrats" is a common way for people to congratulate others; but it's lazy. For those close to us, it's a good idea to be more specific and personal.

You can modify the above template for just about any personal email of congratulations. I'll give you an example of how I can adapt this template for the purpose of congratulating someone on their new baby:

Subject line: Congratulations!

Dear Jen,

Congratulations on your new baby!

I saw on Facebook that you and Tom just had a beautiful baby boy. I know you've been wanting a baby for some time now. I'm so happy for you.

Please let me know if there's anything I can help you with. You were so good to me when I had my Philip.

Congrats again. I'd love to chat when you get a chance,

Michelle

These are obviously not the same letter, and I've varied it a bit. But you see the similarities: getting straight to the point . . . writing where I heard about the new baby (Facebook) . . . and I make a personal comment—in this case offering help and acknowledging that the recipient was so good to me when I had a child. I then conclude that I'd love to talk to her on the phone when she's not busy.

Again, remember to adjust the level of formality to the nature of the relationship.

Condolences

Condolence is a form of sympathy—in the case of someone having passed away. Here, the thought is what counts.

Here's a template you can base your email on:

Subject line: I'm sorry for your loss

Dear Mary,

Your brother told me about Collin's passing. I'm so sorry to hear that. You have my condolences.

Collin was always a kind man. I remember the time when I was upset about my lab results and Collin comforted me, letting me know everything was going to be all right. He didn't have to take the time to do that, but he did. That's the kind of guy he was.

We're all going to miss him and that calming influence he had.

Thinking of you,

Kelly

Here's what I did:

1. I kept it brief.
2. I expressed my sympathies (don't try to put a positive spin on it).
3. I recalled a brief anecdote or story about the deceased.
4. I reassured her that he would be missed.

Again, I was specific. And I didn't mention anything negative about him. The key is to stay positive but to express that you understand what the person is going through. That's not always an easy thing to do, but the thought is what counts.

Sympathy

Sympathy emails differ a bit from condolence emails. You may wish to send a sympathy email in cases of personal injury, job loss, divorce, and so on.

Here is a template you can base your email on:

Subject line: I'm sorry

Dear John,

I heard from your brother that you lost your job recently. I'm sorry to hear that.

At the same time, I can't help but recall how unhappy you were in that position. I remember you talking about the culture there and how it really stuck it to the employees. Maybe this is an opportunity to find a better workplace and something you're really passionate about.

When I was laid off a few years back, I was angry at first. Then I realized they had done me a huge favor, since I found my current job (which I absolutely love). Turns out it was a blessing in disguise.

Let's do dinner sometime, on me. We can trade war stories.

You'll find something better. I know it. You're sharp and a great worker.

Ryan

Here's what I did:

1. I brought up the event that prompted me to write the email and where I heard about it.
2. I sympathized.
3. I put a positive spin on it (notice I didn't do this with the condolence email).
4. I showed I knew what he was going through by offering the story of my own similar situation.
5. I offered to help or spend time with him.
6. I encouraged him.

Now, maybe you haven't experienced a similar situation. That's OK. Don't act as though you know what they're going through if you don't.

But you can still express how you think you *would* feel if you were in that situation. The key is to show you care.

Get well soon

The purpose of a get-well-soon email is not only to show that you care, but also to bring more positivity into the recipient's life, which can aid in their recovery. A get-well-soon email is similar to a sympathy letter; the distinction is largely in the intention.

With a get-well-soon email, you're mostly seeking to enliven the person's day or attitude. With a sympathy email you're mostly looking to show that you understand and that you're there to help if need be. There's more room for some levity in a get-well-soon email (if you're on familiar terms).

Here's a template you can use:

Subject line: Thinking of you

Dear Aunt Rita,

I know you haven't been feeling well lately. Surgery can take a lot out of a person for a while.

You'll bounce back. I know it. You'll be getting back into the Thursday-night swing dancing very soon. Your moves put me to shame, by the way.

Get well soon. I'm thinking of you.

Love,

Jim

Here's what I did:

1. I acknowledged the sickness or illness.
2. I offered an encouraging word (in this case, I added a little humor—*not* always called for, especially depending on the nature of the sickness and the nature of the relationship).

3. I presented a future scenario for her to look forward to.
4. I reassured her that I want her to get well soon.

Again, depending on the nature of the relationship and the degree of the sickness, you may have to be more formal. But with a get-well-soon letter, the person is recovering, and it's for the purpose of lifting their spirits.

Requesting a favor

If you're requesting a favor from someone, one of the cardinal rules is to appeal to the person's self-interest rather than their charity. It also depends on the degree of the favor and the nature of the relationship. The more serious the favor, the more important this rule is. Asking a person to borrow a book is obviously different from asking to borrow their car. And the nature of the relationship will also dictate how much persuasion or "selling" you have to do.

Here's an example of a moderately large favor request from a person you don't know that well:

Subject Line: Speaking at a High School

Dear Joy:

We met at the Chamber of Commerce meeting a few weeks ago. I'm writing because I know you do a fair amount of speaking at young people's events, and I'm wondering whether you'll be able to speak at my son's upcoming high school graduation party.

This will be a huge party, with hundreds of people, many of whom work in the school system and in business. This would be a perfect opportunity to promote your new book on the education system.

I really enjoy your books and find them extremely inspirational—and I think a speech at his graduation party would be just what he needs to help set him on the right path for college.

You wouldn't need to speak long. Even ten minutes would be wonderful.

Please let me know whether you'll be able to speak. The party is on Saturday June 10th from 3:30 p.m. to 9 or so.

Thanks,

Cathleen

Here's what I did:

1. I made sure the person knows who I am or where I met her.
2. Right away I go into what I'm requesting and why—and I do so politely.
3. I bring up what's in it for her. I don't depend on her charity; I explicitly bring up a benefit she'll receive (in this case, she'll get to promote her book to hundreds of people, some of whom are influential in her market).
4. I offer sincere compliments and reinforce why I'm requesting the favor.
5. I give specifics about the request (in this case, date and time).

When you know the person well, or the request is small, you won't have to do as much selling. But it's always good to add something about a benefit the person can look forward to.

Declining an invitation

Ignoring an invitation is a quick way to rupture a relationship. If you can't make it to an event you're invited to, make sure to decline the invitation gracefully. Here's a template you can use for your own email:

Subject Line: Tracy's birthday

Dear Tom:

Thanks for the invitation to Tracy's birthday. It's a big day for her.

Unfortunately, due to a prior commitment, I'm not able make it that Saturday. If it's all right with you, I'd love to have dinner with you and Tracy sometime this month. I have a gift for her I'd like to give her.

Thanks again for inviting me, and I'm sorry I can't make it.

Jamie

Here's what I did:

1. I got to the point right away, thanking him for the invitation and mentioning the event specifically.
2. I made a supportive comment to show that I'm not just writing the person off and that I value the relationship.
3. I write that I can't attend because of a "prior commitment." I could have gone into details about what that prior commitment is, but I didn't have to.
4. Since I actually want to see them, I offer another opportunity for us to get together.

I'm taking the time to send this email in order to salvage the relationship and show respect. If I wanted to break off the relationship or not see the person again, I wouldn't suggest an alternative occasion in which to meet, but I'd still answer the invitation if I could.

Letter of complaint

Dale Carnegie's first rule in *How to Win Friends and Influence People* is to never complain. And generally speaking, this is a wise rule. Unfortunately, complaining is sometimes necessary in personal communications. Fortunately, there's a way to do it in a tactful, respectful way.

There are no guarantees that the recipient will take it kindly and won't be offended; but there are ways to write letters of complaint that make it more probable that the person will take your complaint seriously and will not be personally offended.

Here's a template:

Subject Line: An incident with Christopher

Dear Jim:

I hope you're well. As you know, Christopher spent the weekend at our place this past weekend. I considered not even bringing this up, because we love having Christopher over. But I think it's important for you to know we heard Christopher using foul language in his conversations with Pauli.

Marcy and I have a serious policy against that kind of language in our home, and Christopher knows that. We were disappointed to hear him talk like that, especially since he's such a smart kid.

I hope you can have a talk with him about what is acceptable behavior in our home. We certainly look forward to having Christopher come over again soon. In fact, we'd love to get lunch with you and Susan sometime just to catch up.

Thanks,

Todd

Obviously in this situation, the complaint is about the son, but you can adapt this for complaints directed at the recipient directly. Here's what I did:

1. I began with a pleasantry to blunt it a bit ("I hope you're well").
2. I brought up something positive about him.
3. I explained what happened specifically. In some cases, it may be appropriate to go into more detail and even offer proof of the incident.
4. I reiterated or added a positive about him.
5. I offered what I hope or expect him to do about this situation.
6. I ended by mentioning that I want to continue the relationship.

The key here is to raise the complaint in a way that is tempered with positives and is reassuring. When you're overly negative or rude, the recipient won't listen—or worse, could become enraged. Make your request in a productive, positive way.

Apology

Apologizing in writing has numerous advantages—among which is the ability to carefully choose your words. In person, you may let slip something that you wished you hadn't said. In writing, you can plan carefully.

Here's a template you can adapt for your own purposes:

> Subject Line: About the other night
>
> Dear Evelyn:
>
> I realize now that my comment about your job was insensitive and hurtful. I'm really sorry for saying that. We were in a joking mood, and I meant it as a joke. I wasn't being serious, and I certainly didn't mean to upset you. I should've chosen my words more carefully.
>
> You're a smart, capable employee. I recognize that, of course. Again, I'm sorry. I hope we can put this behind us and still have fun together.
>
> Jill

Here's what I did:

1. I identified the incident, what was said or done.
2. I acknowledged that it was hurtful and apologized simply and unconditionally.
3. I explained the circumstances of why I said it (in this case it was appropriate to clarify the true meaning behind the statement).
4. I reiterated the apology.
5. I made it known that I want to continue being friends.

The degree of the offense is going to dictate how much explaining is necessary. And you don't want to *excuse* the behavior. Take responsibility for it. If you don't acknowledge the fault, the person will likely not feel well-disposed toward you and won't accept the apology. Also I advise against the phrase, "I apologize if I hurt you." The problem with this phrase is the "if." It doesn't own the fact that you hurt them. Acknowledge that you hurt them *in fact* rather than stating it as though it were hypothetical.

But if you apologize with this spirit, the person will probably forgive you.

Answering tough questions

Occasionally, someone will question you over something—an incident, a position, etc.—that is difficult to answer. It can happen in cases in which the person has simply overstepped their bounds, or in cases in which they're legitimately curious. I'm sure you've probably asked tough questions at times.

Here's a template you can use:

Subject Line: Your question

Dear Emily:

You recently asked me a question about my separation, and I was a little standoffish. As you can probably understand, it's a sensitive and difficult issue for me.

To answer your question, the decision to separate was mutual. We both see the value in an amicable separation.

I hope that this situation doesn't make things too awkward and that we can continue to be friends.

Best,

Kim

Here's what I did:

1. I acknowledged the question.
2. I explained that this is a sensitive issue.
3. I chose to answer the question with enough generality to protect our privacy.
4. I showed that I cared about continuing the relationship.

However, it's not always necessary for you to answer a tough question. It may be that the person has no right to the information, in which case, you may choose to mention that it's "personal." "Personal" is usually a socially acceptable way of telling someone, "Don't ask me about this anymore." In this case, I answered the question because I want to inform my friend and maintain trust. In some cases, failing to answer a tough question may result in a loss of trust.

Giving unsolicited advice

Giving advice is almost always tricky. Unsolicited advice is even trickier. You always run the risk of offending the person by implying that their work or what they've done is unsatisfactory, as though you could do better. Giving unsolicited advice must be handled delicately.

Here's a template you can use:

Subject line: Your client issue

Dear Shannon:

You mentioned the other day that you think your clients are walking all over you and you're frustrated by this.

I was thinking of some ways you might be able to turn this around. I've had this issue myself in the past. May I make a suggestion?

You're doing a fine job with your projects. You're quick and reliable—and your work gets results. Then again, your contract gives too much away to the client. For instance, I'd put a clause in there stating you want half the payment up front. And another stating that they aren't allowed to use the work until they've paid you the second half.

In my opinion, these kinds of clauses will help gain you the respect you deserve and get you your money more quickly.

I hope I haven't overstepped my bounds here, but I know how frustrating that situation can be and thought I'd give you a couple pointers.

Best,

John

Here's what I did:

1. I raised the specific issue.
2. I pointed out that I've gone through that issue (if I really have).
3. I asked whether I may make a suggestion.
4. I complimented her on a specific strength.
5. I gave my advice.
6. I raised the benefits of taking the advice.
7. I acknowledged that I hope I didn't overstep my bounds and showed I wanted to help.

There's no guarantee that giving unsolicited advice will work. And on most occasions I don't recommend it. However, there are times when giving unsolicited advice is the right or necessary thing to do, particularly when you can see an easy fix to a situation or when the person is undergoing something in which you'd feel badly if you didn't speak up.

Holidays

When holidays roll around, you may choose to send emails. If the recipient hasn't heard from you in a while, you may want to relay some of the major events of the year, particularly those involving children or major events. If the recipient is accustomed to hearing from you, you should omit these, as presumably they already know about them. You may choose to send an "e-card" with this message attached, or send a plain email.

Here's one for Christmas you can adapt to Easter or other holidays:

Subject Line: Merry Christmas!

Dear Eugene and Family:

We want you to know we're thinking of you at Christmas time. We were just thinking of the time at the Christmas party when Katie's dog seemed to be doing that little dance in the kitchen. To this day it's the cutest thing we've ever seen!

You're in the loop mostly, but you should know that Bill's birthday is on January 11th, and we'd love for you to come.

Merry Christmas and Happy New Year!

-Bridget and Family

Here's what I did:

1. I let them know we're thinking of them.
2. I brought up a time we had fun together.
3. I updated them a bit on a family happening and invited them to a future event.
4. I ended by wishing them Merry Christmas and Happy New Year.

As I said, if you haven't seen them for a while, you may choose to inform them about more events that have happened lately. Otherwise, you can keep it short like I did. This is also a great time to use humor if you'd like, or, if you have shared religious beliefs, to share something religious with the other person.

Giving thanks

Showing gratitude for a gift or favor received is important. By showing that you appreciate what the person has done for you, you show that you value the relationship and that person. Failing to thank a person for a gift or favor can jeopardize the relationship. Even if it doesn't seem as though the person cares, they will certainly feel slighted if you fail to offer some kind of acknowledgment of the good they did.

Here's a template you can use:

Subject Line: Thanks for the book

Hi Joe,

Thank you so much for thinking of me at graduation. I'm really looking forward to reading the book.

I've read a bit by Fitzgerald. In fact, *This Side of Paradise* is one of my favorite novels of all time. The imagery was incredibly poignant. I'm sure I'll enjoy his short stories.

Thanks again. Let's get together soon.

Katie

Here's what I did:

1. I started off by thanking him specifically.
2. I described how the gift was meaningful to me.
3. I thanked him again.

It's a pretty simple formula, and it works. Just show that the gift is appreciated. It goes a long way. What if you don't like the gift or didn't want the favor? Find something good about it anyway, and express your appreciation nonetheless.

Invitations to events

While certain more formal events are best left to invitations by postal mail (such as weddings), many invitations can be extended via email—birthdays, graduations, parties, and so on. Here's a template you can use:

> Subject Line: Dinner party on the 18th
>
> Hi Tim,
>
> We'll be having a dinner party at our place on Saturday, September 18th. Lots of food and drinks. Alan and Rosalyn will be there. It's been a while since we've all gotten together, and we'd love if you and Amanda joined us. We'll have a blast.
>
> It's at 6 p.m.
>
> Let us know!
>
> Jo

Here's what I did:

1. I announced the event with time and date.
2. I described some benefits (food and drinks).
3. I let him know some mutual friends would be there (if this is the case).
4. I gave a reason for the get-together.
5. I expressed that I'd like to see him.

An informal invitation like this does not require the solemnity of a formal wedding invitation, for instance. Be conversational and lively. And make sure to include all relevant details about the location of the event, time, date, etc.

Personal updates

Sometimes, if you haven't seen someone in a while, it's a good idea to send an "update" on your life since you last spoke or corresponded. If appropriate, you can send an update on your children and what's going on in their lives. This strengthens the relationship and shows you're thinking of them. Here's a template:

Subject Line: How's it going?

Hi Carrie,

Just want to see how you're doing and give you a few updates on the drama in my life.

I quit that job at the law firm (yes, the one I was complaining about) and started my own business as a freelance paralegal. So far so good! I can't believe how smoothly it's going. I have a couple clients who pay me reasonably well. I'm much happier.

Also, John is getting baptized soon. I'm going to be sending you an invitation in the mail.

How are things with you?

Lucy

Here's what I did:

1. I gave as the reason for writing the intention to see how she's doing and to share personal news.
2. I described my updates.
3. I asked how she's doing.

Pretty simple. Keep it informal, and don't be afraid to let your personality shine through.

Request for status update

Sometimes you may want to ask how something went in the person's life. Perhaps they got a new job, started a new school, or the like. You want to know what happened and to show you're interested in the outcome. Here's a template:

Subject Line: Your last year

Hi Marjorie,

It's so exciting that this is your last year of high school! You're a senior now (just don't treat the juniors too badly!).

I'm just wondering where you think you may be applying to college, and what you're majoring in. You were always really strong in math and sciences, but I'd love to hear what's on your mind.

Best,

Mary

Here's what I did:

1. I expressed interest in her life event.
2. I asked her for the information I was seeking.
3. I gave her a little insight into my perspective (since it was appropriate).

In some situations, you may not want to pry, particularly if the information is sensitive. Use your best judgment of what is appropriate to request an update on.

Granting a request

We've discussed emails that refuse requests. Now we face an easier and more pleasant task: granting a request. People may ask you for a variety of things, such as a recommendation or to borrow something. Here's a template:

Subject Line: Your request

Dear Gerald:

You recently asked me for some writing advice for your letter. I'm happy to help you with that. You're a good friend, and I think you're completely right about this issue. I'd like to see a positive outcome.

Please email me any information you have, including anything you've already written, and I'll get back to you as soon as I can.

Harold

Here's what I did:

1. I identified the favor request.
2. I granted the request right away (when delivering good news there's no reason to linger and justify beforehand).
3. I explained why I'm helping.
4. I asked for additional information (if needed).

You may also ask them to keep you updated on the issue if that's appropriate. In this case, I simply needed more information in order to complete the request. Make sure to follow through on your commitment.

Suggesting a get-together

Sometimes you just want to get together with someone, for coffee, dinner, or some other occasion. Here's a template for a friendly get-together:

Subject Line: Let's meet up

Hi Alejandra,

I was just thinking of you! I watched *The Godfather* again, and I remembered the time we watched it over at Jim's place when he had that "problem" with his ex. Good times.

It's been too long. I'd love to get together for coffee and hear about your new job.

Let me know!

Jill

Here's what I did:

1. I let her know I was thinking of her.

2. I reminisced about a previous time together.
3. I expressed that I would like to get together and talk about something that interests her.
4. I asked her to let me know (at which point we can arrange a time and place).

These kinds of emails are informal. Make sure you show your personality and be natural.

You'll notice that I've used a couple different salutations, for instance "Dear John" and "Hi John." You're free to choose what you'd like to use. "Dear" is more formal than "Hi" and in some cases may come across as awkward. But it's mostly up to you.

Subject lines are also a matter of preference. With personal emails, when the person knows you and recognizes the "From" address, the subject line isn't quite as important for open rates. I've chosen subject lines that get right to the point, summarizing the email and leading into the body.

There are many different ways to write a personal email. These are merely guidelines for writing more effective ones. Try using them, and I think you'll agree.

CHAPTER 12.

Business Emails for Every Occasion

Email in business can be used in many ways: intracompany communications, marketing, and coordinating with partners, suppliers, and customers. Speed is the overwhelming advantage of email; when you need to get an important message to a client or business associate, one of the fastest ways to do it is by email.

However, because sending poorly crafted business emails can damage working relationships and ultimately undermine your career, immediate delivery can become a liability.

The Basics of Business Writing

In all written business communications—including email—there are only three things you need to remember: Keep it simple; keep it free of grammar and spelling errors, and keep it professional. This means your business communications are infused with consideration, respect, and honesty. A well-crafted business email reflects your competency and projects a positive image.

Here are some tips for writing more effective business emails:

1. Before writing the first draft, organize your main idea and supportive information into an outline.
2. Get to know your reader. For example, what is their job title and level of education?
3. At all costs, avoid using language which is more complex than the concepts it attempts to communicate ("corpora-tese"). Eliminate clichés and keep technical jargon to a minimum. Write naturally.
4. Use an active voice. That's where the action is expressed directly, as in "Mary gave the introductory speech" instead of "The speech was given by Mary."
5. Keep sentences and paragraphs short. Most of us like information in "bite-sized" chunks. Sentences should be between fifteen and twenty-five words and paragraphs in letters, emails, and memos should have three to five lines.[50]
6. Focus on specifics whenever possible. Instead of "high performance," for example, state the quantifiable proof, as in "97.3 percent efficiency."
7. Ensure your writing is concise. Few of us have the time, or the desire, to wade through a bunch of dull, wordy prose. Whenever possible, use one word, instead of three. Here's an example. Instead of writing "in many cases," use "often." Make sure every word has value to the reader.
8. Closely examine punctuation, formatting, and capitalization. Stay clear of overpunctuation (as in too many exclamation

---

50 See SMU Communication 101, http://smucomm101.wikifoundry.com/page/Business +writing+%28essentials%3B+sentence+length%2C+paragraph+length%2C+ jargon%2C+and+more%29.

or question marks). Strive for very few exclamation marks, and don't reduplicate other punctuation marks, like question marks; even if they are in their proper place). Excessive use of either can lend a note of desperation or instability to your message or, at the very least, make your email look spammy.

Keep presentation clean: don't choose "fancy," difficult-to-read fonts and format your emails with lots of white space for easier reading.[51] Avoid using emoticons, and text message acronyms and lingo. One more thing: don't put your message in all caps because it can be misconstrued as yelling.

9. Always project a professional attitude. This means a few different things: you should avoid humor, as it could easily be misconstrued. Second: make sure you've given the reader all the necessary information—and that it's accurate.

10. When you receive a reply to your email, don't put off responding. You don't like waiting days for a reply and neither does anyone else.

11. State your main point in the subject line in an engaging way. Instead of "Warehouse deliveries" (too general), grab attention with something like "Attention: Warehouse deliveries rescheduled."

12. When sending attachments, limit their size. The default maximum quota for receiving is 50 GB, but Office 365 limits size to 25 MB (any files larger are prohibited). If you're sending a file to someone you don't know well, it can help to let them know what software was used to create the file.

13. Use a formatted set of signature lines. It should include your name, job title, company name, physical address, phone/

---

51 See *The Encyclopedia of Business Letters, Faxes, and Email*, Bly and Kelly, page 26.

fax number(s), email address, and a link to your website. It should do all that, but be less than ten lines.

14. Use bulleted lists to simplify your presentation and make it easier for the reader to skim and scan the content.

15. Proofread every email before you send it. A major part of writing effective emails involves careful proofreading. Read your email aloud to yourself, checking for spelling and grammar mistakes. Ask yourself two questions:
    - Could there be any misunderstandings?
    - How would this sound if I were the recipient?

16. Delete any unnecessary words, clauses, sentences, or paragraphs as you proofread. (Many pairs of words imply each other. For example, "finish" implies *complete*, so the phrase "completely finish" is redundant.) Here are some words and phrases that can often be removed to make sentences clearer:[52]

basically	really	for all intents and purposes
definitely	actually	generally
individual	specific	particular
kind of	sort of	type of

Write more concisely and clearly by paring down these commonly used phrases to their essence:

Redundant Pairs or Categories	Change to:
past memories	memories
past history	history
various differences	differences
each individual _____	individual _____
basic fundamentals	fundamentals

---

52 Source: "Eliminating Words," Purdue University Online Writing Lab, https://owl
.english.purdue.edu/owl/resource/572/02/.

free gift	gift
true facts	facts
important essentials	essentials
future plans	plans
terrible tragedy	tragedy
end result	result
final outcome	outcome
large in size	large
often times	often
of a bright color	bright
heavy in weight	heavy
period in time	period
at an early time	early
economics field	economics
of cheap quality	cheap
honest in character	honest
of an uncertain condition	uncertain
in a confused state	confused
unusual in nature	unusual
extreme in degree	extreme
of a strange type	strange
round in shape	round

17. Before attempting a first draft, ask "is email the right channel for this communication?" Would what you're saying have more impact if sent in another form, such as a letter or memo? If email is the way to go, then it's time to start writing.

Focus on the First Paragraph

Because it's the reason why the reader will choose to continue reading your email, you've got to make sure the first paragraph does three things:

tell the reader what this is about, who it is for, and why they should be interested. If you want the reader to click a link, then you'll also need a clearly written and persuasive call-to-action compelling him or her to take the desired action. From there, you'll write to support the statements within that first paragraph.

This focus on the first paragraph, where your main point is clearly stated—and then supported in the following paragraphs—is the earmark of what's called the "inverted pyramid approach" to writing. It's effective because it enables the reader to know immediately why the message was sent. Even if he or she decides not to read further, they still have the important information.

Now, let's look at some examples of well-written business emails to see how the inverted pyramid approach, coupled with a thought-provoking first paragraph, work together. (Feel free to use any one of these samples as a template.) The first category we'll look at involves communicating with colleagues—those people you work closely with most often.

Note: As formatting of email messages—the To/From/Subject Lines and the use of a series of "signature lines"—was covered previously; in order to remain focused on email body content, only the first example includes these features.

Personal Introductions

Networking: people either love it or hate it. Either way, there's no denying in today's world, professional networking leads to more business opportunities, and generally improves the quality of work and increases job satisfaction.[53]

---

53 See "Learn to Love Networking," *Harvard Business Review*, https://hbr.org/2016/05/learn-to-love-networking.

The first sample is an email drafted to introduce the writer to the reader and asks the reader to accept an invitation to become better acquainted, with the intention of doing business together.

Essentials:

1. Begin by introducing yourself.
2. Follow the introduction with the reason why you're contacting them.
3. Extend the invitation to connect.
4. End on a cheerful note.

Here's an example of an introductory email which does all four things:

To: John Houseman <j.houseman@ sova.org>
From: Peter Boglioli <p.boglioli@oregontours.com>
Subject: How We Can Bring More Revenue to Southern Oregon

Dear Mr. Houseman,

My name is Peter Boglioli. I am the senior director of sales for Oregon Tours.

As you and I have never met, I asked Mark Handler from the Seattle Convention and Visitors Bureau to give me your email address.

I did so because I wanted to contact you, as Director of the Southern Oregon Visitors Association about an exciting online opportunity to promote your region of the state. As you're aware, the Seattle-Tacoma area gets a lot of attention all year round . . . not only from tourists, but from convention hosts and attendees.

I think it's time to shine a spotlight on Medford, Bend, Eugene, and Salem—and I bet you agree!

This is why I've developed a six-month content marketing plan which takes advantage of high-profile online publishers like *Huffington Post*,

---

The Daily Beast and *Salon*. The good news is it won't cost your agency—or mine—a dime.

Would you have time to chat next week?

Kind Regards,

Peter Boglioli
Oregon Tours
1234 High Street
Grants Pass, Oregon
(514) 345-8763
Website: oregontours.com

Post-Meeting Follow-up Messages

Let's say Mr. Houseman replied to the email sent by Mr. Boglioli, stating he was available for a meeting on Tuesday, March 30th. The meeting was held and now it's Peter's time to send a follow-up email. Here his job is to thank Mr. Houseman for his time, remind him of who he is, reiterate what was discussed in the meeting and suggest a time when the two could connect again.

Essentials:

1. Start with gratitude: "Thank you so much for your time" or "It was a delight to meet you."
2. In a concise fashion, detail what was said during the meeting.
3. Share a helpful tip or resource.
4. Provide the reader with a reason to make contact with you in the future.

To: John Houseman <j.houseman@ sova.org>
From: Peter Boglioli <p.boglioli@oregontours.com>
Subject: Following-Up on Our Meeting

Hello, again, Mr. Houseman,

I so enjoyed meeting you yesterday in your Medford offices. Thank you for taking the time to speak with me—and an extra "thank you" for the unexpected tour. I found it both interesting and insightful.

As you asked, I've attached the revised copy of the content marketing strategy we discussed to this email.

I'm planning to be back in Medford in July of this year and would like to take you to lunch while I'm there. Please reply with the best date and time for us to meet.

All the best,

Peter Boglioli
Oregon Tours
1234 High Street
Grants Pass, Oregon
(514) 345-8763
Website: oregontours.com

Requests

Being able to ask for help is one of the many benefits of networking. You might need a favor or perhaps you're looking for information, a referral, or a recommendation.

Whatever your reason for writing, be cordial and clear about what you need. If there's a benefit to the reader in granting the request, tell them.

Essentials:

1. If necessary, introduce yourself (or remind the reader of who you are and where you met).

2. Make the request. Be as specific as possible.
3. Provide the necessary background detailing the need for your request.
4. Offer to do something in return.

From: Marsha Smith-Jones <msmith.jones@awp.org>
To: Dave Bower <d.bower@rightthinking.edu>
Subject: A Special Request

Hello, Dave,

I have a favor to ask. The AWP is currently putting together the AWP Vendor Directory to be distributed to our members next year. Considering your experience, any insights you could provide would be valuable to us. Would you be willing to write a short (600-900 word) introduction to the Directory?

We can pay an honorarium of $500. In addition, you'll be given 150 copies of the Directory and a by-line, so you can add it to your list of publications.

Please reply to confirm your interest. We can then set up a time to discuss the project further.

Sincerely,

Marsha Smith-Jones
Event Coordinator
Association of Web Professionals
1031 Franklin Avenue, Suite 318
Sarasota, Florida 34230
(941) 346-12134
Website: www.awp.org

Asking for a Referral

Referrals are the best leads you'll ever get, which means it's smart to take the time to ask for them. As always, there's a right way to do it.

Essentials:

1. Keep it short.
2. Remind the reader of what he or she liked about your service or product.
3. Ask for the referral giving the reader simple instructions: provide the contact details of friends or colleagues who would benefit from doing business with you.
4. Let them know how much this favor means to you. And always say "thank you."

To: Marsha Smith-Jones <msmith.jones@awp.org>
From: Dave Bower <d.bower@rightthinking.edu>
Subject: A Referral Request

Hello, Marsha,

I'm writing you to ask a favor. Do you know anyone who would benefit from receiving a complimentary copy of my new book, *16 Ways to Wow a Corporate Audience*? (I recently sent you a copy and hope you enjoyed it.)

In 2018, I was the keynote speaker at your AWP convention, held in Sarasota, Florida. (The email you sent thanking me for my presentation made me feel like a million bucks—thank you!) My goal for next year is to add three speaking engagements to my teaching schedule and know you can help me to meet—or even exceed—my expectations.

Please reply to this email with the contact details of those individuals or organizations you feel would be "a good fit" for my speaking services.

I'd like to mention your name when contacting your referrals. If there's a problem with that, please let me know.

As always, thank you for your time.

Sincerely,

Dave Bower
Right Thinking
1216 Main Street, Suite 109
Salinas, California 95071
(323) 478-5690

Requests for Information

If you want information on a product or service, it's best to make the request in writing (as opposed to over the phone). In writing, you help the reader better understand what you need and tell them how to comply with your request. This way, you get what you need, when you need it.

Essentials:

1. Be specific and accurate. Provide the reader with a detailed list of the information you need.
2. If you ask a question, do so in a way that requires a detailed response.
3. Acknowledge how busy the readers is; and inform him or her how it will take only a few minutes to comply.
4. Clearly and warmly share your appreciation.

Here's an example of an email requesting product information:

To: Frank Harvey, <f.harvey@writestylesoftware.com>
From: Marsha Smith-Jones
Subject: A Request for Information: "Perfect Writer"

Dear Frank,

Your company has recently launched Perfect Writer which, according to online reviews, "makes a word processor more of a creative writing tool."

I am truly impressed by the features and interested in buying the same, but before that I would like to have detailed information on use and operating system compatibility. I regularly purchase your software and have been totally satisfied with every product I've bought over the years.

I would be very thankful to you if you could send me a detailed catalogue regarding the product, so that I can reassure myself before buying the same.

I hope you can send me the details as soon as possible.

Thanking you
Yours sincerely,

Marsha Smith-Jones
Event Coordinator
Association of Web Professionals
1031 Franklin Avenue, Suite 318
Sarasota, Florida 34230
(941) 346-12134
Website: www.awp.org
Email: msmith.jones@awp.org

Requesting a Meeting

The most common reason to request a meeting is so you're better able to discuss an issue in greater depth. It could be a new idea, a new opportunity, a problem, to brainstorm something, reach a decision about something or any number of things. Whether it's a request for a face-to-face meeting or a phone conference call, the request needs to be sent in a timely way, allowing the reader adequate time to respond.

Ask the reader to respond whether or not he or she will be able to attend. If you've requested a meeting on a specific day and time and the recipient is unable to attend, ask for alternatives that would work with their schedule.

Essentials:

1. Clearly state who you are and *why* you'd like to meet.
2. Be specific as to the time frame.
3. If necessary, include a "please respond by" date so you can know your request was received and read.

To: Charlie Maxwell <c.maxwell@clearwaterpromotions.net>
From: Marsha Smith-Jones <msmith.jones@awp.org>
Subject: Can We Chat?

Dear Mr. Maxwell,

Do you have time to meet with me during the next week to discuss how the AWP can partner with your organization to reach our respective business goals? I promise to take no more than 17 minutes of your time.

I am the Events Coordinator for the Association of Web Professionals. (You may remember we met three months ago at a regional conference sponsored by the AWP.) I was very impressed with your extensive knowledge and experience and hope we can create an effective partnership.

I will call you in a few days to discuss any details or questions you may have and arrange an alternative time if required.

Sincerely,

Marsha Smith-Jones
Event Coordinator
Association of Web Professionals
1031 Franklin Avenue, Suite 318
Sarasota, Florida 34230
(941) 346-12134
Website: www.awp.org

Accepting Requests or Invitations

In business, as in life, you're bound to get invitations or requests for your time. Some you'll be forced to decline; others you'll want to accept. Fortunately, the basics elements are the same in both cases.

Essentials:

1. Express your pleasure in accepting the offer.
2. Repeat the event details (place, date, and time).
3. If necessary, inquire about particulars.
4. Close with an expression of pleasure to attend.

To: Henry R. Hobart <hrhobart@businessventures.net
From: Dave Bower <d.bower@rightthinking.edu>
Subject: Your Proposed Meeting

Dear Mr. Hobart,

I received your email suggesting the 28th of October, at 9:00 a.m. as a suitable time for us to meet about the business proposal presented three months ago.

I accept your suggestion with pleasure.

And I look forward to meeting you at your offices then. We can discuss everything in detail and finalize a final contract to which we can both agree to.

Yours faithfully,

Dave Bower
Right Thinking
1216 Main Street, Suite 109
Salinas, California 95071
(323) 478-5690
Website: rightthinking.edu

Declining Requests and Invitations

Sometimes it can't be helped; you simply don't have the time (or the interest) to accept a meeting request or invitation. As with every business communication, you'll want to be courteous and polite in your rejection.

Essentials:

1. Start with an opening compliment. It helps to ease the reader into the (negatively charged) conversation.
2. Thank the individual for the invitation or request, stating exactly what was requested.
3. Mention how much you value your relationship with the sender.
4. State "no" clearly (without being rude). You want there to be no doubt in the reader's mind.
5. Include a statement that "leaves the door open" for future get-togethers.
6. A warm close, thanking the reader for the invitation and wishing them success in their endeavor.

To: Henry Nightingale<h.nightingale@strategicjobhunting.com
From: Marsha Smith-Jones <msmith.jones@awp.org>
Subject: Your Invitation

Dear Henry,

I was delighted to receive the signed copy of your newest book, *How to Get Hired: 101 Proven Job-Hunting Strategies*. Thank you so very much for thinking of me; I truly look forward to reading it.

Unfortunately, I am unable to accept your invitation to celebrate its release with you on the 23rd of March, as I have a prior commitment (I'll be in South Africa on business for the month.)

Again, congratulations on your newest publication. As you were my trusted mentor in my own job search, I'm confident it will make a big difference for many people in search of gainful employment.

All the best,

Marsha Smith-Jones
Event Coordinator
Association of Web Professionals
1031 Franklin Avenue, Suite 318
Sarasota, Florida 34230
(941) 346-12134
Website: www.awp.org

Thank You Emails

William Arthur Ward, one of America's most quoted inspirational authors, wrote of the power in making the act of saying "thank you" a habit: "Gratitude can transform common days into thanksgivings, turn routine jobs into joy, and change ordinary opportunities into blessings."[54]

You'll find there will be many occasions when it's appropriate to say "thank you" via email—and doing so will help you to stand out in a crowd.

Not only that, it's been found saying "thank you" in marketing or lead-gen follow-up messages actually increases email response rates. "Thanks in advance" generated the highest email engagement with a 65.7 percent response rate. "Thanks" followed with a 63 percent response rate, while "thank you" garnered a 57.9 percent response rate, according to a 2017 survey.[55]

---

54 Source: Brainy Quotes, https://www.brainyquote.com/quotes/quotes/w/williamart 676240.html?src=t_gratitude.

55 See, "Forget 'Best' or 'Sincerely', This Email Closing Gets the Most Replies," http://blog.boomerangapp.com/2017/01/how-to-end-an-email-email-sign-offs/.

Every single day, both in the workplace and outside the office, there can be dozens of opportunities to express gratitude. Unfortunately, email isn't always the best way to get the job done: if you really want your "thank you" to make an impression, a handwritten card or letter is better. Still, email *can* work in certain situations, like when responding to the previous referral or favor requests. (Here's a tip: Save the draft of your thank you email to use as a template for future.)

"Thank You" for a Favor

It's important to express your gratitude for the favors they've done in writing—how else will they ever know what they've done has made a difference? They may even think you're ungrateful (making them less likely to help you in the future). Don't procrastinate! Such expressions of gratitude need to arrive in a *timely* way.

Essentials:

1. State exactly what you're thankful for.
2. Assure the reader he or she will have no regrets regarding their assistance.
3. Make the offer to help them out any time in the future.

To: Blaine Meier <b.meier@extraordinarykidstories.com>
From: Mark Hopkins <m.hopkins@sincerelyyourspriniting.com>
Subject: My Gratitude

Dear Blaine,

I almost want to shout "thank you!" from the rooftop! I spoke with Lynn today. She told me you hired her to complete the illustrations for your new children's book, *Terence the Terrible Turtle*.

I'm so glad you did! She's a talented artist and I'm very thankful you gave her this opportunity. From past experience, I know her creative energy will enhance the creative process for you both.

If there's ever anything I can do for you, just ask.

Thanks again,

Mark Hopkins
Sincerely Yours Printing
235 Highway 9
Boulder Creek, CA. 95006
(831)212-4567
Website: sincerelyyoursprinting.com

"Thank You" for a Referral

Essentials:

1. A clearly worded statement that says "thank you."
2. The name of the referred person(s).
3. An assurance the reader will not regret making the referral as you will do your very best work for this person.

To: Mildred Barclay <mildredb@smythebros.com>
From: Sally McKenzie <s.mckenzie@gmail.com>
Subject: Your Kindness

Dear Mildred,

It's always heartwarming when someone takes the time to help another, as you did when providing me with three referrals.

I contacted each individual last week and have already scheduled follow-up meetings with Paula Johnson and Albert Wiggins. Your third referral has been out of the office since the 12th and is not due back until the end of the month. I will contact him then.

Thank you for the trust you've placed in me; I will do all I can to provide each of these people with the same high-quality service you've come to expect over the years.

Warmest Regards,

Sally McKenzie
(831)246-2835

Collection Email Series

The first set of three emails is intended to collect money owed; you'll notice "personality" isn't part of the body content in any one of the three in the collections cycle.

Essentials:

1. A statement of how much is owed and how long the account has been in arrears.
2. The means to resolve the debt immediately (online/phone payment options).
3. A statement of "what will happen" if the debt is not paid.
4. A request asking the reader to contact you with any questions or concerns.

Email #2

To: Joe Joachim <j.joachim@webinnovations.com>
From: Isaac White <isaac@bestwhitepapers.com
Subject: Payment Overdue

Dear Joe:

Just a reminder . . .

. . . that payment for the white paper I wrote for you (see copy of invoice attached) is now past due.

Would you please send me a check today? A self-addressed stamped reply envelope is enclosed for your convenience.

Regards,

Isaac White
Best White Papers
2742 East Cliff Drive
Santa Cruz, CA. 95060
(831) 234-5678
Website: bestwhitepapers.com

Email #3

To: Joe Joachim <j.joachim@webinnovations.com>
From: Isaac White <isaac@bestwhitepapers.com
Subject: Invoice #5673

Dear Joe:

I haven't gotten payment for this invoice yet. Did you receive my original bill and follow-up letter?

If there is any problem, please let me know. Otherwise, please send me a check for the amount due within the next few days.

Thanks,

Isaac White
Best White Papers
2742 East Cliff Drive
Santa Cruz, CA. 95060
(831) 234-5678
Website: bestwhitepapers.com

Email #4

To: Joe Joachim <j.joachim@webinnovations.com>
From: Isaac White <isaac@bestwhitepapers.com
Subject: An Overdue Payment

Dear Joe:

This is the third notice I've sent about the enclosed invoice, which is now many weeks past due.

Was there a problem with this job I don't know about? When may I expect payment?

Sincerely,

Isaac White
Best White Papers
2742 East Cliff Drive
Santa Cruz, CA. 95060
(831) 234-5678
Website: bestwhitepapers.com

Email #5

To: Joe Joachim <j.joachim@webinnovations.com>
From: Isaac White <isaac@bestwhitepapers.com
Subject: 10-Day Notice

Dear Joe:

What do you think I should do?

Despite three previous notices about this invoice, it remains unpaid.

I haven't heard from you, and you haven't responded to my letters.

Please remit payment within 10 days of receipt of this letter. I dislike sending you these annoying notices, nor do I like turning accounts over to my attorney for collection. But you are leaving me little choice.

Sincerely,

Isaac White
Best White Papers
2742 East Cliff Drive
Santa Cruz, CA. 95060
(831) 234-5678
Website: bestwhitepapers.com

P.S. Please be aware that the copyright on the copy I wrote for you for this assignment does not transfer to your company until my invoice has been paid in full.

Renewal Notices

Let's say you have a contract, subscription, policy, or agreement with an individual which is about to expire. Again, it's most advantageous to use a series of emails, often beginning months before the expiration date.

Renewal Email # 1

The first email, called "the early bird," presents an offer of a reward for early renewal.

Essentials:

1. The name of your company or product.
2. The announcement of an "early bird" discount.
3. The benefit of renewing now rather than waiting.
4. A review of the features and benefits of your service (why it's the best).

5. Ask the reader to take immediate advantage of the early bird offer while it is still on the table.

To: Henry Hinckley <hhinckley@snarlingdoginvestments.com
From: Sally Mercator <s.mercator@entrepreneuracademy.org
Re: [Entrepreneur Academy] Renew Now and Save $160

Dear Mr. Hinckley,

If you're enjoying the benefits of membership to the Entrepreneur Academy, you'll want to renew now to get our "early bird" discount of $160!

Accept this offer and you'll get another year of round-the-clock access to our team of small business advisors and educators—at a savings of 27%!

As you already know, the Entrepreneurs Academy is the #1 online resource for ambitious, goal-oriented entrepreneurs like you.

This is a one-time offer. To accept, please call 1-800-456-6788 during regular business hours. One of our representatives will process your renewal immediately—ensuring you won't be locked out of your account.

Sincerely,

Sally Mercator
Entrepreneur Academy
7890 Center Street
Sarasota, FLA 54678

Renewal Email # 2

The second will be sent thirty days (give or take) after the first email. It's a gentle reminder but it also presents a financial incentive for contract renewal.

Essentials:

1. An attention-grabbing introductory statement.
2. A review of the benefits of your product or service.

3. A clear request for a renewal order.
4. A reminder your product or service will make a major difference in the professional (or private) life of the recipient.

To: Steven Martin <s.martin@tempusfugit.com>
From: Mary Kinder<m.kinder@bbfonline.org>
Re: [The Businessman's Best Friend] Last Chance for Big Renewal Savings!

Hello, Mr. Martin,

It's time to act! Your subscription to the archives of The Businessman's Best Friend is about to expire.

As you're aware, the archive is packed with valuable resources for today's businessman. Every article has been written by top experts in subjects like management, team building, and how to get the most from your employees. These are available to you 24 hours a day, 7 days a week—giving you a big advantage over your competition.

Here's the deal: in two weeks, our membership prices are going up. If you renew today, you'll save $49.00 on a one-year membership. If that sounds good, you'll really like my next suggestion: renew for 2 years, and we'll give you 50% off your second year of membership.

Act now and save! Click here to renew.

Cordially,

Mary Kinder
Membership Specialist
Businessman's Best Friend
(232)456-7890

Renewal Email #3

The third email steps up the pressure in that it reminds the reader he or she is in the last thirty days of service, and without timely renewal, service will terminate.

Essentials:

1. The date of expiration (in bold face).
2. An opening statement of regret the contract has yet to be renewed.
3. A statement of concern the reader will "miss out" on continued services.
4. Clear renewal instructions and a reminder that they must renew immediately to avoid suspension of service.

To: Sam Simmons <s.simmons@clearwaters.com>
From: Ron Harvey <ron@bffonline.org>
Subject:Membership Expiration Notice

Dear Mr. Simmons,

I've just been told you've not yet renewed your membership to the archives of The Businessman's Best Friend. This concerns me because it makes me wonder if you did not get my previous emails. If that is the case, I apologize.

However, you should know that your membership will expire in 22 days. In just over three weeks, you'll no longer have access to the resources and tools which put entrepreneurs like you ahead of the pack.

Don't wait. Click on the link below to renew your membership now. Count me in!

If I can be of assistance in renewing, please call me at (345)234-0987 or simply reply to this email.

Sincerely,

Ron Harvey
Membership Specialist
Businessman's Best Friend
Website: bffonline.org
(232)456-7890

Email #4

The fourth and final email is sent on the expiration date, notifying the client or customer that service has been terminated. This is your last chance to retain the customer.

Essentials:

1. A boldface "Final Notice" statement.
2. A one-time courtesy offer to renew the expired contract at the same rate.
3. An explanation that after this time, the rate for renewal will be higher.
4. One last request to "renew now" as no other renewal requests will be sent.
5. A postscript repeating your final offer, letting the reader know that, if unaccepted, his or her name will be removed from your active accounts.

To: Sam Simmons <s.simmons@clearwaters.com>
From: Ron Harvey <ron@bffonline.org>
Subject: Final Expiration Notice

Dear Mr. Simmons,

Before we say "goodbye" I would like to extend a one-time courtesy renewal offer. Reactivate your expired membership to The Businessman's Best Friend now and you'll receive our low renewal rate.

Wait just 24 hours to renew and you'll pay 27% more for your annual membership.

Why delay?

Renewal takes just a few minutes. It can be done over the phone by calling me directly at (345)234-0987, or through our online payment portal.

Thank you for your time,

Ron Harvey
Membership Specialist
Businessman's Best Friend
Website: bffonline.org
(232)456-7890

P.S. This is the final notice you'll receive. In 48 hours, your name will be removed from our mailing list and your membership will be deactivated.

Email Response to Classified Job Listing or Posting

If you're looking for employment using Monster.com or any of dozens of similar job-listing sites, you'll want to make sure your email presents your qualifications in a compelling way.

Essentials:

1. State where you read the listing.
2. List your specific qualifications and experience relating to the position.
3. State your availability for an interview.

To: Jacob Martin <j.martin@smartsolutionspress.com>
From: Sally Macomb <s.macomb@gmail.com
Re: Your job-listing

Dear Mr. Martin,

Your listing for a junior copywriter in the *San Jose Mercury News* caught my interest. You're looking for a candidate with a background in writing for the funeral service industry–and I'm delighted to say this field is my specialty.

In addition to writing for individual clients, I've worked with three of the top website providers in the field: FuneralOne, FrontRunner Professional, and Funeral Innovations.

I have attached a portfolio of samples for your review.

Please, at your earliest convenience, let me know what you need to see next, in order to move me through the hiring process. I am available for phone conversation Monday–Friday, between normal business hours.

Cordially,

Sarah Jones
(245)367-4589

Unsolicited ("Cold") Email Seeking Employment

Sometimes you'll want to inquire about employment opportunities without having any idea a position exists for you to fill. You're writing to pursue a "cold" lead, basically.

Essentials:

1. Do your due diligence. Visit the company website to find out the name and email address of the most suitable person to contact.
2. Include a bit about the company to illustrate your familiarity with its operations.
3. Be specific and concise about yourself and the job you seek. No more than a paragraph about who you are and why you think you'd be a good fit for this position.
4. Ask for an interview.

To: Mary Reilly <m.reilly@abccompany.com
From: Henry Agassi <h.agassi@gmail.com
Subject: An Interview Request

Dear Ms. Reilly,

It pleased me greatly to read "How ABC Company is Leading the Way in Plastics Recycling" in today's *Wall Street Journal*. You must be very proud of the environmental impact your company has had just this year!

I'm writing to ask if I could interview with you for a position as a junior content and copywriter. I have a degree from UCSC in environmental science and have extensive experience in plastics. Together, my education and experience make me a good candidate for the position. (For your convenience, I've attached my résumé and curriculum vitae to this email.)

I would welcome the chance to explore career opportunities with ABC Company. Please let me know what the next steps would be to obtain an interview with you.

Thank you,

Henry Agassi
211 Nellie Lane
Sacramento, CA. 94567
(931)245-8970

Employer-Employee Emails

As an employer, you'll have reason to draft email messages which review employee performance (either good or bad). When doing so, you'll need to be detailed and specific.

Essentials:

1. List the basic job requirements and duties.
2. Document specific instances of excellent performance (or failure, depending on the situation).

3. State your appreciation for excellence as clearly as you'd state your disappointment, should that be the case.
4. State the consequences, if any, of their performance.

Recognition of Excellent Employee Performance

Writing an email praising employee performance is one of the perks of management. It's a chance for you to build a deeper relationship with a valuable employee.

To: Harriet Franklin <h.franklin@investmentresearch.org
From: Ted Robinson <t.robinson@investmentresearch.org
Subject: Your Stellar Performance

Dear Harriet,

I want to take this opportunity to congratulate you on your successful completion of the Rockefeller Project. By single-handedly managing this challenging project you have set a benchmark for yourself and have taken our company to new heights.

I and the rest of the company are proud to have such a dedicated and hardworking member like you with us on board. You have consistently proved your worth and have not failed in any of the endeavors.

The company has received many compliments for you from our clients and we are delighted to have such a valuable staff like you with us. Your determination to always go an extra mile has brought a lot of fame to this company. With your significant contribution, we have attained many new customers and are also retaining a big number of existing loyal customers.

On behalf of the entire organization, I earnestly express gratitude towards you and wish you all the best for all projects you handle in the years to come.

Sincerely,

Ted Robinson
Investment Research
8723 March Street
Newbury, MI. 45678
(245)456-7890 X 123

Critique of Poor Employee Performance

It's unfortunate, but you may find yourself having to write an email detailing how an employee has failed in their duties. Tact and diplomacy are important, but so is clarity.

To: Hank Henry <h.henry@capitalchemicals.com
From: Sam Stotermeyer <s.stotermeyer@capitalchemicals.com
Subject: Your Recent Performance

Good Morning, Hank,

As you know, your responsibilities include ordering lab supplies. We have had several discussions over the past few months about determining what supplies need to be ordered as well as your timeliness in placing the orders. You agreed that you would establish more frequent inventory and be more diligent in placing orders at the beginning of the week.

Unfortunately, while inventory levels have improved; a great deal of improvement is still needed in placing supply orders timely. More specifically, on May 16th, 2017, there was a delay in starting Phase II of our project because you did not place the special order for flasks and pipettes. This delay could have easily been avoided.

Given the continuance of performance issues, I am giving you a written warning. Your performance must improve immediately or further disciplinary action, up to and including discharge, will result.

If you wish to appeal my decision, please contact my secretary to arrange an appointment. I will be happy to hear your side of the story.

Sincerely,

Sam Stotermeyer
Quality Control Supervisor
Capital Chemicals
6789 South Street
Corollitas, CA. 98212
(481)239-7281 x 567

Closing Thoughts

There are two thoughts worth sharing.[56] The first is from James Thurber, American author and cartoonist, who said: "Precision of communication is important, more important than ever, in our era of hair trigger balances, when a false or misunderstood word may create as much disaster as a sudden thoughtless act."

The second comes from Samuel Clemens, better known as Mark Twain: "The difference between the right word and the almost right word is the difference between lightning and the lightning bug."

Together these statements reinforce the need for accuracy in wording, syntax, and tone. In other words, to avoid complicating misunderstandings, every email you write should be reviewed with a keen eye.

---

56 Source: "Leading Thoughts," http://www.leadershipnow.com/communicationquotes .html.

CHAPTER 13.

Email Marketing
That Sells

Email marketing: a form of direct marketing, where products or services are sold directly to the public. Instead of using traditional methods (mail order and telephone solicitation), business owners use electronic mail (email) to communicate with a targeted audience. Email marketing is the king of the marketing kingdom, with a 4400 percent ROI and $44 for every $1 spent.[57]

This overwhelming success may be due to the widespread popularity of electronic mail; back in 2012, researchers found 77 percent of consumers chose email over other online communication channels.[58] Even though there are those who claim email marketing is on the way out,

---

57 See "70 Email Marketing Stats Every Marketer Should Know," Campaign Monitor, January 6, 2016, https://www.campaignmonitor.com/blog/email-marketing/2016/01/70-email-marketing-stats-you-need-to-know/.

58 See "77 Percent of Us Want to Get Marketing Messages via Email & There's No Close Second Place, Study Says," Marketing Land, April 5, 2012, http://marketingland.com/77-percent-of-us-want-to-get-marketing-messages-via-email-theres-no-close-second-place-study-says-9420.

Marketing Land reported 80 percent of marketers argue email is "the strongest performing media buy" way ahead of search engine marketing and traditional display marketing strategies modified for the digital world.[59]

In this chapter, you'll learn how to create emails for a wide range of marketing offers, including e-commerce, lead generation, upselling, PayPal and credit card orders, webinar invitations, subscription marketing, new product announcements, sales and discount offers, product upgrades, and emails to reactivate dormant accounts.

The Basics of Email Marketing

When you create your website, then you must get people to come to your site, meaning they have to know that you exist first. One of the most popular ways is to put out marketing or advertising that lets potential buyers know something about your site and that you also have something to offer them if they visit. This can be a newsletter, free report, or something else, that reflects what your website is about.

Ideally, putting out an email newsletter once a week, or even every two weeks, means that people must sign up for it to get the news you have to offer. You, then, are building your customer base which provides the means by which your business stays alive and is successful.

Sending emails to people on your list who have opted in and, therefore, given you permission to email them, is not SPAM, and you may email them whatever you want and any number of emails you want. However, if you send too many emails for their taste, or too many emails that are just sales pitches and not useful content, they will stop opening and reading your emails. Many may also unsubscribe, a request for you to take them off your list. In his book *Launch* (Morgan James), Jeff

---

59 Ibid.

Walker says the most important thing you need to make money on the Internet is an opt-in e-list.

You can also rent email lists from list brokers to help build your list of potential customers. Make sure first that those who signed into these lists are opt-in subscribers before you rent it. The seller must show you that proof, or the list may be suspect.

It is inappropriate to "harvest" email addresses by collecting them off websites or social media sites. If you email to harvested names, you do not have their permission, and are therefore spamming. Even if you are not spamming, according to the legal definition (see chapter 3), the recipients will view it as spam. If your Internet service provider (ISP) receives too many spam complaints about you, they may shut down your email account without warning.

Writing Emails to Your List

The first part of your email as a marketer should show your name or your business name in the box indicating who the email is from. The next box down shows the name of who the mail is being sent to, preferably an actual recipient name. The subject box in your email should always use strong words that closely reflect what the reader will be seeing an answer to in the email, or that provides more information that they want to know about.

The body of the email must start out with a good lead that addresses a problem that many on your list might be interested to know more about. The rest of the body of writing provides the information, usually with two to three paragraphs, and can use bullet points for special information highlights. The next section shows where to go to get a report, a book, a video, using a link that the reader clicks on to get there. In essence, you are asking your readers to do something, take an action, or make a purchase if they like what they see.

The closure to the email can also be an add-on opportunity that if the reader clicks on the link now, an extra report is sent for free, or some other product or service is offered, as part of clicking on the link to make a purchase or signing up for something new. Then your name is included at the end, with contact information where you can be reached.

At the bottom of the email, always include a standard text message with an unsubscribe opt-out link, that if people no longer wish to receive the weekly message, they can go and remove themselves from the list. Make sure your system does exactly that. You can also put that standard message at the top, before you present the body of the message, but it is usually better at the bottom.

Certain types of emails must also have disclaimer messages added in, such as those offering any medical advice, legal advice, or financial letters of investment, for example. This is very important to have as a standard on your emails, to avoid being a pest or having people file a complaint with your ISP.

You can also add a notice to have the recipient forward the email to someone who might be interested, but you cannot offer an incentive to do so. You would be violating regulations of the CAN-SPAM Act. Asking people to share your email is known as viral marketing. The more interesting, useful, or entertaining your email, the more viral distribution it will get.

You might suggest that recipients "whitelist" your email, so that the recipient's email provider is set up to "know" your email address and it won't be put into the spam box by accident. This is generally done by having the readers manually add your email address (the one that is in the "From" box) to their contact folder. They can add more information there to make it a more valid contact. Email providers may have different ways of doing this, so it is best to just say that they should "whitelist" your email. Other ways involve going into "settings" and then "filter" to add in the email address for the "inbox."

The idea behind direct email marketing is simple: it's more profitable to send attractive, professional, and compelling ads to a smaller group of recipients who've shown interest in receiving such messages than it does to send thousands of people (many of whom have never heard of you) unsolicited commercial email (UCE) messages. In direct email marketing, having permission to send your marketing messages is paramount. Permission is granted when a site visitor "opts-in" by exchanging their contact details in order to get a discount or other special offer. Once the original offer is received, the business owner can keep on sending the material or messages until the recipient chooses to opt-out.

Never expect email marketing to be all you need. Instead, think "big picture": compliment your email campaigns with promotional efforts in other arenas. Always consider how search engine optimization (SEO) and marketing (SEM), social media engagement, and targeted, strategic, lead-nurturing content creation can work together.

What is an email campaign? Unlike a single "stand-alone" email, a campaign is a coordinated set of email marketing messages delivered at specific intervals which are intended to "escalate a persuasive argument" ultimately motivating the reader to make a purchase.[60]

Email Marketing Do's and Don'ts

Do . . .

Go beyond the ordinary.
Instead of tracking standard metrics like click-through rate (CTR), track (and pay attention to) unique metrics like where prospects went on your website, the number of visits and their frequency, and social sharing. Then combine standard segmentation criteria with this behavioral data

---

60 See "Email Campaigns," GetResponse, https://www.getresponse.com/resources/glossary /email-campaign.html.

to create more complex segmentation. Once you have a better idea of what your different segments find interesting, you can make sure your offers are more customized to fit their needs.

Tailor the message.

Use campaigns to tailor your messages according to the prospect's profiles, interests, and actions. Send different emails/messages to the different segments of your list when appropriate. Make sure you are including value-added content so your readers are more apt to engage with your emails.

Whenever possible, automate.

Utilizing automated email marketing and drip campaigns can make a huge difference in your bottom line. Drip campaigns are essentially lead nurturing; they involve sending marketing information to prospects repeatedly over longer periods of time in order to move them through the marketing funnel.[61] B2C marketers who leverage automation have seen conversion rates as high as 50 percent.[62]

Get creative: use a mix of styles and methods.

To avoid having your email campaigns underperform, consider mixing up campaign styles and methods. By always keeping your content and methodology fresh, you will have a better chance of keeping readers engaged. This creativity should be fueled by the consumer awareness you've gotten from testing responses to different email components and any surveys you've conducted.

---

61 See "Drip Campaign," Track Maven, https://trackmaven.com/marketing-dictionary /drip-campaign/.
62 See "70 Email Marketing Stats Every Marketer Should Know," Campaign Monitor, January 6, 2016, https://www.campaignmonitor.com/blog/email-marketing/2016 /01/70-email-marketing-stats-you-need-to-know/.

Test everything.

Test before sending to confirm deliverability (and that all links go to the right pages). Test subject lines along with standard A/B testing (where changes are made in body content used, images, the location of the call-to-action, or button color and position, for example) to ensure the highest response.

Analyze results.

Leverage the reporting dashboards in your marketing automation solution to understand prospect interaction and improve future campaigns.

Always use social share buttons.

If you include easy social functionality for readers, you encourage them to "evangelize" your message.

Write engaging subject lines.

You've got to grab attention with a great headline to get your readers to open your email. Readers are unlikely to open an email unless there is a clear benefit in doing so; if your subject line doesn't captivate and communicate the benefit of opening the email, then open rates.

Structure your email for scanners.

According to a study conducted by the Nielsen Group, people scan emails very quickly, and the only areas they give any appreciable amount of time to at all are the initial copy and headlines to look for elements that pique their interest.[63] In order to get your message across, you need to make sure your automated email campaign is structured for scanners.

---

63 See: "Email Newsletters: Surviving Inbox Congestion," https://www.nngroup.com/articles/email-newsletters-inbox-congestion.

When writing promotional emails, rely on a tested copywriting formula.

There's no need to reinvent the wheel: fall back on the body of knowledge gleaned by copywriters over the years. Give both the Problem-Agitate-Solve (PAS) model[64] and the BAB ("Before-After-Bridge)[65] formula a try. Subscribe to the newsletters of top copywriters to learn new ways of engaging your audience. For useful case studies and best practices data on Internet and integrated marketing, visit Marketing Profs and Marketing Sherpa.[66]

Always use a call-to-action (CTA) button.

Studies have found that including a CTA button (rather than text-only links) increases conversions. These should feature striking and action-oriented text on a brightly colored background. While green and orange buttons are reported to perform best, contrast is essential, as is the size of button text. (It should be large enough to read easily.)[67]

Always include unsubscribe links. Each of your emails must contain an unsubscribe link. And because it's a requirement of the CAN-SPAM Act, automated email service providers include unsubscribe links in all their email templates.

Don'ts . . .

Here are some basic things to avoid when leveraging email marketing:

- **The color red**—red is a loud color and is used a lot by spammers. It could potentially set off spam filters.

---

64 See: "Master This Copywriting Formula to Dominate Any Social Media Platform," http://www.copyblogger.com/problem-agitate-solve.

65 See: "Increase Your Email Click-Through Rate Using This Simple Copywriting Formula," https://www.campaignmonitor.com/blog/email-marketing/2014/10/increase-email-click-through-copywriting-formula/.

66 URLs for MarketingProfs (https://www.marketingprofs.com) and Marketing Sherpa, (http://www.marketingsherpa.com).

67 See: "17 Best Practices for Crazy-Effective Call-To-Action Buttons," http://www.wordstream.com/blog/ws/2015/02/20/call-to-action-buttons.

- **Misleading subject lines**—from blank subject lines to ones that don't even match your copy, be careful using them because they are a big part of the spam algorithm email providers employ.
- **Capital letters**—avoid using all capital letters within your email or subject line.
- **Excessive use of symbols**—avoid using too many question marks, dollar signs, and exclamation marks . . . especially in a row.
- **Too many hyperlinks**—ideally you shouldn't use more than two or three links.

Using Graphics, Animation, or Videos

Some emails, depending on what is being offered, can be enhanced with a video that shows more about the message, such as testimonials, or showing how a product works. It is a judgement call as to how to design your message for your unique product or service. Most personal emails are text only, eliminating unnecessary distractions while the recipient is reading the email.

If you are selling a book or offering a free white paper or other lead magnet, showing the cover of the book or lead magnet can help generate more sales or downloads. The cover image should hyperlink to the book sales page or lead magnet download page. CD and DVD covers are also good to include in the message if you are offering those. Artists will want to include a picture or two of their work, but be sure that the photography is professional and appealing, with proper lighting and framing.

Get to Know Your Metrics

What numbers should you be concerned about when reviewing the results of a stand-alone email or an email campaign? Here are the most important email metrics to measure:

Bounce rate

The percentage of total emails sent that could not be delivered to the recipient's inbox, a phenomenon known as a "bounce." Use this metric to uncover potential problems with your email list. There are two kinds of bounces to track: "hard" bounces and "soft" bounces. Soft bounces are the result of a temporary problem with a valid email address, such as a full inbox or a problem with the recipient's server. Hard bounces are the result of an invalid, closed, or nonexistent email address.

Delivery rate

The percentage of emails that were actually delivered to recipients' inboxes, calculated by subtracting hard and soft bounces from the gross number of emails sent and then dividing that number by gross emails sent. Look for a delivery rate of 95 percent or higher. If your delivery rate is slipping over time, you may have list-quality problems. If one particular email or campaign has a lower than average delivery rate, there may have been some element flagged as spam by the recipients' service provider.

List growth rate

The measurement of how fast your email list is growing. Calculate growth by subtracting opt-outs and hard bounces from the number of new email subscribers gained in a given period. Then, divide that number by the original list size. Email list growth rate is important because many of the addresses in your list will "go bad" over time, and to be an effective email marketer your list will need to be refreshed with new names. According to MarketingSherpa, the annual "churn rate" of an email list can be 25 percent or more.[68]

Click-through rate (CTR)

This metric represents the number of readers who clicked on one or more links contained in an email message. Calculate CTR either by dividing unique clicks by the number of emails delivered, or by dividing total clicks, including multiple clicks by the same recipient, by the number of emails delivered. Monitoring email CTR is essential because it's an indicator of content /offer relevancy and quality.

Email sharing

This is the percentage of recipients who clicked on a "share this" or "forward to a friend" button to post/share content. Sharing rates are another indicator of the value and relevance of your email messages. By watching this metric, you'll learn what content and offers are "share-worthy" and use that knowledge in the future when developing new campaigns.

Conversion rate

The percentage of readers who followed a CTA by clicking on a link within an email and completed the desired action (such as making a purchase or filling in a form). Unfortunately, conversion is dependent on more than just your email content; the quality of the landing page is also a significant factor.

Revenue per email sent

This is calculated by dividing the total revenue generated from the campaign by the number of emails sent.

---

68 See: "10 Ways to Reduce Churn with Email Campaigns," https://www.campaign monitor.com/blog/email-marketing/2016/10/10-ways-reduce-churn-email-cam paigns.

Open Rate

This is a measure of how many people open (or view) a particular email campaign. Unfortunately, this metric is unreliable, mainly because of the large percentage of email users who have "image-blocking" enabled on their email client.An email is only counted as "opened" if the recipient also receives the images embedded in that message. Even if such a recipient opens an email, it won't be included in the calculation.

Unsubscribe rate

As lots of people don't bother to formally unsubscribe (choosing to just ignore your emails or send them directly to the Junk folder), this is another unreliable metric of email marketing success. When should you worry about your unsubscribe rate? Experts say if you receive less than a 2 percent unsubscribe rate, you're about average.[69] Paying close attention to your click-through and conversion rates is a far better way to monitor list engagement and interest.

E-Commerce

It's obvious e-commerce involves buying and selling online. What may not be apparent are the dozens of actions—like abandoning an online shopping cart—that can trigger an email response. These transactional, or triggered, emails, offer marketers valuable opportunities to nurture the relationship and drive sales.

There are many transactional email message formats: welcome emails, educational and problem-solving emails, order status emails, shopping cart abandonment emails, reorder emails, list reengagement emails (helping you to maintain a clean list), birthday, anniversary and holiday, emails; newsletter emails, sales announcement emails, cross-selling and

---

69 See: "What is a reasonable unsubscribe rate?," https://help.campaignmonitor.com /topic.aspx?t=55.

upselling emails, event emails, and lead-nurturing emails. Despite the array, e-commerce email marketing is really all about creating (and maintaining) a relationship between sender and receiver which is profitable to both parties.

Welcome Emails

When new contacts subscribe to your list, you want to welcome them to the group with an inviting email. The welcome email is one of the most important tools in your email marketing toolbox.

Your welcome email should not only include a warm, personalized introductory message, it must also:

- reinforce the perks of your list (reaffirming they made the right decision in subscribing
- offer an exclusive deal or gift available only to list members
- include one clear call-to-action ("shop now," "start exploring," "show me," or "get my gift!")

Consider using supportive images to better engage readers. Research has given us two good reasons to do so: 65 percentof us are visual learners and 83 percent are more likely to remember text-based content when it's supported by a picture.[70]

When crafting your welcome email subject line, attempt to do three things: catch the reader's attention, thank them for signing up, and give them a reason to open the email. Here's simple subject line which does all three: "Thanks for signing up. Now what?"

---

70 See: "Lessons from an Epic Analysis of 50 Welcome Emails," https://customer.io /blog/welcome-email-best-practices.html.

Don't be afraid to be creative or funny. For example, the subject line of Workflowy's welcome email reads: "It's 6 AM. Do you know where your brain is?" It's both clever and engaging.[71]

Here's another example: When someone clicks on "Sign up to Receive Bob Bly's FREE E-Newsletter" on the home page of www.bly.com, he or she is taken to a landing page (http://www.bly.com/reports) with a persuasive offer and headline: "Get 4 FREE Special Reports from Bob Bly Worth Over $100!" He makes it simple to accept the gift, as he requires only the email address from the user. There's a drawback to this spare approach to list building: it makes email personalization impossible. His welcome email follows.

Center for Technical Communication
From: Bob Bly <rwbly@bly.ccsend.com>; on behalf of; Bob Bly <rwbly@bly.com>
To: kim@thefuneralcopywriter.com
Subject: Here are the reports you requested

Thanks for subscribing to Bob Bly's free e-zine, The Direct Response Letter

Dear Direct Response Letter Subscriber:

Thanks for subscribing to *The Direct Response Letter*.

As a subscriber, you'll be getting practical, utterly pragmatic tips and ideas to help improve your copywriting skills, increase your marketing results, and achieve greater success in your freelance career or small business.

As promised, here are your 4 free bonus reports. Just click on the link below to download:

http://www.bly.com/reports/download.htm

These informative reports—containing over 167 pages of valuable marketing advice—normally sell for—$ 116 on my website.

---

71 See: "The 9 Things Successful Welcome Emails Have In Common," https://medium.com/@Chargify/the-9-things-successful-welcome-emails-have-in-common.

But as a new Direct Response Letter subscriber, you get all 4 absolutely FREE!

If you're a freelance writer . . . copywriter . . . information marketer . . . small business owner . . . consultant . . . coach . . . speaker . . . content author . . . or anyone else who needs to generate more leads, orders and sales . . . you'll find the tips in these reports—and my newsletter—invaluable.

Your subscription brings you one regular monthly issue, usually at the beginning of the month, plus one or two supplementary messages each week. These supplementary messages are typically either free tips or personal recommendations for information products on marketing or related topics. Note: I review products before recommending them and in many cases know the authors.

Click here to download your 4 free special reports now:

http://www.bly.com/reports/download.htm

Sincerely,
Bob Bly

P.S. We do not rent or share your name with anybody.

Since the reader's been waiting for offer fulfillment, the subject line is compelling. And in saying "thank you" at the start (twice!), Bob lets the reader know he appreciates them. He reinforces the value of the offer and fulfills his promise by providing a download link within the email. He also tells them what to expect and guarantees the security of their contact details in the postscript.

Upsell Emails

Upselling typically involves trading up to a better version of what's being purchased. Email upsell messages should include:

- A personalized greeting
- An image/description of the recent purchase
- Product or service recommendations
- A request for help in modifying recommendations

Here's an example of an upsell email message with a twist. It doesn't promote a better version of the original product; instead, it promotes an additional purchase. It is sent automatically to my customers who have just purchased my Twitter e-book, on the logic that if they are interested in social media, they are interested in Facebook as well as Twitter.

From: Bob Bly <rwbly@bly.ccsend.com>; on behalf of; Bob Bly <rwbly@bly.com>
To: Mark Smeaton <mark.smeaton@gmail.com
Subject: Your one-time upgrade offer

Dear Mark,

You'll want to know about this chance to upgrade your order. This option will NOT be available again at this incredibly low price. If you take action right now, you will save 60% off the regular retail price.

Get a copy of my e-book *How to Make Money with Facebook Ads and Boosted Posts*, which regularly sells for $49 . . . for only $19.00. If you'd like to add this to your order, simply scroll down and click on the "Buy Now" button below.

Three Reasons to Love Facebook Advertising

Here's why many of today's savviest—and richest—online marketers absolutely love Facebook advertising:

** FIRST, Facebook is the most targeted online advertising medium in existence: It enables you to deliver your ads to specific groups of people . . . based on age, interests, behaviors, buying preferences, and other metrics . . . to a degree Google advertisers can only dream about.

** SECOND, because it is targeted and the rates are so reasonable, Facebook is extremely affordable, even if your online marketing budget is miniscule. The low cost also allows for more testing for fewer dollars.

** THIRD, Facebook offers greater flexibility than Google and other online ad media in terms of ad design, character length, images, and videos.

And with approximately 1.28 billion active users monthly, no wonder Facebook is the second most visited website, behind Google. That's a lot of eyeballs on your ads.

So . . . if you are an online marketer, copywriter, or consultant, and you are not actively testing Facebook for your products or clients . . . you are leaving money on the table.

In this 80-page ebook, my coauthor James Palmer and I pull back the curtain—and show you how to make thousands of extra dollars online with winning Facebook ads and boosted posts.

To preview *How to Make Money with Facebook Advertising* on a risk-free 90-day trial basis, just click here now:

I totally guarantee your satisfaction with my ebook, *How to Make Money with Facebook Ads and Boosted Posts*. My guarantee is ironclad—and unconditional: If you are unhappy for any other reason . . . or for no reason at all . . . just let me know within 90 days. I'll give you a full and prompt refund of every penny you paid. And on top of that, you can still keep the e-book free—with my complements.

That way, you risk nothing. You can't lose!

But I urge you to hurry. This special LOW PRICE of only $19 (a $30 discount off the $49 cover price) is only valid if you take advantage of this offer right now—it will not be repeated again.

So what are you waiting for? To order *How to Make Money with Facebook Ads and Boosted Posts* on a 90-day risk-free trial basis . . . and save $30 . . . just click here now:

Sincerely,
Robert W. Bly, Director
CTC Publishing

P.S. Order *How to Make Money with Facebook Ads and Boosted Posts* today and you get a FREE 50-page Special Bonus Report, Writing for the Web (list price: $29). Best of all, this bonus report—a $29 value—is yours to keep FREE . . . even if you request a refund on the ebook! To order *How to Make Money with Facebook Ads and Boosted Posts* . . . and get your FREE Special Report . . . just click below now:

Order-Generating Emails

An order-generating email is one which solicits a direct order. The prospect clicks on a hyperlink in the email going either to a sales page or directly to a shopping cart which allows him or her to order with a credit card or digital wallet. Here's an example which illustrates the finer points of asking for a sale.

From: Bob Bly <rwbly@bly.ccsend.com>; on behalf of; Bob Bly <rwbly@bly.com>
To: Jane Smith <jsmith1956@gmail.com>
Subject: Make $9,821 an hour talking on the phone

Dear Direct Response Letter Subscriber,

What's the easiest—and most profitable—information product to sell on the Internet?

It's not ebooks . . . or CD albums . . . or DVDs.

It's "teleseminars."

Your prospects will pay anywhere from $29 to $179 to listen to a 60- or 90-minute phone call.

You don't have to write anything: you can just interview a subject matter expert—or have a moderator interview you about your specialty.

I've earned as much as $9,821 to present a one-hour tele-seminar . . . and others are making even more.

It's the easiest money I've ever made in my life.

To find out how you can make $1,000 to $5,000 an hour or more promoting and producing your own tele-seminars, click below now:

http://www.teleconferenceprofits.net

Sincerely,
Bob Bly

Subscription Marketing

The subscription business model is where a customer must pay a subscription price to have access to a product or service. Pioneered by magazines and newspapers, the model is now used by many businesses and websites.[72] Think of BarkBox (https://www.barkbox.com), or The Beauty Box by Ipsy (https://www.ipsy.com), examples of the "surprise box" subscription model.

Here are eight types of subscription models in the market:[73]

- Knowledge membership: website allows unlimited access to information

---

72 See: "Subscription Business Model," https://en.wikipedia.org/wiki/Subscription _business_model.
73 See: "Eight Subscription Models and Five Best Practices for Your Offerings," https://www.marketingprofs.com/articles/2017/31608/eight-subscription-models -and-five-best-practices-for-your-offerings.

- Buffet content: streaming services like Netflix
- Peace of mind: monitoring websites, like LifeLock
- Front of the line: works well with complex products or services that are complex and require specialists to fix (such as IT services
- Consumables: automatic renewal delivery of items that typically run low—such as office supplies, coffee, household goods, diapers, razors
- Network: sharing services such as Zipcar, Lyft, and BeatsMusic
- Private club: product or service that is limited in supply, like American Express Centurion

How should you promote a subscription service/product using email? Subscription services require marketers to stay involved with customers. Rather than marketing a product or service, they're initiating a long-term relationship. Engagement marketing, or the concept of continuously connecting with individuals based on what they do and wherever they may be, becomes a new and critical strategy.[74]

Here's an example email message promoting a SaaS (software as a service) subscription service.

From: The BackUp Genius Team
To: Karen@abcwebsite.com
Subject: Your BackUp Genius trial is over. Subscribe today to pick up where you left off.

Dear Karen,

Thanks for giving BackUp Genius a try!
Your free trial has expired but you can keep on using BackUp Genius with a paid subscription.

---

74 See: "3 Ways for Marketers to Take on the Growing Subscription-Based Economy," http://blog.marketo.com/2015/07/3-ways-for-marketers-to-take-on-the-growing -subscription-based-economy.html.

The world's most popular online backUp tool

Over 1,000 small business owners sign up for BackUp Genius every day making it the #1 data protection tool.

Subscribe now to keep using BackUp Genius.

- Pick up where you left off–all your data is still there.
- Anyone you've invited during the trial will still have access.
- Subscribing takes just 60 seconds.

Did BackUp Genius work for you?

We'd love to hear why. We're always looking for ways to get better. If you have feedback you think would be useful, please take our brief, anonymous survey.

Prefer to cancel your account instead?

We'll be sorry to see you go. Once your account is canceled, your information will be immediately and permanently deleted. To cancel your account, please visit:
(hyperlink)

What types of payment do we accept?

Currently we accept Visa, Mastercard, and American Express. For U.S. customers subscribing to the Annual Plan, we can accept paper checks. We do not accept PayPal. For all monthly plans we only accept payments online so we will not be able to accept a P.O., invoice you, or take an order over the phone.

Have questions or need help?

Our customer service and support is here to help you any way we can. Please visit <hyperlink> to get in touch.

Thanks again for using our products,

The Crew at BackUp Genius
http://backupgenius.com

New Product Announcements

According to the Direct Marketing Association, 66 percent of consumers have made a purchase as a result of an email.[75]As the most effective tool you'll want in your promotion warehouse, developing an email product launch strategy is essential. Planning includes:

1. Establishing the rhythm of your launch campaign messages. How often do you plan on emailing your subscribers and what will that content include?
2. Highlighting the problem your product will fix early in the cycle. Get people thinking about that problem, and the solutions available to them. (And why your solution is best.)
3. Identifying a clear and consistent call to action (CTA). Think about what action you want your subscribers to take after reading your email. Are they signing up to a separate list for exclusive product updates/announcements? Should they spread the word on social media? Do they have the option to preorder?
4. Integrating your product launch email series with the rest of your launch promotion plan. In addition to email, your plan could include website updates, social posts, blog posts, and press releases; make sure your messaging is consistent across all channels.

There email types used in product launches include: the survey email, a giveaway email, the interest list email, the anticipation email, the offer, a common questions email, and the closing email. [76] Here's an example of an offer email.

---

75 See: "Saturday Stat Series: The Influence of Email Marketing Messages," https://thedma.org/data-driven-marketing/saturday-stat-series.
76 See: "7 Amazing Product Launch Emails [Tried-and-Tested Templates]," http://blog.teachable.com/product-launch-emails.

From: Alex<alex@buildingyourlist.com>
To: Henry Holt <h.holt@gmail.com>
Subject: The Guest Blogger program is LIVE!

Good Morning!

This is an exciting moment for me—as of midnight last night, we've gone LIVE!

I was awake all night getting ready for today. Sometime around 2:00 a.m. I thought of some more bonuses for new members. Things like:

Unlimited email consulting

15-minute phone strategy session

And . . . as a special gift to everyone who eagerly awaited launch day, both membership levels are 15% off for the next 24 hours! Just use the code MOVERANDSHAKER at checkout.

To get all the details on the program and enroll, click here.

Sincerely,

Alex Morin
2167 Harper's Place
Monterey, CA. 93949
415-245-4567

Sales and Discount Offers

A sales email should have three simple sections:

- The Introduction. The subject and the first few sentences have to be an attention grabber. It's the difference between getting opened versus getting ignored or blocked.
- The Value Proposition. This is the main point of your email. Keep it focused on value and solving a problem for your prospect. Why should they care about you? If there is a clear

and concise benefit to the prospect, you'll get a response. If not, you're dead to them.

- Call to Action. This is the crucial point where you tell the recipient exactly what you want them to do. As you'd expect, this can make or break everything.

The following two sales emails form a short series of automated messaging. The first is an announcement of a sale; the second time-sensitive reminder creates urgency in the reader.

Email #1

From: Karen Meyers <karenm@awfp.com>
To: kim@thefuneralcopywriter.com
Subject Line: Don't miss this! Up to 50% Off . . . EVERYTHING!

Dear Kim,

Have you checked out AWFP's 20th Anniversary Sale yet?
Until Wednesday, May 31st, you can take advantage of up to 50% savings on all of our most popular programs—even our Masters Level programs . . . EVERYTHING is on sale.

You can access the full list here.

If there's a course or program you've had your eye on, now is definitely the time to get it!

All the best,

Karen Meyers
Executive Director, AWFP

P.S. Remember, at midnight ET on Wednesday, everything will flip back to full price. So don't delay! Go here now to check out AWFP's 20th Anniversary Sale.

For questions or requests: contact us online.
Trouble viewing this email? View in your browser, here.

Email #2

Subject Line: Only 72 Hours Remain: Up to 50% Off!
From: Karen Meyers <karenm@awfp.com>
To: kim@thefuneralcopywriter.com
Subject Line: Only 72 Hours Remain: Up to 50% Off!

Dear Kim,

This is just a courtesy reminder . . .

Until Wednesday at midnight ET sharp, you can take advantage of the 50% savings on some of AWFP's most popular programs.

You can access the full list here.

You'll be able to save BIG on a program that will give you everything you need to succeed as a professional optimism advocate.

Take advantage and save—and have everything you need to super-charge your career this year.

Click here for AWFP's 20th Anniversary Sale

We want 2017 to be your breakthrough year!

To your success,

Karen Meyers
Executive Director, AWFP

Product Upgrades

There are a few things you want to do when promoting a product or service upgrade by email. First, make your message relevant: personalize it with names and pertinent details, such as how much time is left in a trial or based on certain user activity, to make your message feel relevant and timely. You'll also want to:

Specify features that people will gain or miss out on when upgrading.

- Include plan pricing details to help people making a purchase decision.
- Use social proof to persuade.
- Make it easy to keep in touch. People might not be ready to upgrade or want to cancel, but that doesn't mean you should say goodbye to them forever.
- Make your call to action stand out. Most CTAs in upgrade emails are basic, such as "Upgrade Now!" Try A/B testing copy that is benefits-focused.

From: Richard Sturdivant <r.sturdivant@videomarketingonline.com>
To: Frank Hardy <f.hardy@endlessdreaming.com>
Subject: Your Video Marketing Mastery Test Drive is Ending

Hey, Percy,

The premium features on your Video Marketing Mastery account are coming to a close and it will soon turn back into a free plan.

You have 3 days left.

We hope you've had a chance to explore some of our favorite premium features, like audience tracking and video integration.

If we've done our jobs right you've already gotten a good feel for what we can do for you.

Ready to Upgrade?

You've still got 3 days left to try out our premium features. If you decide you want to upgrade, it's totally painless. Our premium plans start at just $25.00/month and includes 24-hour access to exclusive lead-generation tools and our award-winning support team.

If you're not ready to upgrade, that's okay. You can keep using the free plan . . . forever!

Have questions? Just reply to this email. We're happy to help.

<See Upgrade Options>>

Sincerely,

Richard Sturdivant
Director of Sales
Video Marketing Online
831-245-3456
http://videomarketingonline.com

Shopping Cart Abandon Emails

Abandoned cart email messages are sent to customers who have added products to their cart but, for one reason or another, failed to check out.

It isn't always because the customer changed his or her mind about the purchase; it could have been because the website crashed, because the process was complicated, or because the site timed out.

Shopping cart abandon emails can be remarkably effective as a sales recovery tactic. According to a recent study, nearly half of all abandoned cart emails are opened and over a third of clicks lead to purchases back on site.[77]

Here are two examples. Both depend largely on a picture of the abandoned product and are text-light.

From: Judy Simmons, The Online Bedding Shop <judys@onlinebshop.com>
To: Horace Walpole <h.walpole212@gmail.com>
Subject: We're Still Holding the Roses & Butterflies Duvet cover for you.

Hello, Horace,

Act fast if you want it.

(show product picture)

<Buy now>

Have questions or need help with your purchase?

I'm here to help.

<phone number>

Sincerely,

Judy Simmons
Customer Support Representative
Online Bedding Shop

---

77 See: "Cart Abandonment Stats [Infographic]," http://www.getelastic.com/cart-aban donment-stats-infographic/.

> From: Nancy Drew-Hardy <n.hardy@sweetshopdelights.com>
> To: Marilyn White (m.white@gmail.com)
> Subject: Complete Your Purchase
>
> Hello, Marilyn,
>
> Your shopping cart at Sweet Shop Delights has been reserved and is waiting for your return. In your cart you left:
>
> *(product picture(s) and mouth-watering descriptions)*
>
> But it's not too late!
>
> Click on this link to complete your purchase:
>
> <hyperlink>
>
> Thanks for shopping!
>
> Enjoy the rest of the day.
>
> Sincerely,
> Nancy Drew-Hardy
> Sweet Shop Delights

Lead Generation and Lead-Nurturing Emails

Lead generation describes the process of identifying and cultivating potential customers for a business's products or services. Lead nurturing is also a process, where a marketer works to develop a relationship with prospects and buyers. It focuses marketing and communication efforts on listening to the needs of prospects, and providing the information and answers they need.[78]

Let's talk lead generation first. According to recent research, email came in as the number one most effective online tactic for lead generation in Ascend2's 2016 State of Lead Generation report.[79]

---

78 See: "What is Lead Nurturing?," https://www.marketo.com/lead-nurturing.
79 See: http://ascend2.com/home/research-reports.

So how do you generate leads online? We've seen the most common example of an email-based lead-generation strategy earlier, in the form of Bob Bly's Direct Response Newsletter welcome email. His offer of four free reports led to a user trading his or her contact information in return for access to these valuable resources. This action resulted in an automated response (effectively opening the door to lead nurturing).

This is the heart of email marketing. This is when you work to move these unqualified leads deeper into the sales funnel.

Email marketing experts suggest you:

- keep lead-nurturing emails concise and engaging
- use images to reinforce your copy and more quickly deliver your message
- incorporate social media sharing links into your emails to promote sharing
- use e-books, videos, and slide shares or videos to educate leads on your product or service
- use action words in your calls-to-action: attend, download, register, read, and try now

Because of something called the familiarity principle (the more times we're exposed to a stimulus, the more likely we are to think favorably of it), lead nurturing requires you provide consistent, relevant content to your audience. This next example does just that.

From: Bob Bly's Direct Response Letter <rwbly@bly.ccsend.com>; on behalf of; Bob Bly's Direct Response Letter <rwbly@bly.com>
To: Keith Richard <k.richard@gmail.com>
Subject: Why I am an "Essentialist"

Dear Direct Response Letter Subscriber:

In his bestselling book *Essentialism: The Disciplines Pursuit of Less* (Crown Business), Greg McKeown preaches his philosophy of Essentialism as the path to having a better and more rewarding life.

After reading it, I am a born-again Essentialist!

The core idea of Essentialism is, in McKeown's words:

"There are far more activities and opportunities in the world than we have the time and resources to invest in.

"And although many of them may be good, or even very good, the fact is that most are trivial and few are vital.

"Only when you give yourself permission to stop trying to do it all, to stop saying yes to everyone, can you make your highest contribution towards the things that really matter."

If you know people who pursue a primary goal, activity, or mission with laserlike focus—whether it's building a business, mastering the violin, or accumulating wealth—they are almost surely, with rare exceptions, Essentialists.

If you know people who volunteer for everything, have a calendar filled with diverse activities, pursue a dozen hobbies and interests, and volunteer for every committee in every worthwhile organization under the sun—I can virtually assure you that they are not Essentialists.

I only came across McKeown's book a couple of months ago. But I have been an Essentialist my entire adult life.

I focus, to the exclusion of almost everything else, on just the few things that matter most to me—my business and my clients, writing, and my family.

Yes, I would like to do more. But as McKeown correctly points out, our time, attention, energy, and bandwidth are shockingly finite.

So if you try to do everything, you accomplish—and get good at—almost nothing.

"The overwhelming reality is: we live in a world where almost everything is worthless and a very few things are exceptionally valuable," McKeown writes.

"We can choose how to spend our energy and time. We can't have or do it all."

He quotes John Maxwell: "You cannot overestimate the unimportance of practically everything."

Marcus Aurelius says it this way: "If thou wouldst know contentment, let thy deeds be few."

The way I put it is this: If you are someone who is "all over the place," you will never really get to the one place you want to go.

The key to Essentialism is laserlike focus on one or two things. Steve Martin said:

"I did stand-up comedy for 18 years. Ten of those years were spent learning, four were spent refining, and four were spent in wild success. The course was more plodding than heroic."

I have always described myself as a plodder, too. If you write, as I have, 12 hours a day, 5 days a week for more than 3 decades, you can't help but get better at it!

Sincerely,

Bob Bly

P.S. My Essentialism does not mean I make zero contribution to worthy causes outside my small number of core activities.

But I do so in the most time-efficient manner—by donating money rather than my time to these worthy causes.

By focusing just on my business, I make more money . . . which in turn enables me to make bigger contributions to curing cancer, feeding the hungry, and other things that are important but that I do not have the bandwidth to participate in directly.

Bob Bly
Copywriter / Consultant
31 Cheyenne Dr.
Montville, NJ 07045
Phone 973-263-0562
Fax 973-263-0613
www.bly.com

Follow Bob:

I welcome your feedback! Did you like today's message?

What other topics would you like to see covered in my emails?

Please let me know at: rwbly@bly.com

As always, please feel free to forward this email to a friend!

If you liked this essay, and want to read 75 more just like it, get my book *Don't Wear a Cowboy Hat Unless You are a Cowboy—and Other Grumblings from a Cranky Curmudgeon*, which you can order here: www.bly.com/KindleCowboy

Disclaimer: The Direct Response Letter only recommends products that we've either personally checked out ourselves, or that come from people we know and trust. For doing so, we sometimes receive a sales commission.

Webinar Invitations

Naturally, electronic webinar invitations work best when your email includes everything the reader needs to know. Of course, you'll need to include the webinar title, date, and time of the event, and cost. But you should also introduce the people presenting and "drive home" what people will learn, what problems attendance will help them to solve, the logistics of the event, and what attendees can expect. There should also be prominently placed "Register Now" buttons to facilitate registration.

Promoting your webinar via email all hinges on getting your webinar invite right. As with all marketing emails, the first two things you'll need to get right are the "From" line and the subject line.

From: Bob Bly <rwbly@bly.ccsend.com>; on behalf of; Bob Bly
<rwbly@bly.com>
To: Mark Smeaton <mark.smeaton@gmail.com>
Subject: "Attend" my content marketing workshop without leaving home!

Dear Direct Response Letter Subscriber:

Just a quick note to let you know I'll be giving a talk on "The 4 Levels of
Content Marketing" at the virtual Summit on Content Marketing.

www.bly.com/CMSummit

All the talks will be prerecorded and available on streaming video
through June 2, 2017. But you have to click the link above to register.

Recent research from Havas has found that some 60% of the content
created by the world's leading 1,500 brands is "just clutter" that has little
impact on consumers' lives or business results. I call this phenomenon
"content pollution."

In this Summit, dozens of speakers—including my friends Ilise Benun,
Gordon Graham, and Steven Slaunwhite—will show you how to avoid
content pollution . . . and create content marketing campaigns that
generate opt-ins, clicks, conversions, leads, and sales by the truckload.

For more information on the Summit . . . and to register and grab the
$100 Early Bird discount while it is still available . . . visit:

www.bly.com/CMSummit

Bob Bly

Copywriter / Consultant
31 Cheyenne Dr.
Montville, NJ 07045
Phone 973-263-0562
Fax 973-263-0613
www.bly.com

I welcome your feedback! Did you like today's message?

What other topics would you like to see covered in my emails?

Please let me know at: rwbly@bly.com

As always, please feel free to forward this email to a friend!

Disclaimer: The Direct Response Letter only recommends products that
we've either personally checked out ourselves, or that come from people we
know and trust. For doing so, we sometimes receive a sales commission.

The next email is a time-sensitive discount promotion for a webinar:

From: Bob Bly <rwbly@bly.com>
To: kim@thefuneralcopywriter.com
Subject: 50% discount on e-book training expires at midnight

Dear Direct Response Letter Subscriber:

There's no product easier to create or sell online . . . than a simple, straightforward instructional or how-to e-book:

<hyperlink>

Why are e-books the perfect information product to sell on the Internet?

>> 100% profit margin.
>> No printing costs.
>> No inventory to store.
>> Quick and easy to update.
>> No shipping costs or delays.
>> Higher perceived value than regular books.
>> Quick, simple, and inexpensive to produce.
>> Each e-book is a unique product—no one else has it.
>> Prices below $50, they sell well, even in a recession.

My very first e-book, published in November 2004, has generated $46,819 in sales so far.

My labor: almost zero. I didn't write any new material for it. The book is simply a collection of existing articles I had written for and published in various writers' magazines.

My total cost to produce it: $175 to a designer setting the articles into a nice PDF layout.

That's a 26,394% return on my investment. By comparison, the S&P 500 generated a total return of 87.9% during the same 14.5-year period.

The bottom line: investing the $175 in my fledgling information marketing business beat what others made in the stock market by 300 to 1!

Now, I want to show you how to make an annual six-figures passive income creating and selling simple e-books—in my AWAI course:

"Bob Bly's Ultimate Guide to E-book Writing Success: A Comprehensive Program to Writing and Selling E-books for Profit."

For more information . . . or to register for our home study course on how to write and sell e-books for fun and profit . . . just click below now:

\<hyperlink\>

Sincerely,
Bob Bly

P.S. In 2015, worldwide sales of e-books exceeded $9 billion. Why not grab your share of these enormous revenues for yourself? Register today and you get the program for half off the regular rate. But I urge you to hurry, as the 50% discount expires at midnight on March 10, 2017:

\<hyperlink\>

Bob Bly

Copywriter / Consultant
31 Cheyenne Dr.
Montville, NJ 07045
Phone 973-263-0562
Fax 973-263-0613
www.bly.com

Reactivation or "Win-Back" Emails

Reactivation (or reengagement) is when marketers reach out to people who have previously expressed interest, made a purchase, or subscribed to a list, but have since become inactive. A 2014 study looked at 33 email reactivation campaigns, from which came a set of **best practices for reengagement emails:**[80]

---

80 See: "Awaken the Dead! How to Re-Engage Your Audience with Reactivation Campaigns," https://blog.marketo.com/2015/06/awaken-the-dead-how-to-re-engage-your-audience-with-reactivation-campaigns.html.

1. The best subject lines to use for reactivation campaigns are personalized and include "Miss You."
2. Don't just send a single email. Instead, send a short series.
3. End the series with an incentive, such as a discount. When doing so, your subject line should state the exact dollar amount of the discount given, rather than the percentage of the discount. (They were found to be almost twice as successful!)
4. Reengage early—think about sending reactivation emails every 30/60/90 days, and never go longer than 180 days before contacting the subscriber to affirm continued interest.

Here's an example of a reactivation email.

From: Frank Smith, Ridgefield Customer Relations Specialist
To: Kim Simon <k.simon@happinessblogger.com>
Subject Line: We Miss You, Kim

Greetings!

It's been months since we've seen or heard from you and well . . . we miss you!

We wanted to check in to give you a really special reason to come back: a promotional code worth $25.00 off your next order.*

Remember why you joined us in the first place? You found out we deliver exclusive handpicked offers and discounts sent directly to your inbox–on the schedule you preferred.

When you come back, be sure to check out our Spring Home Decoration Sale page for extra savings.

Sincerely,
Frank Smith
Customer Relations Specialist

*One discount code per person. Offer valid through January, 2018.

CHAPTER 14.

The Role of Email in Content Marketing

Content marketing—giving away free information to build your brand, increase response to marketing campaigns, convert more online traffic, and educate the prospect on your technology, methodology, products, and services—is one of the hot trends in marketing today. Other marketing methods increasing in usage today include online video, social media, quick response codes (QRCs), search engine optimization (SEO), live online chat, and infographics. This chapter shows how to use free content offers that increase response to email marketing campaigns, which means greater conversion rates and more leads generated, as well as how to drive traffic to your existing content with emails.

The term "content marketing" may have been coined in 1996 at a roundtable for journalists held at the American Society of Newspaper Editors by John F. Oppedahl. That would mean the name content marketing is about twenty years old. But in fact, content marketing has been used for far longer than that. It's only the name that is of recent vintage, not the method. I personally have been doing content marketing for nearly four decades, and some marketers have been at it even longer.

I did my first content marketing campaign in 1980. At the time, I was advertising manager of Koch Engineering, an industrial manufacturing company owned and run by David Koch, who then, despite running for vice president of the United States on the libertarian party ticket, was relatively unknown. Today he is a household name as one half of the infamous "billionaire Koch brothers."

One of the products we sold were various "tower internals," and one type of internal was the "tray." These are circular metal disks with capped openings on their surfaces. The trays are placed inside refinery towers to enhance the distillation of crude oil into kerosene, gasoline, heating oil, jet fuel, and other petroleum-based products.

Specifying the correct configuration for the design of trays for your particular refinery is a highly technical task, and the engineers who worked in the refineries needed instruction on how to do it correctly.

To assist and educate them, we produced a design manual which we dubbed the "tray manual." The tray manual was wildly popular—by far our most requested piece of literature. But back then, we didn't call it "content marketing." We called it "giving away free information." The practice was the same. We just didn't have a name for it.

Content marketing has been used for well over a century. To test response to print ads, Claude Hopkins (1866–1932) offered free informational booklets in many of his ads.

And in 1916, Campbell's began promoting its soups with content marketing by offering free booklets of recipes that used Campbell's soups in the dishes. It not only offered useful instructions for making meals, but because a can of soup was a key ingredient in every recipe, it encouraged consumers to cook with and buy more cans of Campbell's soup.[81]

---

81 http://www.splendidtable.org/recipes/spaghetti-a-la-campbell, *The Splendid Table*, an American Public Media (aka NPR) talk program: "Spaghetti à la Campbell."

Back in those days, this free content was simply called "free booklets." In the later part of the twentieth century, marketers referred to them as "bait pieces," because the booklet or other free information offer helped "hook" prospects and turn them into leads.

Today the preferred term for free content is "lead magnet," the idea being that the tempting offer of valuable free information is like a magnet that draws people into your ad and gets them to respond and request the white paper or other free content.

There are all sorts of published opinions and tests on the effectiveness of content marketing. But let me sum up my experience in just two simple points.

First, I can't remember the last time I did a B2B or B2C marketing campaign without a free content offer.

For B2B, the lead magnet is often the primary offer and what drives prospects to respond. For B2C, the free content is often a bonus report given as an added gift with purchase of the product.

Second, on average, adding the offer of a lead magnet to a B2B lead-generation campaign can often double the number of inquiries—and often much more—versus the same campaign without the free content offer.

Plus, according to FierceCMO (10/3/2016), a poll of more than four thousand Forbes readers found that branded content was 9 percent more effective than paid advertising at getting consumers to consider buying a particular brand.

In the "good old days" of B2B marketing, our primary offer was a "free color brochure" filled with sales copy about the product. It worked then. But today, prospects respond better if you also promise to send them free information that will be useful to them in their job.

The Challenge of Content Marketing

According to Fig. 14-1, three of the top six challenges in B2B content marketing are producing engaging content, and doing so consistently and in sufficient variety.

Fig. 14-1. Top content marketing challenges.[82]

Producing engaging content is number one on the list, with six out of ten marketers surveyed citing it as a problem. And no wonder: According to an article in eMarketer (4/26/17), a recent UK study found that eight out of ten prospects who see branded content forget what they have seen within three days, with roughly half unable to remember a single detail about it.

The solution, writes Josh Althuser in an article in *Ragan's PR Daily* (6/23/17), is not to create more content unless you have a good reason

---

82 *B2B Content Marketing - 2016 Benchmarks, Budgets and Trends—North America,* 6th Edition.

for doing so: "Before you even open Word and start typing, ask yourself why you're writing. Too much content is produced without consideration for its purpose. What will this piece of content achieve? Why is this content so important? By answering these questions, you'll give your content purpose and focus. That means you'll create better content."

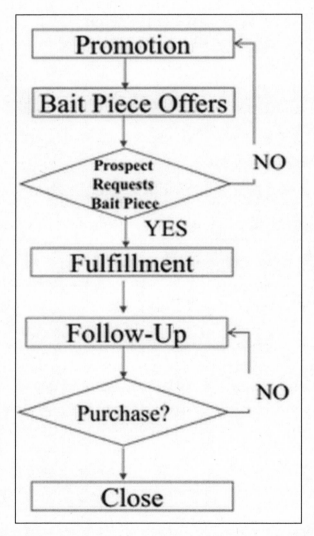

Fig. 14-2. Use of free content offer in online lead generation.

One thing free content offers do particularly well is boost open rates, click-through rates, and conversion rates in email marketing campaigns. The process, as shown in Fig. 14-2, is to first send out an email (identified as "promotion" in the diagram, because an online ad, postcard, or other marketing vehicle can also be used) with a bait piece offer.

If the prospect downloads the bait piece, you fulfill his request, then follow up to convert the inquiry to a purchase. Follow-up can be via email, snail mail, phone calls, or any combination. For those prospects who do not respond, we continue to email them this offer, or send the same offer through other channels, or try different lead magnets and offers, until they do respond. As a rule of thumb, I would say that having a bait piece offer in a lead-generating email marketing promotion on average produces double or more the response than the same email without the free lead magnet offer.

The Importance of Content in Email Marketing

When I started in marketing in the late 1970s, you could send a letter that was just about your product or service and how it could help the buyer. And people would respond.

In today's era of content marketing, just talking about your product or service, or even offering information on it, is no longer enough. To get maximum response from letters, both postal and especially email, you must include some sort of lead magnet or free content incentive to respond.

The following are some of the content offers most commonly used as lead magnets in email marketing campaigns.

White paper
A white paper is sort of a hybrid between an information article and a product brochure. Companies publish them as lead magnets to offer

in marketing and thereby attract potential customers who respond to download the white paper.

White papers are abundant in marketing enterprise software to IT professionals, and you can find countless examples of software and technology white papers at www.bitpipe.com. But they are used in dozens of other industries and product categories as well. Prospects are familiar and comfortable with white papers, and if the topic looks interesting, will download yours.

Ebooks

An e-book typically has even less product information than a white paper and may even be written and designed to more closely resemble a real book.

E-course

The prospect clicks on a hyperlink in your email, which takes him to a landing page. He signs up for your e-course by entering his email address and clicking submit. The e-course is a series of five to seven lessons, with each lesson delivered as a text email in an autoresponder series, usually one a day or every other day. Marketers who offer e-courses as lead magnets say the conversion rates are higher than with white papers.

Teleseminar

A teleseminar is a lecture or seminar, typically sixty to ninety minutes, delivered live to attendees over a telephone conference line. The invitation is sent by email, which has a link the recipient can click to go to a registration page and sign up.

One effective tactic is to record the teleseminar, burn it onto an audio CD, and then offer the free audio CD as a lead magnet in email and direct mail campaigns. For example, by adding the offer of a free audio CD recording of a teleseminar to a direct mail campaign, a computer company generates six times greater response than the same letter without the free CD offer.

Webinar

A webinar is similar to a teleseminar except, in addition to the audio component, attendees can watch the speaker's PowerPoint or videos on their computer screen. Webinars are more popular than teleseminars today. You need a special webinar service or software to do one, and the leader is www.gotomeeting.com.

Survey

Send an email inviting participants to take part in a survey on a topic that is of interest to them and the outcome of which they might be interested in learning. The incentive for them to respond is that if they complete the online survey, you give them the survey results free. The leading tool for online surveys is www.surveymonkey.com.

Brochure

Though strictly speaking, brochures are sales copy rather than informational content; but if you put enough technical information in a brochure, recipients will perceive it as having educational value. This is especially true with brochures on high-tech and industrial products. For some reason, mentioning that it is a color brochure increases response versus just saying brochure. Saying it is illustrated and has reference tables and product data also makes it more attractive and increases click-through rates and conversions. Brochures, catalogs, and information kits, like white papers, can be color PDFs, allowing for immediate download.

Catalog

Some consumers in particular enjoy catalogs, so offering a free catalog will generate inquiries. Use a title that increases the perceived value. ATS, a company selling software made in the United States to companies overseas, printed its catalog cover with this headline: "The ATS Directory of United States Software: A Guide for Overseas Buyers." "Catalog" sounds salesy, but "directory" and "guide" imply utility and value.

Military Issues, a catalog marketer of military collectibles and toys, sends its customers an email (Fig. 14-3) notifying them that the company's mail order catalog has been sent via the U.S. Postal Service and to look for it in your mail box. This gives them a double-hit: it encourages readership of the print catalog, and also allows the customer to click on

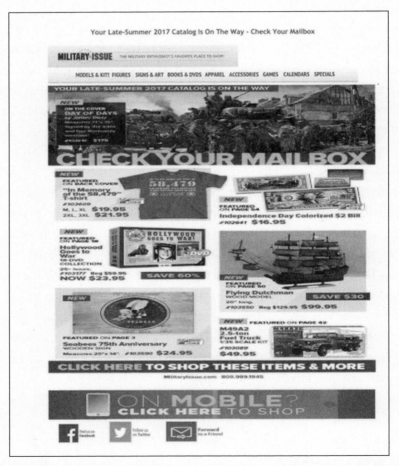

Fig. 14-3. Email alerting customer that a catalog has been sent via postal mail.

a hyperlink in the email to browse products on the website and order online.

Information Kit

If the sales literature you send to prospects has multiple components—such as a brochure, a DVD, and a price sheet—call it an "information kit." A kit implies value and that you are getting a lot of stuff and is more attractive to prospects than a brochure only.

7 Tips for Better Content Marketing

In a survey of *Target Marketing* readers, 83 percent said content marketing either works in tandem with traditional marketing communications (71 percent) or that content is replacing traditional marketing as the primary selling tool (12 percent). Only 15 percent of marketers said they don't really do content marketing. None of those surveyed agreed with the statement content is a waste of time. Joe Pulizzi of Content Marketing Institute says that the average business marketer spends thirty percent of the company's marketing budget on the creation and execution of content, and that 56 percent of marketers increased their content marketing spending last year.

But content marketing isn't just publishing information. There's way too much information available today. Your prospects are drowning in information. But they are starved for knowledge, for ideas on how to solve problems and methods for doing their jobs better.

In addition, you're not in business to publish and give away content; you're in business to sell your products and services. Unless publishing content helps you achieve that goal, it's a waste of your time and money.

Here are 7 guidelines that can help make your content marketing efforts more productive and effective:

1. **Narrow the topic.** There is no benefit to cramming every last fact and bit of information about a subject into your white paper or other content marketing piece; the prospect can get all of the same data and sources using Google.

   Content marketing works best when you narrow the topic. The narrower the topic, the more in-depth and useful your content can be.

   For instance, let's say you are an industrial gas manufacturer creating a ten-page white paper on safety for plant managers. If the title is Plant Safety, you cannot hope to cover that topic in even the most superficial way; entire books have been written on that subject.

   On the other hand, you could produce a very useful white paper on Safety Tips for Handling Compressed Gas Cylinders. It's a topic plant personnel want and need to know more about. And with your vast experience, you can probably offer some tips and methods that are new to the reader.

2. **Target the prospect.** The more narrowly you target the audience for your white paper or other content marketing piece, the better able you are to deliver content that is truly useful to them.

   For our example of the white paper on tips for handling compressed cylinder gas, are you targeting plant managers or plant operators? Plant managers might be more interested in cylinder inventory and control, while plant operators want nuts-and-bolts tips for handling the cylinders. A CFO would want to look at reducing costly gas cylinder accidents, while the CEO might be concerned about liability.

3. **Determine the objective.** Remember, we are not in the business of giving away free information for our health. There

has to be a purpose for the content we are spending time and money to produce—content no one pays us for.

For instance, a software publisher found that when he lost sales, it wasn't because prospects bought a competitor's products with better features and benefits. It was because the software in that category is expensive, and prospects, even though they wanted the functionality the software delivers, couldn't cost-justify its purchase.

To solve this problem, the marketer published a white paper titled Calculating Return on Investment for Purchase of XYZ Software. It demonstrated that, even though the software was expensive, the time and labor savings it provided could pay back its cost in six to eight months. Salespeople used the white paper to overcome the objection of it costs too much.

4. **Educate the reader.** Years ago, Duncan Hines ran an ad in women's magazines about its chocolate cake mix. The headline was, "The secret to moisture, richer chocolate cake." Why was this headline so effective? Because it implied you would learn something useful just by reading the ad, regardless of whether you bought the product.

Generic advice won't cut it in content marketing today. The prospect does not want to read the same old tips he's seen a dozen times before repeated in your white paper.

Chances are, you possess proprietary knowledge about your products and its applications. Share some of this knowledge in your white papers. Give your reader specific advice and ideas that everyone else isn't already telling him.

Don't be afraid that by telling too much, you'll eliminate the prospect's need for your product or service. Quite the opposite: when they learn the effort that solving their problem entails and see that you clearly have the needed expertise, they will turn to you for help.

5. **Deliver value.** When you can, include some highly practical, actionable tips the prospect can implement immediately. The more valuable your content is to prospects, the more readily your content marketing program will achieve its stated objective. It's like fast food stands giving away food samples at the mall: the better the free food tastes, the more likely the consumer is to purchase a snack or meal.

6. **Set the specs.** Outline the characteristics, features, and specifications the prospect should look for when shopping for products in your category. If you do this credibly, the prospect will turn your white paper into a shopping list. And of course, the requirements you outline fit your product to a tee. For example, if your white paper title is ten things to look for when buying a static mixer, your mixer naturally will have all ten characteristics, while the competition won't.

7. **Generate action or change belief.** Content marketing is successful when it gets prospects to take action or changes their opinion, attitude, or beliefs about you and your product as it relates to their needs.

When writing white papers, I always ask my client, "What do you want to happen after the prospect is finished reading our white paper?" I often end the white paper with a final section titled "The next step" that tells the reader what to do and how to do it.

CHAPTER 15.

Device-Specific Email Design

According to Litmus.com's latest report, *The 2017 State of Email Report*, the market share of emails opened on mobile phones was at 54 percent, higher than Desktop (16 percent), and Webmail (30 percent) (p. 35). Email marketing campaigns should take this into consideration when designing emails that are more likely to be opened on mobile phones than on desktops.

When deciding how to format your design layout, the focus should be with the iPhone or Android mobile phone in mind first. The phone application (app) makes it easy to access emails without having to open a browser to get to the email service, such as Yahoo! or Gmail accounts, and sign in to access messages.

If an email is designed with responsive elements to fit the window of a phone app, then it is as likely to translate well over browsers, according to Salesforce Canada, so long as email width is set at min-width 300 px (mobile) and max-width 600 px (browsers). It is wise, however, to always test a new layout design by sending the email to your email address first and looking at it over the phone apps and in different browsers.

The visual appearance of emails on mobile phone apps should be pleasing to the reader's eye and not be crowded with excessive text. Use graphics and images sparingly and make sure they relate directly to your email subject matter.

Every major email provider has developed their own mobile phone email app, which can be downloaded from either the Google Play Store, or from the Microsoft Store, with most apps being free. This includes the Google Gmail, Yahoo! email, Microsoft (MS) Outlook for the MS Office software programs (not free), and Microsoft Live email.

There are other hybrid phone apps for email which can be used and new ones are arriving on the marketplace nearly every day. However, it would hardly seem likely that one should, or could, test an email design every time a new email app shows up. So, when using Cascading Style Sheet (CSS) and Hyper Text Markup Language (HTML) to build email layouts, the language structure must include certain responsive elements that will allow for being viewed on just about any app, device, or browser. The responsive element in coding the email layout must translate through these changes over any platform device.

Before mobile phones and email apps, consumers opened their emails on their computers, laptops, and tablets, using different browsers of choice. Currently, the big browser brands in use are Google Chrome, Mozilla Firefox, Opera, and MS Edge. MS Internet Explorer (IE) is also still in use, but Edge is considered the new replacement browser that overcomes many issues that IE had. Edge rolled out during the Windows 10 upgrade in 2015 and continues to evolve.

Many consumers still use browsers on computers to open emails in the morning while drinking coffee before going to work or in the evening after work is over. Many people, including me, find it is easier to respond back to personal emails using a standard keyboard to type out messages.

Throughout the day, however, email recipients are more likely to often turn to their phones to quickly pick up emails and texts while on the go and, when necessary, shoot back short messages using the phone's keyboard.

In today's business standards and code of etiquette while at the office, an employee is not allowed to use a company laptop or desktop to access personal emails, mainly for security reasons. Hence, the mobile phone becomes essential for most people to access personal messages and to get the latest news about product and service specials directly from their emails.

The Short Message Service (SMS) is the texting application that mobile phone users access when sending off short messages to family, friends, and coworkers. Virtually all smartphones have this capability and it is used more for two-way personal messaging, rather than email applications, which have a more formal style in delivering information.

It is essential that email marketers make the email design layout easy for recipients to respond back, such as easy-to-read text flow and best sized response buttons for call-to-action (CTA) access. Here are a few design tips along with guidelines for size standards, making it easier to send one email successfully across multiple platforms.

Media Query

A term commonly used when referring to CSS components in web pages and emails, is "media query." CSS is a style sheet language that describes through its components how a web page in a markup language, such as HTML, should be laid out and presented, based on set rules. CSS is the use of adaptive or responsive language that recognizes what device it is appearing on, and sets the page to correct screen size.

The media query, in the case of emails, is the switch or trigger to change the style sheet, based on the screen's set of rules. One could visualize this as a ping, and the response gives back the information needed to display or adjust the page, or email to the target screen. Consequently, CSS language components should be placed at the head of an email within the designed language on the email sheet.

The difference between simply using HTML alone and then HTML with CSS is that HTML does not make those dynamic adjustments by itself. It is a more static layout and not responsive to screen changes. Incorporating CSS language with HTML gives the trigger that makes the web page or email responsive to the screen it lands on. This is essential for mobile phones and their small screens. Of importance is the CSS focus on column widths in container tables to make those adjustments to the targeted screen, particularly for mobile phone screens.

Be aware, though, that Gmail was updated to include responsive design and media queries, and that there are still some issues involving media query within the mobile app version for Gmail. While the Android mobile phone platform did not need a complete update for the Gmail app, the iOS for Apple iPhones and iPads did. The iOS on Apple iPhones, therefore, must be at least version 5.0.0 and later versions.

If you find that your email designs are not responding properly in Gmail, you can test an alternative solution such as removing the flexible percentages in max-width and min-width. Other alternative solutions address MS Outlook issues and older rendering engines, and Apple issues, using conditional statements within a fluid/hybrid solution.

Using the following design layout presented below, will eliminate the majority of potential problems you may encounter that concern sending emails over multiple platforms, devices, and the mobile phone.

Email Page Layout Structure

While two- or three-column layouts in newsletters (650 px to 700 px in width each) were common when opened on computer or tablet screens, they do not translate well on small-screen Android and iPhones. The screen opened with one of two columns which you could read downwards, but you would have to scroll over to the right and up to start reading from the top of the adjoining column.

For busy on-the-go readers, having to scroll horizontally over to the next column can be annoying, time-consuming, and breaks the mental flow of receiving ideas in reading comprehension. Readers may just decide to "view it later" and hit the "back" button so they can read other emails. You have then lost the reader and the first element of interest.

Instead, create a single text container column, sized 320 pixels (px), with 480 px at the largest dimension, which safely covers every platform from phone viewing to browser viewing. Note that when referencing px, this applies to a fixed unit measurement, not the resolution of a screen. It is also considered a radial measurement, as opposed to a linear measurement. Its function is to measure the screen size, not an image resolution.

Using CSS and HTML language components, however, means that if you wanted to do two or more columns of text or pictures, the language should describe where horizontally aligned columns would, instead, roll down sequentially under the first column. On a mobile phone screen, this looks like a single column; but on a desktop screen, the three-column formatting is still in place.

If using a preset form, as developed by bulk email services, you may not have to worry about setting border widths, but you will if building your own original form using HTML and CSS. Of particular note, is the use of the CSS *call* function with which the width, the min-width (minimal), and max-width (maximum), responds to the device platform on which the email is viewed. This CSS descriptive language keeps the column properly sized for the device screen.

Once your column borders are set, add your logo on the page, either on the left side or in the center, in the header section. Next, you add those pieces of content which will be there every time you do a send out. This includes your company name and all contact information, such as address, phone, fax, and email, and is placed in the footer. Underneath that, you can add all your social media links, such as Facebook, Twitter, LinkedIn, Pinterest, and others, that you think your readers may be interested in, including your business website link.

Set into place the necessary disclaimers, opt-in or out statement and link, which is usually best placed at the bottom of your communication. While the HTML version may lay these boxes of information horizontally across the page bottom, CSS can have those boxes move to a vertical placement, one box on top of the next box of information. These can be set above or below your contact information, which should also be in its own container box.

You can also add in a statement at the bottom that encourages your readers to pass on your email to any of their friends that may also be interested in your subject content. It is very important that you do not offer compensation of any kind for them to do this, as you can get into legal trouble with the Federal Trade Commission (FTC) because of the CAN SPAM Act.

Once your form is set up, then save it in your online email provider account with a name that is easily recognized so you can use it repeatedly, renaming each new send out by date and subject title. You may build several forms over time for different campaigns, but having the first template set gives you a ready-made tested format to build on.

If creating original email layouts, create a main folder which will have multiple subfolders, each with a different type of email layout design for specific send outs. That way, you can keep your CSS and HTML language structure intact and make only minimal changes to the body of the email and to the subject line. It also saves you a lot of time with having the necessary language already in place.

Body of the email

Start your content with the main header, stating the reason why your readers are receiving the email from you. Your subject box should be a teaser to this information, so that the reader is drawn to opening the email and learning more. A subheader, in a smaller size font, can be added on underneath this header, as a further emphasis in your email regarding your product or service.

Begin your main content inside the first container table with the most important information regarding why you are sending this email to your subscribers. Use only the words you need to convey your message, making it interesting, concise, and fast to read. You can start with a short lead that enforces why your product or service will be what your subscribers need.

All text should be aligned to the left side and do not indent highlights or sections of text as these will tend to be skewed when changing platforms, particularly when viewing on a phone screen. Instead, use left-aligned bullet points to show highlight information, such as benefits, features, or other points of interest.

Offer your first call to action (CTA) after the first or second paragraph, using a large button-styled graphic that is easy to tap on, or a simple link to the purchase or subscription page. These CTAs engage your reader by asking for the reader to take an action, such as "Buy Now," "Click Here to Sign Up,"or "Click Here to Know More."

CTA buttons are usually rectangular in size to accommodate text and should be no larger than 44 x 44 pixels. These are set between paragraphs and stand out to the reader, prompting them to click on it. Then create the second paragraph with content that adds more interesting information.

You can also use text links instead, as a CTA, but make sure there is enough white space above and below the link to easily tap on it with a finger so it activates properly. You will need to ensure there is enough white space above and below the CTA. Add the proper placement language so that on a mobile phone, the link text does not slide up against a paragraph of text.

Many mobile phone users suffer from "fat finger" syndrome, meaning that when they click on one part of an email or web page displayed on their mobile screen, they accidently hit an adjacent part. For this reason, buttons are preferable to text links for CTAs.

Content text should be easy to read, so use two to three sentences at the most for each paragraph, and then insert a break between paragraphs. One-sentence paragraphs, traditionally avoided by many people in offline business writing, make email extremely readable and add a breezy tone. Make text easy for recipients to read and stay engaged in the message you want to convey. A measurement guideline for a sentence would be 45 to 75 characters per line, which includes letters, characters, numbers, and spaces.

You can alternate paragraphs with your secondary headers that give further points of interest. Bullet points are also useful for listing benefits and features of the product or service. Maybe add the CTA button after the first two paragraphs, then again after another two paragraphs, and finally at the closing point. You can offer an incentive for clicking on the last CTA button, such as a free bonus report, and outline a few benefits of receiving the report.

When the phone is held upright (about six inches in height for a Samsung Galaxy J7), the email body of content may look exceptionally small, unless the text is sized larger. Users can flip the phone sideways (90 degrees) to read across the six inches instead, but it is still small, unless they can resize it by touch-spreading the page.

Include only the graphics and images necessary to convey your message and focus on the text. A linked button image, set to the middle of the page in between paragraphs, would be all that you need for a CTA to subscribe or purchase something that is being offered.

Plan a test run of your sample email send out, using only a few email accounts first, preferably those that you own, or those of colleagues or friends willing to help you with feedback. If you do not have an Apple iPhone, ask a friend who has one whether you could send them the test email, and then look at the result on their phone. The same is true for Android phones. Your friend could send you a screen shot or picture of the email so you can look at it and make any adjustments in the layout.

When opening email phone apps to click on a message, you may be asked to click on a message box, asking if you want to see the graphics. Look at it first without graphics to see how the content flows on the page. Then click on it and then look at the whole message to see how it all visually comes together.

If any graphics outweigh the content on the page, then you must go back and resize the graphics to be smaller. Reset them in a different place so the images do not interfere with the text flow. The goal in setting up your email page is to keep it simple and without any clutter, particularly when viewed on the mobile phone screen.

Fonts and Font Size

The recommended size for the text font is 22 points (pts) for your headlines, and 14 pts for your main writing of the body content. Any size smaller or larger is going to cause problems somewhere in the platform chain, such as with Apple devices, which may cause sentences to not wrap correctly. Any smaller fonts (such as 10 pts) will also be resized to 12 pts automatically, so make it a rule to just use 14 pts to be safe.

Use a black sans serif typeface font, such as Arial, as a starting point. You can experiment with different fonts later on. You can also use text in bold or italics, to highlight certain points, but not the whole page. Keep it simple.

Sans serif fonts are used for online web text and these fonts do not have the small decorative flourishes on the end of the strokes, like the serif fonts, such as New Times Roman. Unlike print materials that use serif fonts for easier reading at a resolution of 1,000 dots per inch, computer monitors have a resolution of only 100 dots per inch. Some popular sans serif fonts are Arial, Helvetica, Optima, Futura, Apercu, Gotham, and Frutiger.

Be mindful that many readers may not have 20/20 vision, particularly older people, making it hard to read small text on a mobile phone.

They will avoid it altogether if there is too much eye strain and discomfort.

Avoid using font colors other than black, as people with eyesight problems may have trouble reading the text when the text is recolored to grey or blue. Never use a dark background in an email. Ever.

Image Sizing

Inserting your company logo is an easy way to be recognized and identify your brand. There are size rules for images on websites and emails, and you may need to resize your logo and other images before you can use them in emails. Use only those graphics which are essential to your message, such as your logo and social media links, a picture of the product, or something that conveys an emotion, such as a desire to have that product or service. In the email layout, center images and graphics between paragraphs with enough surrounding white space.

Most email providers such as Yahoo!, Google, and Microsoft Outlook, give their clients the choice to activate images when the email is opened, whether through a browser on a PC, or by phone app. If the reader chooses not to turn on images, then any white spaces will be consistent in space size while reading down the page.

For people who choose not to view images and graphics, text descriptions of the image can be provided. This is done through the alternative (ALT) text attribution, or "alt tags," that shows up when graphics or photographs are blocked by default by the email provider. That way readers can see what the images were about, and can also choose to change the setting to show graphics and images.

The use of CSS descriptive language can be applied for a more responsive outcome when tagged to your email graphics and images. When placed, it allows changes in font, style, color, weight, and size, and enhances your branding scheme when seen sequentially over multiple emails.

If you are skilled in working with Adobe Photoshop, you can edit your image until you are satisfied with colors and proper size. Save it first with the Photoshop extension to retain any layered changes, then export and save the image as a JPEG, PNG, or GIF file.

When saved in Photoshop, you can always come back and reedit it, particularly with layers and colors, and then export it again. The dimension size should be 480 x 480 pixels for insertion into the content body. Depending on which editing software you use, you can go to the "Edit" or "View" menu and click on the dimension or size to reduce it down.

The resolution, when saving the image, should be a maximum quality at 72 dpi, using RGB color values, instead of CMYK. Once exported and saved in a jpeg format, you cannot edit that work. In total, the jpeg file size should be less than 1 MB. You can check this by hovering your mouse over the file, which brings up the file properties off to the side. Note the size as KB, along with the dimension pixel size.

If you do not have Photoshop, these settings can also be carried out using other programs, such as Paint, Pixlr, Canva, and PicMonkey. Animated gifs are also useful in emails, although there may be issues with them showing up properly in MS Outlook, depending on which version the reader has.

Animated gifs should also be 480 x 480 pixels, or less, and use only ten frames or less. Create your own buttons, or check with your email provider to see what they have. The general size for button images is 44 x 44 pixels, and is generally designed as a rectangle, as previously stated, but can be any shape you wish to make. Remember it must be easy to click on with a thumb or stylus.

While your emails can be read on any device and browser platform, the reality is that more people are opening emails on their phones. Design and create your emails with the phone in mind, and you will have greater success in reaching your audience.

"Read More" Blocks and Anchor Tags

A table box in an email contains the beginnings of a story, but provides a place to add a link in a block (or button) containing the words "Read More." When clicked, the action result takes the reader to a website, where the complete story is replicated on a web page, along with supporting images. Anchor tags, or links in a newsletter, function like index links which, when clicked, takes the reader to another location in the newsletter to read the article.

Your Email Signature

You may choose to sign your emails and newsletter with simple text, in what is known as a "sig file." But you can also create your signature to be recognized as specific to you, whenever seen. If you want to include a logo with your name and contact information, then you would need to create an HTML container table box which will hold your logo and your signature, plus the contact information. Your name can be script font, like a handwritten signature, with everything else in plain text. Instead of your logo, you can also add your photograph to make it more personalized. Any required disclaimers should be placed after the signature.

Using Html and Css Versus Commercial Bulk Email Provider

In most cases, you will not need to use extensive descriptive and markup languages to create your emails, unless you are using your own styles, as opposed to premade forms offered by commercial email service providers. Most service providers today will already have the necessary coding and language at work behind the scenes. You work only with developing content on the front side, using their preset templates.

However, in case you wish to create unique forms that respond to different devices, including mobile phones, then find a good free online validation service that will help with making sure that your language is going to work. Start first with your provider to find out what they use on their platform, as CSS, for one, may not be used through their platform.

One free service is W3C Markup Validation Service, found at validator.w3.org. This way, you can perfect your coding layout before you do the test run. Once you have run the test, if there is a problem with an image, for example, that is out of place, then you know where to look in the coding layout to make changes. If using a bulk email service provider, they can also help with setting up the right coding layouts, and help you with any concerns about how to custom design for the right outcomes.

If you are new to creating bulk emails for your growing list of readers, it may seem like there is much to learn before you even send out the first one. The above guidelines will help overcome any initial fears in building your email pages.

New ways of using the CSS and HTML languages are in continual development as devices continue to upgrade as well. The use of these languages, in conjunction with the design rules, is crucial to ensuring that emails will successfully translate to all browsers and devices without incident, including mobile phones as the most important goal for email campaigns.

CHAPTER 16.

Integrating Email into a Multichannel Communications Program

Emails are just one of dozens of marketing communications channels available to us in the twenty-first century. And we are said to live in an age of "multichannel marketing," because almost all promotional campaigns today include many, not just one, of the channels—with email being one of them more often than not.

But how do you make the decision whether to send an email, make a phone call, leave a door hanger on neighborhood homes, send a postal letter, run a banner ad, mail a postcard followed by three email blasts, send a drip campaign (series of postal mailings or emails), or hold a Facebook Live conference, and then run Facebook boosted posts or ads?

In this chapter, we look at the most effective ways to integrate email into an overall multichannel marketing campaign. To begin with, let's take a look at what makes up multichannel marketing programs and how marketing uses the various platform capabilities to strategically attract customers.

Multichannel Marketing Fundamentals

In the early days of marketing campaigns, before the Internet, ads were placed in trade journals, consumer magazines, and newspapers. It was a simple process, and when interested readers asked for more information by phone or letter, the advertiser mailed them a pretty four-color sales brochure on the product or service. Or the ad had a coupon for a discount on a purchase he could use when coming to the store or showroom.

Direct mail campaigns, conducted through the U.S. Postal Service (USPS), were also a way to attract attention from targeted prospects, such as business-to-business (B2B) executives who made purchasing decisions or consumers who bought products by mail. There were a few other marketing vehicles: cases studies, press releases, and articles published in trade and consumer magazines.

The Internet universe in today's marketing environment requires a more complicated strategy for reaching potential customers. You must first decide, when building an acquisition campaign to bring in more leads and sales, how you will make first contact, and how you want leads to respond to your message. Will you send out a direct mail package and business reply card, or give a toll-free number for them to call you directly?

Alternatively, can you give them a landing page URL, where they can submit an electronic form online to get more information, or request contact from a sales representative. One point to remember about offering website and landing page addresses on hard copy documents: use simple addresses that can be easily typed by hand into the browser URL box. If you have long, complicated addresses, the reader may give up when a simple error prevents him from reaching your site or page on the first attempt. Always think about making it as easy as possible for the customer to reach you.

When your leads have signed up to receive emails from you, the decision must then be made about how many emails there should be in a sequence, particularly if it is to lead them to make a purchase. You can send a series of email with linked videos (see chapter 7), which explain a new system or service that would help them with their business.

Once your viewers receive the first email with the first video, your autoresponder system automatically sends additional emails in the series according to a schedule you set in the software using simple commands; no programming required.

As you can see, an email program design can be complicated and may depend on which branch of your multichannel marketing campaign you received your leads from. While the basics of designing multichannel marketing campaigns are covered in this chapter, you can find more detailed information in my book, *The Marketing Plan Handbook* (Entrepreneur Press).

Funnels

The term *funnels* in marketing refers to the process of guiding customers along a path of actions, leading to the final step of conversion to making a purchase. For example, the first step may be to have customers sign up to receive your emails. From there, the customer receives an email with a link that takes him to a landing page where he gets more information about a product or service. Once the customer decides to make the purchase, the product or service is added to the shopping cart and then the customer goes through the checkout process.

In multichannel marketing, you may also be funneling customers from several different channels, such as Facebook and other social media platforms, online advertisements, direct marketing packages, and emails, all leading to the same campaign landing page. Another way to think of it is like mixing a drink (multiple channels), with each part of the recipe added (attention, interest, desire, action), one at a time, using a funnel that pours the ingredients into a glass to make the final drink.

Emails in Multichannel Marketing Programs

When it comes to marketing strategies and developing campaigns, emails are a valuable tool for interacting with customers and bringing in new ones, such as the "welcome" email received after first registering on the company website. Adding a personal touch by using the new customer's name, begins the process of building trust in the company brand, and letting the customer know the company cares about its customers. Email, at its best, is the glue that can tie together nearly every part of a multichannel marketing system, so that tracking from one touchpoint to the next is more effective, regardless of how nonlinear the customer pathway may be.

The different ways that emails can be used in a multichannel marketing program are: welcome; thanks for your request; thanks for your order; an order confirmation; an upsell; autoresponder email conversion series; email drip campaign; free e-class in a content marketing campaign; "free touch" emails (sent via autoresponder to encourage readership of a downloaded white paper and move the sales cycle along); customer service; customer relationship management (CRM), and others that might need special development as the need arises.

Welcome and thank you for your request

Whenever a reader signs up to receive emails, particularly if joining a group that is focused on a topic (gardening club, woodworkers club, etc.), then each new member receives a welcome email, outlining the kinds of information available in the club, and how often members will receive emails about topics of interest. When people sign up for my online e-newsletter, we send a welcome email thanking them for subscribing and delivering the free bonus reports we give as a gift to new subscribers. Sign up here www.bly.com/reports and you will get that email delivered quickly via autoresponder.

Order confirmation, thank you for your order, upsell

When the order is complete, an automated order confirmation is sent, along with a personalized thank you for your order email. This is a very important part of the purchase, as customers like to be thanked for having spent their money with you. Another email may be sent shortly after, offering an upsell product that the customer might be interested in, based on his recent purchase. There may also be an upsell link within the confirmation email to a related product that the customer may wish to browse. If you offered a bonus report as part of the purchase, then a separate email is sent with a link to download that report.

Email conversion series and email drip campaigns

While the aim for both campaigns is similar (get the customer to sign on), there is a slight difference in how each campaign works. The email conversion campaign leads an interested viewer through a series of messages that reference the product or service, with each giving more expanded details of product features and benefits to the viewer and how it can help him in his business.

The email drip campaign is a series sent to potential customers or clients from whom you want to generate an inquiry. For those who do not respond after the first email, they may receive a second email a day or two later asking if the reader would like more information or would like to schedule a meeting or phone. The third email (after no response) is sent to say that the emailer is sorry to have missed the customer but reinforces the opportunity to schedule a meeting or phone call. The schedule for these automated sequenced emails can span from a week to a month, and may need A/B testing to see which time span works best—every two days, or every four days, or once a week.

"Free touch" emails

A reader browsing the Internet may download a white paper on a new software package. The company giving the free white paper then contacts the reader by email in two days to see if he read it and had any questions, or perhaps to highlight some of the valuable content and encourage the prospect to review it (e.g., see the XYZ technique on page 5 to reduce your data center software license costs up to 30 percent). The email may also include a link to sign up for a trial period so the reader can see the software in action. A phone number is also given, so the reader can call first with specific questions on how that software works under certain conditions. This is part of moving the sales process along. Any email that builds a relationship, offers advice, or encourages usage of the free content without attempting to sell is called a free touch.

Customer service and customer relationship management (CRM)

Whenever there is a problem and a client wants help from the company, an autogenerated case number is given to the issue and customer after making a complaint through a phone call or on the website chat service. This becomes part of the company's CRM system, so that it can be tracked throughout the process of solving the problem. The company can conduct future analyses on similar problems that happen, and may show that a process needs to be fixed or overhauled.

White mail reply emails

White mail is nontransactional correspondence from customers and prospects, mainly questions about products, applications, services, or asking for advice. Some marketers simply respond with a form email delivered via autoresponder that acknowledges the request. Others write personal answers sent via individual, not mass, emails. In my experience customers prefer and appreciate the personal touch in email correspondence, and it definitely helps make them more loyal to the marketer and results in increased engagement and purchase.

Integrating Emails with Other Marketing Channels

In the earlier section, we looked at what types of emails there were and how they could be used under specific circumstances. In this section, you will see the various ways to combine several marketing channels.

Lead generation

If you are looking to generate leads instead of direct sales, you can initiate contact by first sending a postcard as a warmup. The postcard may have your phone number and landing page URL in big, bold type, with copy about what you do. Keep it short because this is a quick visual hit on your future client's eyes. On the back, you can give more content, along with the contact information again (yes, it should be on both sides). If you are planning the follow-up step described in the next paragraph, tell them to watch the mail for a package of helpful material coming their way.

A week or two after sending the postcard, follow up with a direct marketing package, and make sure that the image on the front of the postcard is also front and center in your package, which will trigger the viewer's memory that he has seen this before. Finally, you can send an email directly to your future client asking for a phone call, or to have the client call you or respond by email.

Renewal series

Make it easy for your customers to renew their magazine, newsletter, or service contract subscriptions, memberships, and insurance policies. A few months before a subscription is up, send out the first of five to seven emails to remind subscribers that their subscription is coming to an end. You can also send a reminder by regular mail with a form they can fill out with their charge card number, and send back in the prepaid envelope you provided. If no response, make a phone call and ask for the renewal. Some renewal series also have a phone call as one of the efforts.

A proven renewal strategy is to send one renewal effort very early, say six months before subscription expiration, with a one-time deep discount that is only good if the subscriber renews now. This is called an Early Bird offer. Make clear that this is your best offer, and if the subscriber doesn't take it, it will not be available again.

Driving traffic with Google AdWords

You can drive more traffic to your landing pages by running online ads, using Google AdWords, Google's online advertising platform. Why is this so important? When you build your ad in their Google AdWords account, you set yourself up in the Google Search Network to be found easily, with your Google Ad, using keywords.

You only pay Google when someone clicks on your ad, which is why this is known as pay-per-click (PPC) advertising. Using keywords becomes important in getting only customers who are very interested in buying from you. You do not want to pay fees for people who only have a passing interest in your topic. To find out more about Google AdWords, go here: https://support.google.com/adwords/answer/6080949.

Webinars again . . .

This begins an email sequence, as we have discussed before, where first the registration confirmation is sent to the customer, which includes the link for auto-connecting the event to the online calendar of choice. Then a reminder email can be sent the day before to ensure the customer has remembered to set that time aside for the webinar.

Another email reminder is sent the day of the event, just as a backup and includes the link to deregister, if the customer cannot make it. This may become important to the webinar platform you are using, as they may need to know what server resources to distribute to your webinar, based on number of people attending.

Your email sequence continues after the webinar is over by sending out a link to the recording, in case the customer wants to see it again. You can also add on special bonuses for having attended, including upsells that enhance the purchase if made within 24 hours.

For those who did not attend the webinar, an email can be sent out saying that you were sorry they missed the webinar, and you can still give the replay link, in case they want to go now to view it. Remind them that the replay will only be up for another two days and then it comes down, and they will not be able to sign up for whatever it was you were offering.

Free e-class

As discussed in chapter 14, e-classes are a series of written or video lessons delivered via autoresponder. These e-classes offer significant information to the customer and, while they are a lot of work to create, typically produce better results than just offering a conventional white paper.

An email is sent out to notify readers that a free e-class is being offered about a topic of interest to most readers. The class can reference a point of interest to many, such as how to get that book the reader wants to write or already has written into the kindle format and onto the Amazon platform for sale. Or the class can be how to do the herringbone stitch, while working with #11-size seed beads.

The first email offers information about the class and gives a link to sign up for it. A second email, a last-minute reminder sent a day or two before the event, often gets a lot of additional attendees to register.

The class may be live and many are also recorded for later playback. Included on the signup form or a confirmation email is a link to have the event added to Google calendar or Microsoft Outlook calendar, a very convenient tool for readers who are apt to forget about the upcoming event.

After registering, then the reader receives a confirmation email, along with the link which includes a special ID number, and when the time comes, the reader simply clicks on it to attend the class. There should also be an automated reminder email sent the day of the event to jog the reader's memory that he will be attending that class.

Other Things to Know

Multichannel marketing can be done on many platforms, although you must configure the ad to meet the platform's guidelines of use and appearance. As part of figuring out where clicks on advertising links come from, when using Google AdWords, you can use dynamic tracking URLs which may work with your third-party tracking system, using dynamic search ads (DSAs). The landing page URL must load from the advertisement link you provide, or else it is rejected. You can find out more about how to work with the several options, by going here:

https://support.google.com/adwords/answer/2549100?hl=en

Case Studies in Multichannel Marketing

Starbucks, the Rewards card, and charity

Multichannel marketing can occur in several ways, besides social media, mobile phone alerts, or website advertising. For example, one way for companies to increase brand awareness and loyalty is by promoting charitable giving, such as Starbucks did when partnering with Neighbourly, a charity platform in the United Kingdom, during the Christmas season. Registered customers with the Starbucks Rewards card, who made a purchase of a holiday drink between December 1st and the 24th, then had the purchase recorded on their Rewards card, prompting Starbucks to donate five pence (5p) to charity for each of those recorded drinks.

Emails were sent out to all Rewards members first, giving details of the program, along with a call-to-action (CTA) button to choose the charity of choice. While it is certain that the program was also touted on social media and the company website, sending the email ensured that most Starbucks Rewards customers would receive the notification directly, rather than trusting that customers might go on social media, or the company website, and see the notice there.

With the Rewards card, Starbucks has a built-in process of tracking how successful this campaign is by analyzing the data on customers' Rewards cards. The Starbucks example shows how an email campaign becomes essential in getting the word out to customers about special events of interest to its Rewards customers.

Disney Parks + Make-A-Wish + #ShareYourEars on Facebook

Another case study in giving to charity is the Make-A-Wish Foundation and Walt Disney Parks and Resorts, which showed that social media can be a powerful tool in getting the word out about a charity drive to build donations and awareness.

In 2016, Disney Parks put out the message that for every Facebook profile that showed an image of that person wearing Mickey Mouse ears, or a creative interpretation of ears, Disney would donate $5 to the foundation. All participants had to do was create the picture, using the Facebook photo framer, and then upload/share it to the Make-A-Wish America Facebook page, using the #ShareYourEars. The photo could also be shared on Twitter and Instagram.

While Disney Parks had set a $1 million limit, that amount was changed to $2 million, in recognition of the huge outpouring of customers' support. It was a great success and, like the Starbucks campaign, went a long way in positive customers' perception of the company and brand image, including a higher level of social media visibility.

Under Armour—the Rule Yourself marketing video

Under Armour is a sportswear company started by former athlete Kevin Plank, who began his company because he wanted to find better fabrics to use while working out. Starting with the HeatGear° T-shirt, he then came out with the ColdGear° fabric and AllSeasonGear° lines.

In a 2016 marketing campaign video, Olympic swimming champion Michael Phelps, with twenty-three gold medals, is shown during his extensive physical workout to achieve perfection, while the marketing campaign promotes taking on the challenge of being dedicated to be your best every day.

Viewers were challenged to join one or more fitness challenges via Google Play apps, such as app MapMyFitness Rule Your Fitness Challenge, app MyFitnessPal Rule Your Nutrition Challenge, or to create one on UA Record's website, tailored to the user's needs. Of course, the marketing campaign's goal was to get viewers moving toward better fitness, as well as using Under Armour sportswear for better comfort while working out. It also enhanced the brand as the best to use while working out. If Michael Phelps uses the brand, why not you too?

Tracking Systems

When using a tracking system, such as links, cookies, and affiliate codes in emails, the resulting data can be obtained from the commercial email provider, the webmaster handling your website and landing pages for products and services, or your e-commerce software such as 1shoppingcart or Infusionsoft. If you have Google Analytics applied to your website, then you will be able to pick up quite a bit of information that is also analyzed for you.

There is also data that comes from mobile phone interactions while searching on the web, such as opening emails through phone applications, and from social media outlets. The amount of data can be massive, when coming from several channels. Therefore, you should set up a system that successfully incorporates all the data to link up by an ID key to each customer or registered person that is connected to your business in some way, such as having signed up to receive emails from you, or who made a purchase.

Cookies

A cookie is a small packet of text, sent by a website server, which is placed on your browser on your computer. It contains information about you and your preferences and recognizes you when you make a return visit. Consequently, the server recognizes you and presents you with customized web pages.

Large companies like Amazon, Walmart, and other similar enterprises can track you across platforms using cookies that store a unique session ID from the last time you signed into your account and looked at various items. If you are in your Facebook account, you most likely have seen advertisements on the right side, for items you were looking at on your account in Amazon, just hours, or even minutes, ago. Advertisements you clicked on previously, on non-account websites, can also show up on your browser's home page when you open the browser up.

Whenever you visit a website, that site generates user-specific cookies, which are saved on your computer. While the cookie does not know you by name, per se, unless you are in your account, it knows you by the cookies installed on your computer's browser and that you were there at an earlier point. Whenever you return to that site, the website remembers you by your cookies, whether it is to sign in to your account or if you just want to browse further. While you are there, the website also shows you what you previously were looking at during your last visit.

ISPs and IP Addresses

There is another factor in this journey across multiple channels, and that is the Internet protocol (IP) address you are assigned by the Internet service provider (ISP), such as Time Warner/Spectrum, AT&T, and other ISPs. However, this address defines a specific location, such as working on one computer from home, and the IP number address is that of the ISP's modem, which stays the same until you reboot it for one reason or another. That same IP address covers all other computers and devices that also hook up to that same modem.

Consequently, you can now understand that websites can easily follow your every move across the Internet while you are working on your computer at home. In most cases, cookies on your computer are the dominant tracking tool, rather than your IP address, although that IP address can factor in under certain circumstances.

If you use your employer's company computer at work to access your personal accounts (which you should not do), that will have a different set of cookies tied to you, installed on the work computer and its browser. If you go to a coffee shop with the same computer you use at home and access the shop's free Wi-Fi service, then you have a different IP address when you check your computer but still have the same cookies. The IP address you now see for your computer is that of the modem used by the coffee shop.

Google Analytics, Tracking Pixels, and More About Cookies

When you use cookies and tracking pixels (invisible images placed in HTML), you will see how easy it is to track anyone over the Internet and through multiple channels, making this a marketer's delight when a company wants to see the different points of contact on their multichannel marketing infrastructure. Such tracking data helps marketers decide what processes work better, such as using videos instead of pictures, how successful a Facebook Live chat was, and whether the Facebook or Twitter platform worked better in a return on investment (ROI) analysis, when advertising an upcoming webinar.

Decisions are made, based on the data obtained from these campaigns, which decide how future campaigns will be implemented and on what platform. Supporting corresponding evidence, such as a higher rate of sales, also support these decisions.

Google Analytics is a powerful and useful tool, not just for your website, but across your multichannel infrastructure. To use Google Analytics Multi-Channel Funnels Reporting application programming interface (API), you must first have a Google account and then sign in to create an application to access data, which is registered on the Google API Console. When a request for a range of data is approved, then the application gets a short-term access token. This makes you an authenticated user with the ability to get reports on data concerning how individuals interacted on a conversion path over several sessions.

You can also combine and integrate funnels data with your own data, such as conversion data with your sales and costs of running advertisements. Go here to find out more about funnel reporting: https://developers .google.com/analytics/devguides/reporting/mcf/v3/

When it comes to cookie tracking and Google analytics, the best practice to track users over different browsers and devices is to use the User ID feature, along with a client ID field, in a JavaScript tracking snippet embedded within the cookie infrastructure. The Google Analytics developers website gives significant information on how to change cookies to show unique users over different browsers and devices. You must be an authenticated user to get this data as well.

If you are not savvy in working with cookies, then hire a specialist to get the right ones made for your website. You can also ask your website host provider for what can be used on your website. Google Analytics information on cookies can be found here: https://developers.google. com/analytics/devguides/collection/analyticsjs/cookies-user-id

About tracking pixels

Aside from cookies, you can use tracking pixels anywhere you have a presence: emails, your website, social media advertisements, and in links and CTAs. For example, you can have an email-open tracking pixel in a portable network graphics (PNG) format, which activates whenever a reader opens the email on his browser or on a mobile phone.

The tracking pixel is an invisible (or transparent) 1x1 pixel image inserted within the HTML language. When the pixel is activated, a message is sent back to the collecting data site registering as an open action, and gives the IP address of the device where it was opened.

Tracking pixels can also be attached to images, videos, and hyperlinks. At the end of the day, you can find out how many different IP addresses there were on emails that opened, what cookies were activated, and what links within the email were clicked on. This also includes advertisements on social media, online trade websites where you put your advertisements, and anywhere else you have a touchpoint. If you can get cookies and/or tracking pixels into your HTML settings, then you have a far better chance of learning what your customers do, who they are, what they like, and what they do not like, particularly when using Google Analytics.

Emoticons and Emojis

Below is a partial listing of emojis—the graphic symbols in HTML most commonly used in email and elsewhere online and the meaning and appropriate usage of each. Emoticons are similar to emoji images but are formed using text symbols; e.g. ☺ is a smiley face made in Word. Note: This table is by no means comprehensive, as new emojis are created every year.

FB Definition

😀	grinning face
😁	grinning face with smiling eyes
😂	face with tears of joy
🤣	rolling on the floor laughing
😃	smiling face with open mouth
😄	smiling face with open mouth & smiling eyes
😅	smiling face with open mouth & cold sweat

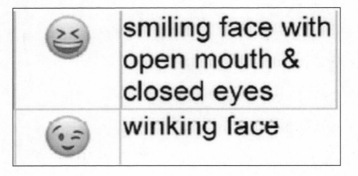

😆	smiling face with open mouth & closed eyes
😉	winking face

	smiling face with smiling eyes
	face savouring delicious food

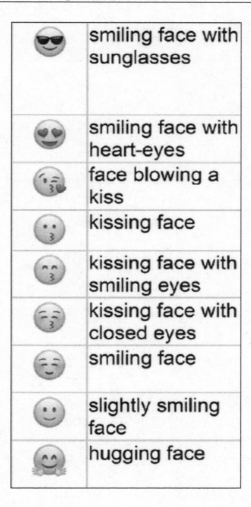

	smiling face with sunglasses
	smiling face with heart-eyes
	face blowing a kiss
	kissing face
	kissing face with smiling eyes
	kissing face with closed eyes
	smiling face
	slightly smiling face
	hugging face

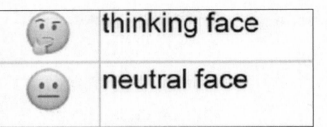

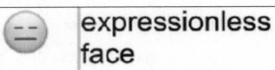	thinking face
	neutral face

	expressionless face

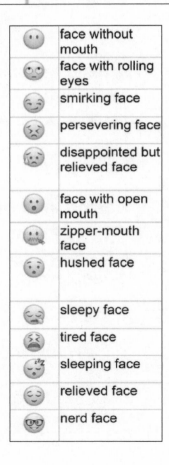

	face without mouth
	face with rolling eyes
	smirking face
	persevering face
	disappointed but relieved face
	face with open mouth
	zipper-mouth face
	hushed face
	sleepy face
	tired face
	sleeping face
	relieved face
	nerd face

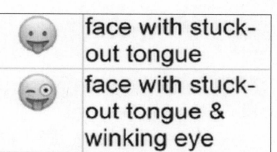	face with stuck-out tongue
	face with stuck-out tongue & winking eye

	unamused face
	face with cold sweat
	pensive face
	confused face
	upside-down face
	money-mouth face
	astonished face

😟	frowning face
🙁	slightly frowning face

😖	confounded face
😞	disappointed face
😟	worried face
😤	face with steam from nose
😢	crying face

Model Email Marketing Messages

Here is a sampling of email marketing messages sent to my own opt-in list. Size of the list during the mail period has grown from 44,000 to 65,000 names. For each example, you get the full text of the email, an analysis of the copy showing why it worked, and the results include open rates, click-through rates, conversion rates, number of units sold, and gross revenues.

Sample Email #1: The Internet Marketing Retirement Plan

Gross revenues: $6,111
Clicks: 1,401
CTR: 3.44%
Conversion rate 4.5%
Opt outs: 21

One method that can work for creating successful information products is to focus the product around the lifestyle the product can deliver, not the product itself.

"The Internet Marketing Retirement Plan" is an introductory program to Internet marketing for people who want a spare-time online income without working their butts off to get it. The goals of the plan: get you to the point where you make $100,000 to $200,000 a year or more selling information products on the Internet, with only an hour or so of active involvement on your part a few days a week—and to reach that level within 12 to 24 months.

Retirement is a hugely emotional issue, and so the simple subject line, "Want to quit working some day?" resonates with readers whether they think they are ready to retire or not.

We continue to promote this product actively, and I believe it is our bestselling audio program.

Subject: Want to quit working some day?

Dear Direct Response Letter Subscriber:

Are you looking for a way to "escape" the 9-to-5 rat race?

Do you feel chained to your desk—at a job you don't like—by the reality of having to earn money?

Most of us trade our time for money.

We may make a very nice living doing that . . . but we are never truly free as long as we punch a time clock—or have a boss telling us what to do.

We have to get up early in the morning every day . . . commute in the cold and dark . . . and put in long hours making money for someone else.

But now, I've discovered a safe, surefire way for you to completely retire—within 18 to 24 months from today—even if you haven't saved a dime for retirement.

In my new audio program, "The Internet Marketing Retirement Plan," I show you how I did it.

By following this plan, I went from zero to $4,000 a week in online income—in less than 8 months.

And to earn that $4,000, I literally spend just 20 minutes a week on my Internet marketing business . . . as incredible as that sounds.

I still work long hours as a freelance copywriter . . . but I do so because I want to, not because I have to.

Wouldn't you like to be in a position where you can do anything you want each day—rather than having to get up early and commuting to work every morning?

To discover the 3 simple steps to building an online "retirement income" . . . and to review the Internet Marketing Retirement Plan risk-free for 90 days . . . just click here now:

http://www.theinternetmarketingretirementplan.com

Sincerely,
Bob Bly

P.S. I guarantee that the "Internet Marketing Retirement Plan" can help you create an online business . . . capable of generating $100,000 to $200,000 a year in net passive income . . . within 18 to 24 months.

If after reviewing the program, you do not agree . . . or are not 100% satisfied for any other reason (or for no reason at all) . . . just return the materials to me within 90 days for a full and prompt refund.

That way, you risk nothing!

To get started, click below now:

http://www.theinternetmarketingretirementplan.com

Sample Email #2: The 22 habits of financially successful writers

Orders: 120
Gross revenues: $3,480
Conversions: 5.2%

This was another email that did well. It's for an e-book that is among my top sellers, *Write and Grow Rich*. This email launched the product. *Write and Grow Rich* was my first foray into Internet marketing and my first product.

When I decided to "test the waters" of Internet marketing, I looked for a way to put together my first product quickly and easily. As it happens, I had written about a dozen columns for *Writer's Digest* magazine on how to earn six figures as a freelance writer. The articles had all been published in the magazine, and I owned the rights to them.

I emailed all the articles to Dennis Rome, a graphic designer who was just starting out in his own freelance business. "Turn them into an e-book, please," I asked Dennis. He did so, and the first edition was born.

I priced the e-book deliberately low—$29—because I had never sold anything to my e-newsletter subscriber list before, and I was worried they wouldn't buy anything expensive. The book sold well. I gave Dennis additional content to make the book more substantial, including some of my cartoons, and released a second edition at $39.

The email shown here offered the first edition at $29, and did very well. Why did it work?

Two reasons. First, it's a short "teaser" email that understands its purpose is to generate a click, not make a sale.

The goal is not to get someone to buy anything. It is to tell just enough to whet their appetite . . . and to click on the link to learn more.

Second, the number "22" habits in the headline arouses curiosity. The reader starts to make a list of qualities of successful writers. He cannot come up with 22, and wants to know what he is missing. Or, he does come up with 22 habits, and wants to compare his list with mine —again, to see what he might be missing.

Subject: The 22 habits of financially successful writers

Dear Direct Response Letter Subscriber:

A recent survey revealed that writers who earn more than $60,000 a year consistently do 22 things that writers who earn less money don't.

To get your hands on this list of 22 habits of highly profitable writers . . . and master dozens of additional strategies for earning six-figures as a freelance writer . . .

click below now:

http://www.freelancewritingprofits.com/

Sincerely,
Bob Bly

Sample Email #3: Getting Your Book Published

Clicks: 840
Conversion rate: 4.8%
Orders: 40
Gross revenues: $3,880
Opt outs: 38

My philosophy as an online information marketer is to focus on subjects that I know extremely well and have lots of experience with. The reasons for that are twofold. First, whether I write the product or hire someone else to do it, my extensive knowledge makes the content stronger and more valuable.

Second, I use my personal experience and track record to establish credibility in the email and landing page copy I use to sell the product.

This being the case, I felt extremely comfortable producing a program on how to write a nonfiction book and sell it to a major NYC publishing house, because I had written and sold more than seventy books. That means I had all the sample documents, war stories, and experience-based knowledge to share with my customers.

The product is an album of audio CDs. As do all my audio albums to date, it sells for $97 plus $6.50 shipping and handling. I do not make money on the shipping and handling; the fee I charge simply covers my cost, which means the buyer—not I—pays for shipping and handling.

My audio products cost on average $10 per unit to manufacture, plus or minus a dollar or two depending on the number of CDs in the program. So my profit is around $90 on every sale.

If you click on the URL link in the email below and go to the landing page for this product, you will see that I do not offer a "full refund" but rather a "full product refund." That means if you buy the product for $106.30 ($97 plus $6.50 shipping and handling, and you return it for a refund, I give you a $97 refund representing the cost of the product. I do not refund your $6.50 shipping & handling. Nor do I, as some direct marketers—most notably Rodale—do, give you a postage-paid return address label for shipping the product back to me if you want to return it for a refund.

In the subject line, I use a variation of my "Ghostwriters urgently needed" formula: "Publisher looking for new book authors."

It gives the impression that I am a publisher— or know of publishers (which is the case)—looking to publish books by new authors. You could argue that it is slightly deceptive, but I don't think it is—and I clearly explain in my email that I am selling a product.

The headline, "Publisher looking for new book authors" is a variation of the long-running ad for the Institute for Children's Literature, "We're looking for people to write children's books."

It too gives the impression that the ad is from a publisher, not a product seller. That it has been running virtually unchanged for decades told me that (a) it works and (b) it passed any legal or consumer scrutiny.

The rest of the email is a standard sales pitch: get attention with the lead—talk about the reader's problem or need—position your product as the solution—give some proof that the product can do as you claim—and ask the reader to click on the hyperlink to find out more.

In the lead, I mentioned that my seventieth book had just been published. This seems at first glance not to be effective, because it starts with me and my ego, not the reader and her needs. But I have found the fact that I have written more books than my age fascinates people and automatically makes them think I am an expert in writing and publishing. So I lead with that fact to establish instant credibility.

In the bullet points, I list the "hot buttons"—what I believe, based on many years of experience teaching "how to get your book published," the top five or so things the reader wants to know.

In many of my email marketing messages, I don't talk about price or guarantee, since that's discussed on the landing page.

But in pure sales pitches where I say "here is a product I think you should buy," I know that pushing a product raises two concerns in the reader's mind:

1. What will it cost me?
2. What if I am not satisfied?

By giving the price and stating the guarantee, I address both concerns up front. So anyone who is still interested enough at this point to click and read further is a more qualified lead—and more likely to buy.

Subject: Publisher looking for new book authors

Dear Direct Response Letter Subscriber:

Early next year, my 70th book will be published by Thomas Nelson, a large and respected publishing house.

Why should you care?

Because after selling 70 books to major publishers, I know how the game is played . . . and I'm qualified to guide you in finding a publisher for the book you are writing or want to write.

Now, my "Get Your Book Published" program can help you:

** Come up with a great idea and title for a book you want to write.

** Write a book proposal agents and publishers will love.

** Get a publisher to pay you a royalty and advance for your book.

** Negotiate the best book deal with your new publisher.

** Write and organize a book that will stay on the bookstore shelves for decades.

Some "author's coaches" charge writers thousands of dollars.

But they don't guarantee your success.

And how many of them do you think have written 70 published books?

My program costs less than $100 . . . and you can inspect it risk-free for 90 days . . . then decide whether to keep or return it.

I guarantee you'll find a publisher for your book with my help—or your money back.

Click here for free details:

http://www.gettingyourbookpublished.com/

Sincerely,
Robert W. Bly

P.S. The first 100 people to reply get a FREE copy of my book, "Getting Your Book Published" (list price: $14.95).

P.P.S. I love books and writers, and really want to help you join me in the ranks of published book authors. Let's get started!

http://www.gettingyourbookpublished.com/

Sample Email #4. Make money as a marketing consultant

Orders: 112
Gross revenues: $4,368
Clicks: 1,216
CTR: 3.02%

Conversion rate: 9.2%
Opt outs: 37

Since the market, not you, determines what it wants to buy, you can increase your odds of success by letting the needs, interests, and desires of your subscribers determine the products you will create.

Virtually everyone on my list is interested in marketing topics, and most people at some time or another get tired of the corporate world and dream of striking out on their own. Combining these, I came up with the idea of doing an e-book on how to succeed as an independent marketing consultant, and commissioned Frank Girard to write it.

The email is only forty-four words long. It does not need to be longer. The landing page does the selling. The email's objective is to get qualified prospects to click on the link to the landing page.

There is no creativity or brilliant writing here. Sometimes, when you have something your customers really want, the best copy approach is to be straightforward and just say what it is.

I did that here, and was gratified to get over a hundred orders within a couple of days.

Subject: Make money as a marketing consultant

Dear Direct Response Letter Subscriber:

Have you ever thought about parlaying your marketing knowledge into a six-figure annual income as a freelance marketing consultant?

Well, now you can. Just click below for details:

http://www.sixfiguremarketingconsultant.com

Sincerely,
Bob Bly

Sample Email #5. Copywriter's Toolkit

Orders: 135 orders

Gross sales: $5,265

Clicks: 1,238

CTR: 2.3%

Conversion rate 10.9%

Opt outs: 36

In this email, we introduced a new product, *The Copywriter's Toolkit*. It is an e-book collection of the forms I use in my freelance copywriting business.

In the world of information marketing, form kits sell extremely well. They have high perceived value, since you can argue that creating each form took $1,000 worth or more of an attorney's or other professional's time. They also have high actual value, since the buyer can save huge amounts of time and money by buying the forms.

Subject: 10 things copywriters ask me for most

Dear Direct Response Letter Subscriber:

Every week, aspiring and newbie copywriters email or call me for help.

Specifically, they want me to send them some piece of paper—a form, letter, document, or contract—I use in my freelance copywriting business . . .

So they can model or even copy it when creating their own version.

http://www.copywritersforms.com

In recent years, the 10 most commonly requested items have been my:

1. Offline copywriting fee schedule.

2. Online copywriting fee schedule.

3. Standard client agreement.

4. Copywriter's information kit.

---

5. Lead-generating sales letter for my freelance copywriting services (generates a 10% response).

6. Kill fee schedule.

7. Marketing communications audit.

8. Copy manuscript format.

9. Nondisclosure and confidentiality agreements.

10. Sales lead tracking form.

The good news is: now you can get copies of all of these items . . .

As well as dozens of other standard forms, checklists, model contracts, and other boilerplate documents.

All of which can help you start—and run—a successful freelance copywriting business.

In my new e-book, *Copywriter's Toolkit* I give you literally every important and useful business tool I've developed during my 25+ years as a copywriter.

These forms, letters, and agreements took me hundreds of hours of trial and error—and thousands of dollars—to create and test.

They've helped me become a self-made multimillionaire solely through my freelance writing.

Now I am practically giving away the complete set . . . yours to use forever, in any way you wish (except reselling them to others) . . . for less than one dollar each.

It's the steal of the century.

For more information . . . or to examine the *Copywriter's Toolkit* risk-free for 90 days . . . just click below now:

http://www.copywritersforms.com

Sincerely,
Bob Bly

Email #6: Marketing with articles

Date: 2/13/07

Orders: 72

Gross revenues: $2,808

Clicks: 800

CTR: 1.98%

Conversion rate: 9%

Opt outs: 32

Sometimes I write my emails around a new idea I am introducing to the reader. But everyone knows, whether you sell online or offline, writing articles is an effective marketing tactic.

So this product does not present a new idea; it simply gives how-to instructions for writing and distributing articles for marketing purposes. The only twist is that it positions article writing as a solution to a major problem Internet marketers have: list building.

Subject: Building your e-list with articles

Dear Direct Response Letter Subscriber:

Everyone says, "A great way to build your e-list is by writing articles for free—and getting them published in e-newsletters that reach your target market."

But they don't tell you *how* to do it.

Now—having published more than 500 articles both online and offline—I'll teach you how easy it is to write and publish articles.

My new e-book, *Marketing with Articles* answers your most important questions about promoting yourself by writing articles—both online and offline.

Including:

** "Why are e-zine publishers—some of whom are my competitors—willing to run my articles?"

** "What is the target word length for the e-zine articles I submit to e-newsletter publishers?"

** "How can I convince an online marketer I don't know to run my articles in her e-newsletter?"

** "In what way does my writing an article for someone else's e-newsletter, and giving it to them for free, help build my own e-list and increase my online sales?"

** "Is there a way to 'automate' submission of my articles to e-zines, rather than approach online marketers one at a time?"

The answers to all of these questions—and much more, including submission guidelines, model articles, and where to submit articles online—are explored in-depth in *Marketing with Articles*.

For more information . . . or to order *Marketing with Articles* on a no-risk 90-day trial basis . . . just click below now:

http://www.getfamouswritingarticles.com

Sincerely,
Bob Bly

P.S. Did you know there are over a dozen websites where you can post your articles—and offer them to online marketers—who come to these sites looking specifically for free content they can run in their e-newsletters?

To get the URLs for all of these "article submission sites"—and begin listing your articles with them—just download your risk-free 90-day trial copy of *Marketing with Articles*. The list of article submission websites starts on page 102:

http://www.getfamouswritingarticles.com

Sample E-Newsletters

Multi-topic e-newsletter

From: Bob Bly
Subject: Marketing help from Yelp

Bob Bly's Direct Response Letter:
Resources, ideas, and tips for improving response to business-to-business, high-tech, Internet, and direct marketing.

You are getting this email because you subscribed to it on www.bly.com or because you are one of Bob's clients, prospects, seminar attendees, or book buyers. If you would prefer not to receive further emails of this type, go to www.bly.com, enter your email address, and hit unsubscribe.

Your subscription brings you one regular monthly issue, usually at the beginning of the month, plus supplementary messages each week. These are typically either free tips or personal recommendations for information products on marketing or related topics. I review products before recommending them and in many cases know the authors.

We do not rent or share your name with anybody. Feel free to forward this issue to any peers, friends, and associates you think would benefit from its contents. They will thank you. So will I.

To write a great headline, write LOTS of headlines

Always have more than one headline ready. Even if the client says he's only giving you one test panel—make sure to have several alternative headlines.

Says superstar copywriter Carline Anglade-Cole, "It never fails that the ONE headline I LOVE the most—is the one that performs the worst! And the headline I'm not thrilled about—becomes the kick-butt winner!"

According to Carline, your job is not to come up with the winning headline. It's to give your clients options—so they choose which one to buy. She adds, "It doesn't matter which headline works best—you're still the winner, because the royalty checks come to YOU."

Action step: Make it a habit to provide 2 . . . 3 . . . 5 . . . or more headlines for every project. It's what Carline does. Me too.

Source: Copy Star, 6/16/17.

Marketing help from Yelp

A new Nielsen study released in 5/17 says Yelp does a better job than Google or Facebook in driving conversion: 92% of people who use online review sites say they made a purchase after visiting Yelp. Action step: register your business on Yelp now.

Source: Today@TargetMarketing, 6/14/17.

Selling to farmers: 'tis the season

Direct mail guru Craig Simpson shares this useful guide: Based on his extensive direct mail testing, the worst time to send direct mail to farmers is during harvest season, because they have no time to read it.

Conversely, Craig gets his best results mailing aggressively to farmers in the off-season, when they are highly responsive. Lesson: timing is everything. So is there logic that dictates timing for your market—for instance, tax season for accountants, holiday season for gift catalogs, or offers affected by students going back to school?

Source: Talon Newsletter, June 2017, p. 1.

Strategic timing for email distribution*

As with direct mail (see above section), consider the intersection of timing and subject matter when scheduling email distributions. For instance, say you're sending an email about coffee consumption. Might it resonate best if sent in the morning, when someone is more likely to be drinking coffee?

Action step: Your email service provider (ESP) may be able to provide details about the best time to send emails based on your industry and unique company data. Ask them!

Source: PR Daily News Feed, 6/14/17.

Boost direct mail response rates with quizzes

A time-tested but now under-used tactic for boosting direct mail engagement, readership, and response is to use a quick at the top of page one of the sales letter above the salutation, on the outer envelope, or both.

It works on two levels. First, people like taking quizzes. So it's an involvement device.

Second, the quiz asks qualifying questions that help the prospect self-identify as someone in need of what you are offering.

Source: Today@TargetMarketing, 6/9/17.

---

3 tips for getting new clients through networking

#1: Start conversations—Go out of your way to get into conversations with anyone and everyone you can, in person, on the phone, or via email.

#2: Ask questions—Find out what they're working on. Also, tell them what you're working on. Anything can come out of a simple conversation: ideas, alliances, connections, referrals, new business, and new opportunities.

#3: Arrive early—If you wait until most of the attendees have arrived at the meeting or event, many of them will already be in conversations and it won't be as easy to break in.

Source: AWAI Golden Thread, 6/12/17.

Which has better ROI: email marketing or social media?

According to a ClickZ article (6/14/17), email continues to have the highest ROI of any marketing channel. So when some smartass tells you email marketing is on its way out, and that you should be doing SnapChat, don't you believe them: Email—not social or CEO—is still the "killer marketing app" on the internet. And that's the fact, Jack!

Quotation of the month

"It is better to be a young June-bug than an old bird of paradise."
—Mark Twain

Reprint my articles—free!

Media, bloggers, marketers, editors, publishers, web masters—need powerful content on your website or blog? You can syndicate or republish any of the articles you've read in Bob Bly Direct Response Letter—for free! To view complete articles, visit our newsletter archives at [LINK]. Republishing our articles is quick and easy. All you have to do is include author attribution (byline/name of author) and the following statement, "This article appears courtesy of Bob Bly Direct Response Letter," and include a back-link to www.bly.com. That's it!

Our 60-second commercial

Bob Bly is available on a limited basis for copywriting of landing pages, direct mail packages, video sales letters, brochures, white papers, ads, email marketing campaigns, articles, blog posts, and web pages. We recommend you call for a FREE copy of our updated Copywriting Information Kit. Just let us know your industry and the type of copy you're interested in seeing (ads, mailings, etc.) and if Bob is available to take on your assignment, we'll tailor a package of recent samples to fit your requirements. Call Bob Bly at 973-263-0562 or email rwbly@bly.com.

Single topic e-newsletter (essay style)

Subject: The last writer starving in a garret

Dear Direct Response Letter Subscriber:

Tomorrow, as I turn 60, I look back and recall how different young writers were in the 70s when I started submitted my stories to magazines for publication—as compared with the new money-focused young wordsmiths today.

Back then, there was some odd notion that many writers had about it being somehow romantic, cool, and even hip to be struggling in poverty and obscurity . . .

. . . eating Kraft mac and cheese for dinner every night—and the proverbial writer "starving in a garret."

The garret for me being my crappy walk-up tenement studio apartment on Manhattan's Upper East Side.

The goals were art, publication, literature, fame, and the best-seller list first . . . and after that, then yes, money.

But for today's writers, who aspire to getting rich in mere weeks by selling information online rather than a novel to HarperCollins (a publisher to whom I sold two paperback books on Star Trek), money is the main thing, front and center.

As is evidence by the astounding popularity of all the high-priced "make a million dollars with information marketing online" programs being sold today.

In my day, you learned your craft in copywriting by reading used copies of Ogilvy and Caples books you bought used for a dollar at the Strand.

Now people of all ages, from all walks of life, hand over their credit card to buy training in information marketing and copywriting for thousands of dollars a pop . . . without batting an eyelash.

But even in my day, the brighter writers were too smart to buy into the "starving artist" mentality that others embraced.

In his book *Factotum*, Charles Bukowski, who was poor for a lot of his life, wrote:

"Starvation, unfortunately didn't improve art . . . the myth of the starving artist was a hoax.

"A man's art was rooted in his stomach. A man could write much better after eating a porterhouse steak than he could after eating a nickel candy bar."

How true!

And, like J. Jonah Jameson in the first *Spiderman* movie—who tells Peter Parker, "Freelance is the ticket"–

–Bukowski, like so many other writers, was an advocate of freelancing . . . and abhorred 9 to 5 jobs (which he was forced to take for decades until he finally started making good money as a freelance novelist and poet).

Bukoswki in *Factotum* again:

"How in hell could a man enjoy being awakened at 6:30am by an alarm clock, leap out of bed, dress, force-feed, piss, brush teeth and hair, and fight traffic to get to a place where essentially you made lots of money for somebody else and were asked to be grateful for the opportunity to do so?"

I get this: when I had a 9 to 5 corporate job, I hated setting and waking up to an alarm, perform morning ablutions, put on a suit and tie, and commute to be at work by 8 or 9 a.m.

Ironically, as a freelancer, I have gotten up every morning at 6 a.m–without an alarm clock–for decades.

Within 3 minutes of getting up each morning, I walk a flight of steps to my desk, turn on the PC, and start writing immediately.

No need to waste valuable time making sure I am clean shaven, my shirt freshly cleaned and pressed, my shoes shined, my pie-hole freshly rinsed with mouthwash, and my hair neatly combed–as I did in my days as an employee in corporate America.

I arise naturally, bright and bushy tailed, eager to dive into the day, because I love freelance writing.

Always have. And hope, think, and am pretty confident I always will.

We'll see.

But now in my 38th year of being a writer–so far, so good.

Sincerely,
Bob Bly

Email Service Providers

Marketing Email Services for Business Use

If you have a list of thousands of customers and prospects and want to email them on a regular basis, you can use one of the business email service providers listed here. Their email distribution platforms are relatively easy to use.

Many of them come with transactional email services and design templates for HTML email. With some, when a customer buys your product, they get a receipt back in the email box, plus a preset note from you saying "Thank You," sent by autoresponder software. Ideally, it is convenient to do all these actions using one company. If you have products for upselling, this can be included during the transaction point and would help you make more money.

Also look for options on getting statistics about your send outs. This can include how many readers opened your email, how many clicked on the link to look at the product, how many made the purchase, total number of orders, and gross revenues generated by the email. Other statistics you could get are: what time of day provided more success in transactions than others as well as results of A/B testing of emails with differing content components, showing which one worked better than others.

Aweber
www.aweber.com

Bronto
www.bronto.com

Constant Contact
www.constantcontact.com

Campaign Monitor
www.campaignmonitor.com

Emma
www.myemma.com

MailChimp
www.mailchimp.com

Pinpointe
www.pinpointe.com

Zoho
https://www.zoho.com/mail/

Personal Email Services for Individual Use

There are many email services providers for personal use by individuals, and the vast majority, including the ones below, are free:

Fast Mail
https://www.fastmail.com/signup/

GMX
https://www.gmx.com/

Google Gmail
www.google.com/gmail

Hush Mail
www.hushmail.com

Outlook
www.outlook.com

Yahoo! Mail
www.mail.yahoo.com

Fifteen Email Marketing Fundamentals at a Glance

Here are fifteen proven techniques for maximizing the number of email recipients who click through to your website or other response mechanism.

1. At the beginning of the email, put a "From" line and a "Subject" line. The "Subject" line should be constructed like a short attention-grabbing, curiosity-arousing outer envelope teaser, compelling recipients to read further—without being so blatantly promotional it turns them off. Example: "Come on back to Idea Forum!"

2. The email "From" line identifies you as the sender if you're emailing to your house file. If you're emailing to a rented list, the "From" line might identify the list owner as the sender. This is especially effective with opt-in lists where the list owner (e.g., a website) has a good relationship with its users.

3. Some e-marketers think the "From" line is trivial and unimportant; others think it's critical. Internet copywriter Ivan Levison says, "I often use the word 'Team' in the "From"

line. It makes it sound as if there's a group of bright, energetic, enthusiastic people standing behind the product." For instance, if you are sending an email to a rented list of computer people to promote a new software product, your "Subject" and "From" lines might read as follows: FROM: The Adobe PageMill Team / SUBJECT: Adobe PageMill 3.0 limited-time offer!

4. Despite the fact that free is a proven, powerful response-booster in traditional direct marketing, and that the Internet culture has a bias in favor of free offers rather than paid offers, some e-marketers avoid FREE in the subject line. The reason is the "spam filter" software some Internet users have installed to screen their email. These filters eliminate incoming email and many identify any message with FREE in the subject line as promotional.

5. Lead off the message copy with a killer headline or lead-in sentence. You need to get a terrific benefit right up front. Pretend you're writing envelope teaser copy or are writing a headline for a sales letter.

6. In the first paragraph, deliver a mini-version of your complete message. State the offer and provide an immediate response mechanism, such as clicking on a link connected to a web page. This appeals to Internet prospects with short attention spans.

7. After the first paragraph, present expanded copy that covers the features, benefits, proof, and other information the buyer needs to make a decision. This appeals to the prospect who needs more details than a short paragraph can provide.

8. The offer and response mechanism should be repeated in the close of the email, as in a traditional direct mail letter. But they should almost always appear at the very beginning, too.

That way, busy Internet users who don't have time to read and give each email only a second or two get the whole story.

9. John Wright, of the Internet marketing services firm MediaSynergy, says that if you put multiple response links within your email message, 95 percent of click-through responses will come from the first two. Therefore, you should probably limit the number of click-through links in your email to three. An exception might be an e-newsletter or "e-zine" broken into five or six short items, where each item is on a different subject and therefore each has its own link.

10. Use wide margins. You don't want to have weird wraps or breaks. Limit yourself to about 55 to 60 characters per line. If you think a line is going to be too long, insert a character return. Internet copywriter Joe Vitale sets his margins at 20 and 80, keeping sentence length to 60 characters, and ensuring the whole line gets displayed on the screen without odd text breaks.

11. Take it easy on the all-caps. You can use WORDS IN ALL CAPS but do so carefully. They can be a little hard to read—and in the world of email, all caps give the impression that you're shouting.

12. In general, short is better. This is not the case in classic mail order selling where as a general principle, "the more you tell, the more you sell." Email is a unique environment. Readers are quickly sorting through a bunch of messages and aren't disposed to stick with you for a long time.

13. Regardless of length, get the important points across quickly. If you want to give a lot of product information, add it lower down in your email message. You might also consider an attachment, such as a Word document, PDF file, or html page. People who need more information can always scroll

down or click for it. The key benefits and deal should be communicated in the first screen, or very soon afterward.

14. The tone should be helpful, friendly, informative, and educational, not promotional or hard-sell. "Information is the gold in cyberspace," says Vitale. Trying to sell readers with a traditional hyped-up sales letter won't work. People online want information and lots of it. You'll have to add solid material to your puffed-up sales letter to make it work online. Refrain from saying your service is "the best" or that you offer "quality." Those are empty, meaningless phrases. Be specific. How are you the best? What exactly do you mean by quality? And who says it besides you? And even though information is the gold, readers don't want to be bored. They seek, like all of us, excitement. Give it to them.

15. Including an opt-out statement prevents flaming from recipients who feel they have been spammed by stating that your intention is to respect their privacy, and making it easy for them to prevent further promotional emails from being sent to them. All they have to do is click on Reply and type "UNSUBSCRIBE" or "REMOVE" in the subject line. Example: "We respect your online time and privacy, and pledge not to abuse this medium. If you prefer not to receive further emails from us of this type, please reply to this email and type 'Remove' in the subject line."

About the Author

B ob Bly is an independent copywriter and marketing consultant with nearly four decades of experience in business-to-business and direct response marketing. McGraw-Hill calls Bob Bly "America's top copywriter" and he was AWAI's Copywriter of the Year. Clients include IBM, the Conference Board, PSE&G, AT&T, Embraer Executive Jet, Intuit, ExecuNet, Boardroom, Medical Economics, Grumman, RCA, ITT Fluid Technology, and Praxair.

Bob has given presentations to numerous organizations including: National Speakers Association, American Seminar Leaders Association, American Society for Training and Development, U.S. Army, American Society of Journalists and Authors, Society for Technical Communications, Discover Card, Learning Annex, and New York University School of Continuing Education.

He is the author of more than ninety books, including *The Copywriter's Handbook* (Henry Holt) and *The Elements of Business Writing* (Pearson). Bob's articles have appeared in *Cosmopolitan, Writer's Digest, The Writer, Successful Meetings, Amtrak Express, Direct, City Paper, Bergen Record, DM News,* and many other publications. Bob is a columnist for *Target Marketing.* The *Direct Response Letter,* Bob's monthly e-newsletter, has over 65,000 subscribers (www.bly.com/reports).

Awards include a Gold Echo from the Direct Marketing Association, an IMMY from the Information Industry Association, two Southstar Awards, an American Corporate Identity Award of Excellence, Marketer of the Year from Early to Rise, and the Standard of Excellence award from the Web Marketing Association. He is a member of the International Association of Business Communicators (IABC), Business Marketing Association (BMA), and the American Institute of Chemical Engineers (AIChE).

Prior to become a freelance copywriter, Bob was advertising manager of Koch Engineering and a staff marketing writer for Westinghouse Defense. He holds a BS in chemical engineering from the University of Rochester and is trained as a Certified Novell Administrator.

Questions and comments on *The New Email Revolution* can be sent to the author at:

Bob Bly
Copywriter
31 Cheyenne Drive
Montville, NJ 07045
Phone: 973-263-0562
Fax: 973-263-0613
Email: rwbly@bly.com
Web: www.bly.com

Index